An American Perspective
on Japanese Law

アメリカから見た日本法

J・マーク・ラムザイヤー

長谷部恭男
宇賀克也
中里実
川出敏裕
大村敦志
松下淳一
神田秀樹
荒木尚志
白石忠志

有斐閣

INTRODUCTION

Introduction

I do not want to be misunderstood.

I do not want anyone to consider this the American view of Japanese law. Rather, these are the views of one American scholar about several famous Japanese cases. I do not represent American professors. I do not hold opinions that are typical to American scholars. I certainly do not share any majority opinion. These are simply my own personal thoughts.

Neither do I want anyone to consider these essays my thoughts about Japanese law in general. Instead, they represent my thoughts about several specific well-known cases in Japan. Some of the cases are typical of a field. But some are instead famous because they are unusual. I did not choose these cases. Rather, these cases were selected by the publisher in consultation with Japanese scholars. I am simply responding to the cases presented to me.

If these essays expand the scope of debate in some fields, I will be pleased. Within any academic community, it is easy for scholars to come to focus on a particular facet of a problem. The focus can often clarify matters, of course, but sometimes it can cause scholars to overlook interesting facets of a problem. I hope these essays will suggest to some readers new problems to pursue.

In writing these chapters, I have tried to follow three principles. First, judges are human beings. They have a job. That job subjects them to a set of constraints and rewards. In turn, those constraints and rewards both affect the people who choose to apply for the job, and shape the work that those who do hold the job choose to accomplish. In several chapters, I explore the career implications judges face for deciding a case in a certain way. I find that judges who decided certain constitutional cases contrary to the position of the LDP suffered in their careers. I also find that -- contrary to some popular complaints -- judges do not suffer career penalties for acquiting criminal defendants.

Second, the facts matter. Judges decide the cases on the basis of the human beings they face, not just on the basis of abstract principles of law. They write their opinions to justify their outcome, however, and for that purpose invoke the abstract principles. In writing the opinion, in other words, they select those aspects of the facts that fit within those abstract principles. As a result, a published opinion in a case is only a partial statement of the facts that a judge encounters. The judge includes the facts that legally justify the opinion he reaches, but not necessarily the facts that were most important to him. Consequently, to understand why a judge decided a case the way he did, one must understand the entire factual context -- including facts that he did not include in the opinion. This is not always possible, of course, but sometimes it is. In several chapters, I find and discuss some of the facts omitted from the published opinion that probably mattered greatly.

Third, cases do not always have the effect that judges anticipated. Understanding the effect that legal decisions have on the larger world is the realm of social science. Yet coming to their jobs from legal training, judges often lack the social science that they need to understand the impact that their decisions will have. In several chapters, I try to show the disastrous effects that can follow when judges ignore social science. This is particularly pronounced in labor and landlord tenant law.

I enjoyed writing these essays. I hope that you enjoy reading at least a few of them.

September, 2019

Nagano-ken, Nojiri-ko

J. Mark Ramseyer

INTRODUCTION

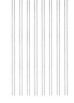

はしがき

　誤解されると困るので，本書に関する私の立場を明確にしておきたい。

　この本は，「アメリカ」から見た日本法ではない。それは，（私という）ある一人のアメリカ人の目から見た幾つかの日本の裁判例に関するエッセー集である。私は，アメリカの法学者の代表でもなければ，典型的な学者でもないし，通説を語ろうとしている者でもない。したがって，本書は，単に，一人の学者の個人的な解釈を集めたものである。

　また，本書においては，日本法の全体的な評価も行われてはいない。少数の有名な判例に関する短いエッセーを集めたものであり，中には典型的な判例もあれば，変わっているからこそ有名な判例もある。また，判例は，私が選んだわけではない。著名な学者と出版社が相談して選択したものであり，私は，単に割り当てられた判例を私なりの考え方で解説しただけである。

　どこの学界でも限られた課題に議論が集中することが多いし，この集中を通して重大な問題が正確に解決されることがよくある。しかし，議論が集中したために他の課題が無視されることも時々ある。これまで見逃されていた幾つかの問題が学界で取り上げられるようになれば，この本を書くことに意味があったということになろう。

　私は，本書執筆に当たり次の三つの原則に基づいて書くことに努力した。第一，裁判官とは，ロボットでもなければ，電子計算機でもない。裁判所内で活動し，給料を貰い，出世を目指している，普通の人間である。もちろん，その勤務には，基本的なインセンティブ制度が付随している。最高裁の事務総局に高く評価されると年収が上がって都会のポストに任命され，低く評価されると年収が上がらず田舎の支部に任命されて10年の任期後にクビにされる可能性さえもある。これこそが，裁判官として書く判例に影響を及ぼすインセンティブ制度であり，裁判所におけるキャリアーを選択する研修生に影響を及す制度でもある。いくつかの章では，事件の解決法によって裁判官の経験する行政的影響を探ることにした。そこでは，重大な憲法事件で与党に逆らった判例を発表した裁判官が不利に扱われたことを説明し

ており，刑事事件の被告を無罪にする裁判官も不利に取り扱われると時々言われることもあるが，この現象がデータに現れないことをも説明している。

　第二，事件の事実関係は，重要である。人間であるからこそ裁判官は，事件の解決に抽象的な法律を機械的に当てはめるよりも，当事者にふさわしい結果を導き出そうとすることが多い。確かに判例には，当該解決を正当化する事実が選択され，抽象的な法的原理が書き込まれたものが多いが，その事実と原理が実際に事件の解決に重要だったとは限らない。判例に書かれた事実は，裁判官の取り扱った事実の一部だけであるので，裁判官がなぜある事件をそのように解決したのかを理解するためには，（判例に書かれなかったことをも含む）全ての事実関係を理解しなければならない。もちろん，裁判に書かれていなければ調べようとしても確認できるとは限らない。しかし，調査が可能な事件もあり，判例に述べられなかった事実が重要だと思われるものを幾つか取り上げることにした。

　第三，判例が裁判官の予想していた影響を及ぼすとは，限らない。法律や判例の影響とは，法学ではなく社会科学の分野にあたり，法学部を卒業した裁判官が十分に理解できるとは限らない。以下の判例の中には，裁判官が社会科学を理解しないで事件を解決したことを通して及ぼした哀れな現象を幾つか取り上げる。労働法と借地借家法の判例は，特に悲惨な結果を導いている。

　この判例評論の執筆に当たり，楽しい時間を過ごすことができたが，これを読んで楽しんでくれる読者が数人でもいることを望んでいるところである。

　2019 年 9 月

長野県野尻湖にて

Ｊ・マーク・ラムザイヤー

AUTHORS

J・マーク・ラムザイヤー（J. Mark Ramseyer）

ハーバード大学教授

主要著作

『法と経済学——日本法の経済分析』（弘文堂，1990年），Japanese Law (University of Chicago Press, 1998) (co-authored with Minoru Nakazato)「戦後日本における租税法の成立と発展」『租税法の発展』（共著，有斐閣，2010年），「累進課税とモラルハザード」『租税法と市場』（共編，有斐閣，2014年），Second-Best Justice (University of Chicago Press, 2015)

解説

PART 1 憲法

長谷部 恭男（はせべ やすお）

解説 ● CASE 1, 2, 3, 4, 5

早稲田大学教授

PART 2 行政法

宇賀 克也（うが かつや）

解説 ● CASE 6, 7

東京大学名誉教授

PART 3 租税法

中里 実（なかざと みのる）

解説 ● CASE 8, 9

東京大学教授

PART 4 刑事法

川出 敏裕（かわいで としひろ）

解説 ● CASE 10, 11

東京大学教授

PART 5 民事法

大村 敦志（おおむら あつし）

解説 ● CASE 12, 13, 14, 16

学習院大学教授

v

PART **5**
民事法

松下 淳一（まつした じゅんいち）

解説 ● CASE 15

東京大学教授

PART **6**
会社法

神田 秀樹（かんだ ひでき）

解説 ● CASE 17, 18, 19

学習院大学教授

PART **7**
労働法

荒木 尚志（あらき たかし）

解説 ● CASE 20, 21, 22

東京大学教授

PART **8**
経済法

白石 忠志（しらいし ただし）

解説 ● CASE 23, 24

東京大学教授

CONTENTS

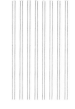

PART 1 憲 法

CASE 1　砂川事件　Sakata v. Kuni — 2
1. The facts — 2
2. The decision — 4
3. Discussion — 4
4. The Naganuma sequel — 5
5. Article 9 and judicial careers — 7

解説 憲法解釈の方法 — 12

CASE 2　三菱樹脂事件　Mitsubishi jushi, K.K. v. Takano — 15
1. The facts — 15
2. The reasoning — 18

解説 憲法の基本権条項は私人間に適用されるか — 20

CASE 3　衆議院議員定数配分規定違憲訴訟　Kurokawa v. Chiba ken senkyo kanri iinkai — 23
1. The facts — 23
2. The decision — 23
3. Discussion — 24

解説 投票価値の較差 — 28

CASE 4　ノンフィクション「逆転」事件　Isa v. Kono — 30
1. The facts — 30
2. The U.S. comparison — 32
3. Protecting fraud? — 35

解説 プライバシーは何を守るのか — 38

CASE 5　非嫡出子法定相続分違憲訴訟　[unnamed parties] — 40
1. The facts — 40
2. The decision — 41

vii

3 Discussion ● 42

解説 非嫡出子の法定相続分 ———————————— 51

PART 2 行政法

CASE 6 武蔵野市長給水拒否事件　Kuni v. Goto　54

1 Introduction ● 54　　2 Classic examples ● 56
3 Municipal administrative guidance ● 58

解説 日本における行政指導をめぐる状況の変遷 ———— 66

CASE 7 強制予防接種事件　Yoshihara v. Kuni　68

1 The facts ● 68　　2 The decision ● 69
3 Infectious disease and vaccines ● 72
4 Vaccine externalities ● 75
5 Government negligence and the disease environment ● 78
6 Government negligence and the state of knowledge ● 79
7 Incentive effects ● 80

解説 強制予防接種の被害者の救済 ———————— 83

PART 3 租税法

CASE 8 サラリーマン税金訴訟（大島訴訟）大法廷判決
Oshima v. Sakyo zeimusho cho　88

1 The facts ● 88　　2 Discrimination ● 90
3 Tax incidence ● 91
4 Deviations from economic income ● 93

viii

5 Administrative costs ● 95

解説 大法廷判決に見る租税政策論と法律学 ——————— 96

9 興銀税務訴訟
K.K. Nihon kogyo ginko sosho shokeinin v. Kojimachi zeimusho cho   98

1 The facts ● 98

2 Why did the government do this? ● 101

解説 興銀税務訴訟が租税訴訟に与えた影響 ——————— 107

PART 4 — 刑 事 法

CASE 10 光母子殺害事件第二次上告審判決 [No names given]   110

1 The facts ● 110   **2** The reasoning ● 111

3 The number of victims ● 113

4 The politics ● 115

5 How mandatory is mandatory? ● 118

解説 死刑の選択基準 ——————————— 119

11 狭 山 事 件   **Kuni v. Ishikawa**   122

1 The facts ● 122   **2** Guilt and innocence ● 127

3 Police misbehavior ● 128

4 Ethnic profiling ● 130   **5** Police discretion ● 132

6 Erroneous convictions ● 136

解説 捜査・訴追の規制 ——————————— 138

PART **5** 民 事 法

CASE

12 サブリース事件　Sumitomo fudosan, K.K. v. Senchurii tawaa, K.K.　142

1 The facts ● 142　　**2** The decision ● 145

3 Discussion ● 146

解説　サブリースと借地借家法 32 条の適用 ──────153

13 学納金返還請求事件　[No name given] v. Gakko hojin Nihon daigaku　155

1 Fees at the Arts and Science Departments ● 155

2 Fees at the Medical Schools ● 157

3 U.S. Universities ● 162

解説　学納金の法的性質と機能 ──────169

14 更新料返還請求事件　K.K. Choei v. Kuroki　171

1 The facts ● 171　　**2** The decision ● 172

3 Discussion ● 172

解説　更新料条項の不当性判断 ──────184

15 懲 罰 賠 償　Northcon I v. Katayama　186

1 The facts ● 186　　**2** The decision ● 186

3 Discussion ● 187

解説　懲罰賠償の意義──陪審制及び裁判官の公選制との関係で ──192

16 松下電器カラーテレビ事件　194
● Taishi kensetsu kogyo, K.K. v. Matsushita denki sangyo, K.K.

1 The facts ● 194　　**2** The decision ● 194

3 The 1994 statute ● 198　　**4** Product safety ● 200

解説　製造物責任の法的意義と社会的影響 ──────204

x

PART 6 　会 社 法

CASE 17

ブルドックソース事件
Steel Partners Japan Strategic Fund (Offshore), L.P. v. Bull-Dog Sauce Co., Ltd.　208

1 The case ● 208　　　2 The substance ● 211

3 The American parallel ● 214

解説　敵対的買収への対抗策 ──────── 218

CASE 18

UFJ銀行事件　Sumitomo Trust Bank, K.K. v. K.K. UFJ Holdings　220

1 The facts ● 220　　　2 The decision ● 223

3 Discussion ● 226

解説　大手銀行の救済に関する買収の協議禁止条項の効力 ── 231

CASE 19

アパマンショップ事件　[Apamanshop Derivative Litigation]　233

1 The facts ● 233　　　2 The decision ● 234

3 Duty of care ● 236　　4 The underlying dispute ● 239

解説　経営判断の法理 ──────────── 241

PART 7 　労 働 法

CASE 20

高知放送事件　K.K. Kochi hoso v. Shiota　244

1 The facts ● 244　　　2 The decision ● 245

3 Discussion ● 245

解説　解 雇 規 制 ──────────── 257

21 秋北バス事件　Yoshikawa v. Shuhoku Bus, K.K.　262

1　The facts ● 262
2　Employment practice ● 263
3　Mandatory retirement ● 265
4　Changes to workplace rules ● 270

解説　解雇権濫用法理と就業規則の合理的変更法理 ─── 272

22 電通事件　Oshima v. K.K. Dentsu　275

1　Suicide and overwork ● 275
2　The case ● 279
3　Did Oshima die from overwork? ● 280
4　Should courts discourage hard work? ● 284
5　Should firms sort applicants by mental health? ● 285

解説　過労死 ─── 288

PART 8　経済法

CASE 23 三井住友銀行事件　In re K.K. Mitsui Sumitomo Ginko, Fair Trade Commission Recommendation Decision　292

1　The case ● 292
2　Discussion ● 294

解説　優越的地位 ─── 301

CASE 24 石油カルテル事件　Kuni v. Idemitsu kosan, and Kuni v. Sekiyu renmei　303

1　The case ● 303
2　The context ● 305
3　Government compulsion ● 307

解説　行政指導と独禁法 ─── 310

あとがき ─── 313

xii

1 PART

憲　法

CASE	
1	砂川事件
2	三菱樹脂事件
3	衆議院議員定数配分規定違憲訴訟
4	ノンフィクション「逆転」事件
5	非嫡出子法定相続分違憲訴訟

CASE

Sakata v. Kuni

13 Saihan keishu 3225 (Sup. Ct. Dec. 16, 1959).

●

砂川事件

(最判昭和34年12月16日刑集13巻13号3225頁)

1 The facts

a. Introduction   For several decades after World War II, the U.S. Air Force operated a base at the site of what is now Showa Kinen Koen in Tachikawa. From 1950 to 1953, it used the base to fight the Korean War. During the 1960s, it would use it to fight the war in Vietnam.

In 1957, the U.S. Air Force decided to expand its Tachikawa runway, and supporters of the Japanese left moved to oppose its plans. For those on left, the time was still one of hope. The Liberal Democratic Party (LDP) that would dominate the government for the next half-century had only formed itself two years earlier. Its opponents on the left could reasonably hope to take control of the government and restructure the country along socialist lines. After all, Kruschev had only disclosed Stalin's atrocities a year before; the mass murder and starvation under Mao's Great Leap Forward and Cultural Revolution were yet to come.

In these years of eager anticipation, left-leaning law graduates joined the courts in large numbers. Many who did so also joined the judge's division of the Young Jurists League (YJL; the Seinen horitsuka kyokai) loosely affiliated with the Japan Communist Party (JCP). Of the judges hired from 1958 to 1969, 28 percent joined the League.

Among the judges on the left, Akio Date would in time become something of a folk hero. During the 1930s, as a judge in Manchuria he was said to have released a large number of Chinese prisoners. By the late 1960s, he had joined the private bar and would file at least one high-profile suit to let Japanese firms sell militarily sensitive equipment to mainland China.[1]

b. The District Court[2] In 1957, Date sat on the Tokyo District Court. There, he heard the case against several rioters arrested for trying to block the expansion of the Tachikawa runway. The government prosecuted them for criminal trespass under a special statute applicable to U.S. military bases. The statute exposed the protesters to a higher penalty than did the standard trespass statute.

Date acquitted the defendants. Article 9 of the Constitution banned military weapons, and the Tachikawa base was nothing if not military. If the government could not maintain its own military, neither could it rent military services from the U.S. by contract. After all, any such contract made Japan complicit in American military adventures —— of which the Korean War was but the first example. Vietnam would soon become the second. Accordingly, the security agreement with the U.S. was unconstitutional, and if the agreement violated Article 9 so did any statute designed to facilitate the U.S. presence under the agreement. Prosecuted under an unconstitutional statute, the rioters were not guilty.

---

[1] 1969 Beijing-Shanghai-Japan Industrial Exposition v. Japan, 560 Hanrei jiho 6 (Tokyo D. Ct. July 8, 1969).

[2] Sakata v. Kuni, 180 Hanrei jiho 2 (Tokyo D. Ct. Mar. 30, 1959).

3

2 The decision

From the District Court, the government appealed directly to the Supreme Court. The Court reversed. It gave several reasons. First, Japan entered its security agreement with the U.S. to ensure its own defense, and Article 9 did not ban self-defense. Second, Article 9 banned a Japanese military force, but the U.S. military (even if under contract to Japan) was not a Japanese military force. Third, the entire question was politically charged, and courts should avoid such questions unless the conduct at stake was obviously unconstitutional.

3 Discussion

a. Preliminary observations   The litigation under Article 9 illustrates several basic comparisions between U.S. and Japanese courts:

(i) Politically motivated litigation occurs in Japan. The point is obvious to anyone in Japan; it is not always obvious to American law students.

(ii) Japanese judges try to avoid politically sensitive decisions, and use some of the same tools as American judges. The "political question" doctrine is exactly such a tool.

(iii) If a trial court decides a case on constitutional grounds, the losing party may appeal directly to the Supreme Court.

(iv) Prosecutors may appeal an acquittal. Both the U.S. and Japanese constitutions ban "double jeopardy," but U.S. courts interpret the ban to foreclose any appeals from a criminal acquittal.

b. Framers' intent.   Japanese judges rarely resort to "framer's intent" in constitutional law. In U.S. cases, justices routinely survey other indices of what the drafters of the Constitution might have meant. For exactly that reason, for example, they routinely refer to the Federalist Papers.

The Japanese Supreme Court seldom discusses "framer's intent." In the Sunagawa case, it interprets a document imposed on the country by the U.S. military. Yet in doing so, it never asks what Gen. Douglas MacArthur might have thought when he forced the Japanese government to adopt Article 9.

To pose the question, of course, is to answer it —— and demonstrates the preposterousness of Date's District Court opinion. MacArthur may or may not have intended to let the Japanese government maintain a modest force for self-defense. He did not intend to ban his own military bases.

4　The Naganuma sequel

a. Case assignment　The Sunagawa and later Article 9 cases illustrate crucial aspects of the Japanese judiciary. Turn to the 1969 dispute over the Self-Defense Force's (SDF) Nike missile base in Naganuma, Hokkaido. To build this base, the SDF needed to redesignate a portion of a national forest. Those on the left opposed the base, and recruited neighboring farmers to contest the forest's redesignation.

The case went to a young (he became a judge in 1959) judge in the Sapporo District Court named Shigeo Fukushima. The chief judge on the court was one Kenta Hiraga, and when he discovered that the case had been assigned to Fukushima, he panicked. Fukushima was a member of the JCP-affiliated YJL, and the JCP opposed the SDF. By the terms of its own organizing document, the YJL was committed to fighting any amendment to the Constitution. Given that the LDP sought to amend the Constitution to delete Article 9, the YJL's opposition to any amendment implied opposition to any military force (including the SDF) as well.

Worried what Fukushima might do, Hiraga sent him a memo. In it, he detailed several legal problems with the plaintiff's claims. Given that the Sunagawa case concerned the U.S. bases rather than the SDF, it did not apply straightforwardly. Yet if the "political question" doctrine suggested that a court should not hold the base unconstitutional in Sunakawa, it suggested the court should not void the redesignation of the forest here. Neither was it clear whether the plaintiffs had "standing" to contest the redesignation. Both factors would have raised problems for plaintiffs under U.S. law as well.

b. The crisis　　Outraged that his chief judge might suggest how he should decide the case, Fukushima mailed a copy of Hiraga's memo to his colleagues in the YJL. Those colleagues leaked the memo to the press, and the press declared itself shocked. The Diet launched impeachment proceedings against both Hiraga and Fukushima, and reprimanded both. In turn, the courts' administrative headquarters ordered all judges in the YJL to resign their membership.

Fukushima himself held the SDF unconstitutional.[3] The High Court reversed, partly for the standing reasons Hiraga had outlined.[4] On remand Fukushima again held the SDF unconstitutional —— this time in a long and militant diatribe.[5] The High Court again reversed,[6] and the Supreme Court affirmed the reversal.[7]

c. The denouement　　The interest, however, lies in what

---

[3]　[Unnamed parties], 565 Hanrei jiho 23 (Sapporo D. Ct. Aug. 22, 1969).

[4]　[Unnamed parties], 581 Hanrei jiho 5 (Sapporo High Ct. Jan. 23, 1970).

[5]　[Unnamed parties], 712 Hanrei jiho 24 (Sapporo D. Ct. Sept. 7, 1973).

[6]　[Unnamed parties], 821 Hanrei jiho 21 (Sapporo High Ct. Aug. 5, 1976).

[7]　[Unnamed parties], 36 Saihan minshu 1679 (Sup. Ct. Sept. 9, 1982).

happened to Fukushima and to other judges who held either U.S. bases or the SDF unconstitutional. After declaring the SDF unconstitutional, Fukushima first found himself reassigned to Tokyo —— for the simple reason that the Supreme Court Secretariat (jimusokyoku) moves all Sapporo (Hokkaido) and Naha (Okinawa) judges back to Tokyo after their time there. In 1977, the Secretariat sent Fukushima to the Fukushima Family Court. By 1989, he had spent 12 continuous years in family courts.[8] He wrote an essay in a newspaper complaining of what he consideed mis-treatment, and abruptly quit.

5 Article 9 and judicial careers

Fukushima's experience was not unusual: the Secretariat regularly punished judges who held that either U.S. bases or the SDF violated Article 9. To investigate this issue, Prof. Eric Rasmusen and I studied all 47 lower court judges who had published an opinion on Article 9 by the late 20th century. Of these judges, 5 had held the bases or the SDF unconstitutional; 42 had held them constitutional.[9]

We then used other aspects of a judge's background to predict his likely success within the courts —— to ask whether judges who held the bases or the SDF unconstitutional did worse in their careers. More specifically, we ran "tobit regressions" with a dependent variable equal to the fraction of time during the decade after the opinion in which the judge held prestigious administrative appointments. Because smart and hardworking judges have more successful careers than those who are less bright and industrious, we included several control variables: (a) whether the judge attended one

---

[8] Nihon minshu horitsuka kyokai, ed. 2010. Zen saibankan keireki soran [Career Data on All Judges]. Tokyo: Nihon minshu horitsuka kyokai, 5th ed. (ZSKS).

[9] J. Mark Ramseyer & Eric B. Rasmusen, Why Are Japanese Judges so Conservative in Politically Charged Cases?, 95 Am. Pol. Sci. Rev. 331 (2001).

of the top national universities (the University of Tokyo or the University of Kyoto), (b) the estimated number of times he failed the entrance exam (the shiho shiken) to the Legal Research & Training Institute (LRTI; the shiho kenshu jo), (c) whether the Secretariat identified the judge as particularly promising and started him at the Tokyo District Court, (d) whether the judge was a member of the YJL, and (e) the fraction of time the judge spent in prestigious administrative appointments during the decade before the Article 9 opinion. The results appear in **Table 1**.

Preliminarily, note several observations.[10] First, judges who attended either Tokyo or Kyoto University have more successful careers than other judges. This result appears in a large number of regressions that Prof. Rasmusen and I report elsewhere. Second,

---

[10] These are observations that Prof. Rasmusen, Prof. Frances Rosenbluth, and I have collectively developed over a long range of publications. See generally J. Mark Ramseyer & Eric B. Rasmusen, Measuring Judicial Independence: The Political Economy of Judging in Japan (Chicago: University of Chicago Press, 2003); J. Mark Ramseyer & Frances McCall Rosenbluth, Japan's Political Marketplace (Cambridge: Harvard University Press, 1993); J. Mark Ramseyer & Eric B. Rasmusen, Political Uncertainty's Effect on Judicial Recruitment and Retention: Japan in the 1990s, 35 J. Comp. Econ. 329 (2007); J. Mark Ramseyer & Eric B. Rasmusen, The Case for Managed Judges: Learning from Japan after the Political Upheaval of 1993, 154 Univ. Penn. L. Rev. 1879 (2006); supra note 9; J. Mark Ramseyer & Eric B. Rasmusen, Why Is the Japanese Conviction Rate so High?, 30 J. Legal Stud. 53 (2001); J. Mark Ramseyer & Eric B. Rasmusen, Why the Japanese Taxpayer Always Loses, 72 S. Cal. L. Rev. 571 (1999); J. Mark Ramseyer & Eric B. Rasmusen, Judicial Independence in a Civil Law Regime: The Evidence from Japan, 13 J. Law. Econ. & Org. 259 (1997); J. Mark Ramseyer, Who Hangs Whom for What? The Death Penalty in Japan, 4 J. Legal Analysis 365 (2012); J. Mark Ramseyer, Talent Matters: Judicial Productivity and Speed in Japan, 32 Int'l Rev. Law & Econ. 38 (2012); J. Mark Ramseyer, Do School Cliques Dominate Japanese Bureaucracies? Evidence from Supreme Court Appointments, 88 Wash. U. L. Rev. 1681 (2011); J. Mark Ramseyer, Predicting Court Outcomes through Political Preferences: The Japanese Supreme Court and the Chaos of 1993, 58 Duke L.J. 1557 (2009); J. Mark Ramseyer, Judicial Independence, in The New Palgrave Dictionary of Economics and the Law (London: Macmillan, 1998); J. Mark Ramseyer, The Puzzling (In)dependence of Courts: A Comparative Approach, 23 J. Legal Stud. 721 (1994).

Table 1　Job Quality by Article 9

Dependent variable:	Good jobs afterward
Unconstitutional	−.397*
Good jobs before	.729*
Seniority	.019*
Flunks	−.018
Elite university	.201*
Tokyo D.C. start	.231
Opinions/year	−.023
YJL	.099

Notes: regression is tobit. * ——statistically significant at 5 percent level, one-tailed test. n=50. For details, see J. Mark Ramseyer & Eric B. Rasmusen, Why Are Japanese Judges so Conservative in Politically Charged Cases?, 95 Am. Pol. Sci. Rev. 331 (2001).

this phenomenon does not reflect any bias within the courts in favor of elite graduates. As I show elsewhere, instead it is because these judges accomplish more work.[11] Third, judges who pass the entrance exam to the LRTI most quickly have more successful careers than others (this result appears in other regressions, but not in **Table 1**). Note that an analogous phenomenon appears among the private bar as well: lawyers who passed the exam most quickly earn higher incomes than others.[12]

　　Fourth, in other regressions Prof. Rasmusen and I find that an initial appointment to the Tokyo District Court correlates with success throughout a judge's career (this result does not appear in **Table 1**). The Secretariat apparently identifies those judges most likely to

---

[11]　Ramseyer, Do School Cliques, supra note 10.

[12]　Minoru Nakazato, J. Mark Ramseyer & Eric Rasmusen, The Industrial Organization of the Japanese Bar, 7 J. Empirical Legal Stud. 460 (2010).

succeed and starts them at the Tokyo District Court. For the most part, these judges do indeed have the most successful careers.

Fifth, judges who were members of the YJL in the 1960s had less successful careers thereafter. Although the phenomenon does not appear in **Table 1**, it appears in a wide variety of regressions I performed with Prof. Rasmusen. These judges spent more time in provincial branch offices and family courts. They spent less time in prestigious administrative offices. They climbed the pay scale more slowly. And they continued to suffer career penalities even as late as the 1990s.

Turn then to **Table 1**: to the regressions on those 47 judges who published an opinion regarding Article 9. The negative coefficient on "Unconstitutional" indicates that those judges who held either American bases or the SDF unconstitutional spent fewer years in prestigious administrative posts in the decade after their Article 9 opinion. The effect is statistically significantly different from zero at the 5 percent level.

The other results are consistent with the effect that Prof. Rasmusen and I find elsewhere. The positive coefficient on elite university attendance indicates that Tokyo and Kyoto University graduates spent more time in prestigious appointments during the decade after the Article 9 opinion. The coefficient is statistically significantly different from zero. And the positive coefficient on "Good Jobs Earlier" indicates that those judges who spent more time in prestigious posts during the decade before the opinion spent more years in such posts after the opinion. The effect is again statistically significant.

The Secretariat punishes judges who take positions that run contrary to those of the ruling LDP. The point has obvious consequences for the character of the court. Most obviously, it makes it less likely that judges will take positions contrary to the LDP.

10

Table 2	Time to sokatsu

Dependent variable:	Good jobs afterward
YJL	.919*
Tokyo D.C. start	−1.383
Flunks	.014
Elite university	.086

Notes: regression is OLS. * statistically significant at 5 percent level, one-tailed test. n=501. For details, see J. Mark Ramseyer & Eric B. Rasmusen, Why Are Japanese Judges so Conservative in Politically Charged Cases?, 95 Am. Pol. Sci. Rev. 331 (2001).

More subtly, this phenomenon implies that LRTI graduates who share the LDP's policy preferences will self-select into judicial careers. Of the judges hired from 1958 to 1969, 28 percent were members of the communist-affiliated YJL. In **Table 2**, Prof. Rasmusen and I asked how long they spent in the courts before reaching "sokatsu" status. Because that posting correlates with their progress along the pay scale, it also measures how fast their salary increased. The coefficient of 0.919 on YJL membership indicates that they reached that status about one year later than other judges with comparable credentials.

In turn, this bias against left-leaning judges in judicial administration will bias the group of LRTI graduates who choose to join the courts. Put most bluntly, after learning what the courts do to leftist judges, left-leaning LRTI graduates will have much less incentive to join the courts. For a communist (or socialist) who takes his Marxism seriously, a career in the courts is simply not much fun. If he writes opinions that indulge his far-left preferences, he will spend his career in provincial branch offices and family courts. Much better to skip the courts and work in private practice.

Finally, note the structural reason for this effect. The effect is distinctly partisan —— but that partisanship follows from the institutional organization of the courts. First, the Prime Minister appoints the justices of the Supreme Court. What is more, he appoints them late enough in life (about age 63 or 64) that they will not change their political preferences before hitting mandatory retirement at age 70.

Second, the Chief Justice of the Supreme Court supervises the Secretary General of the Secretariat. Almost always, he himself worked as Secretary General before joining the Supreme Court. He knows, in other words, how the Secretariat works.

Third, the Secretary General supervises the judges in the Secretariat. And the judges in the Secretariat, in turn, monitor the judges in the lower courts. They evaluate their performance, reward those they favor, and punish those they oppose.

解説 COMMENT　憲法解釈の方法

　憲法の解釈方法論はさまざまである。条文の日常言語上の意味を尊重すべきだとか，積み重ねられてきた判例を整合的に説明し正当化できる理論に基づくべきだ，あるいは憲法全体の構造を重視すべきだ等と言われる。アメリカ合衆国に特徴的なのは，制憲者意思説というアプローチで，憲法典の意味が不確定である場合は，制憲者がどのように考えたかが手がかりになるというものである。そのため，フィラデルフィアの憲法制定会議の議事録や各州での憲法案の承認の際に影響を与えたと言われる『ザ・フェデラリスト』が参照される。日本を含めて他の国には，ここまで憲法の起草や制定にかかわった個々の人物の発言や著作を参照する風習はない。

　憲法案を審議・決定した会議にしろ，各州で案を承認した議会にしろ，本来的に意思を有する個人ではなく多数人からなる会議体であって，その「意思」とされるのは，最終的に会議体としての議決の対象となった文書のみのはずで

ある。審議過程での個々の議員の発言や，ましてや会議外で刊行された文書が，憲法の理解にあたって確かな手がかりになるという発想には，不思議なところがある（ジェレミー・ウォルドロン〔長谷部恭男ほか訳〕『立法の復権』〔岩波書店，2003〕29-32頁参照）。

日本国憲法の当初の起草には，マッカーサー将軍と占領軍総司令部のスタッフがあたった。起草当時のマッカーサーが，将来，日本に米軍が駐留し続けるべきだと考えていたか否かは不明である。沖縄に基地が確保されている以上（沖縄の施政権が日本に返還されたのは1972年5月である），日本本土に米軍が駐留する必要はないと考えていたとの観察もある（Geoffrey Perret, Old Soldiers Never Die: The Life of Douglas MacArthur〔Random House, 1996〕, p. 535）。当時，アメリカが唯一の核兵器保有国であったことからすれば，あながち非合理な態度とは言えない。

日本の司法部，とくに最高裁判所が政治部門との対立を避ける傾向があるとの指摘はしばしばなされる。それは，最高裁判所が違憲判断を示すことがきわめて稀であることに典型的に現れていると言われる。その原因については，さまざまな見方がある。国会で成立する法律のほとんどがいわゆる閣法（法案を内閣が提出したもの）であって，事前に内閣法制局によって綿密な審査を経ており，違憲の疑いのある法律案が提出されることが考えにくいとの観察もある（いわゆる安保関連法については，このことはあてはまらない）。また，最高裁は個別の事件における当事者の救済こそが自身の核心的任務だと心得ており，そのため，当事者の救済のために必須と言い得る場合にのみ憲法判断を示すのだとの観察もある（最高裁判事であった藤田宙靖教授による『最高裁回想録』〔有斐閣，2012〕115頁以下参照）。

他方，日本の司法部は，社会生活の各方面で男女の差別の抑止や雇用の保護のために積極的な役割を果たしてきたのであり，その際，「社会通念」が根拠としてしばしば援用されてはいるが，実際には裁判所があるべき社会通念を想定しつつ民法90条等の一般条項を利用し，社会規範の積極的創造を行ってきたとの観察もある（フランク・アッパム〔岸野薫訳〕「日米における政治と司法の機能」土井真一ほか著『岩波講座　憲法4』〔岩波書店，2007〕）。判例に現れる「社会通念」が事実上のものではなく，最高裁が想定するあるべき社会通念であることは，最高裁自身も指摘している（例：最大判昭和32・3・13刑集11巻3号997頁《チャタ

レー事件》)。

　本件判決が，正調の統治行為論にのっとった苫米地事件判決（最大判昭和35・6・8民集14巻7号1206頁）とは異なり，「一見極めて明白に違憲無効」である場合には，高度の政治性を有する問題についても憲法判断に踏み込むとの姿勢を示した背景については，長谷部恭男「砂川事件判決における『統治行為』論」同『憲法の論理』〔有斐閣，2017〕第13章参照。そこでも描いたように，一国の軍事戦略と憲法の基本原理との間には深い連関がある。

　なお，本件判決は，集団的自衛権の行使を認める根拠となると言われることがあるが，本件では日本による集団的自衛権の行使は全く論点となっていない。片言隻句を文脈から切り離して捉えた暴論と言うしかない主張である（長谷部恭男編『検証・安保法案』〔有斐閣，2015〕4-5頁参照）。

Mitsubishi jushi, K.K. v. Takano

27 Saihan minshu 1536 (Sup. Ct. Dec. 12, 1973).

三菱樹脂事件
(最大判昭和 48 年 12 月 12 日民集 27 巻 11 号 1536 頁)

1 The facts

Upon graduating from the elite Tohoku University in 1963, Tatsuo Takano applied for a job with Mitsubishi Plastics, Inc. Company representatives interviewed him and offered him a job. At the end of his three-month probation, however, they flatly dismissed him. He had lied about his political activities during college, they explained. He had lied both on his application form and in his interview.

Takano had explicitly denied participating in any political organizations. In its application form, Mitsubishi Plastic had asked about membership in political groups, and he had written "none." When interviewed, he had claimed that he had worked long hours in the student cooperative "in order to pay school expenses." He "hadn't had the time to participate in the student movements," he explained. But in truth, he "hadn't had any interest in them anyway."[1]

In fact, the statements were not even remotely true. Takano had spent his college career on the local Central Committee of the militantly New-Left Zengakuren. As part of the group, he had joined

---

[1] Takano v. Mitsubishi jushi, K.K., (Tokyo D. Ct. July 17, 1967), at www.cc.kyoto-su.ac.jp/~suga/hanrei/8-1.html.

15

the 330,000-strong Tokyo protests in 1960 over the U.S.-Japan security treaty. The ensuing riots had left one student dead, Eisenhower's planned trip cancelled, and Kishi's legacy as Prime Minister in tatters.

Takano sued Mitsubishi Plastics for his job. He cited several grounds. Article 14 of the Constitution provided:

> All of the people are equal under the law and there shall be no discrimination in political, economic or social relations because of race, creed, sex, social status or family origin.

He added Article 19:

> Freedom of thought and conscience shall not be violated.

And he cited Sec. 3 of the Labor Standards Act:[2]

> An employer shall not engage in discriminatory treatment with respect to wages, working hours or other working conditions by reason of the nationality, creed or social status of any worker.

The junior-most judge usually writes the opinion for a panel, and the junior-most judge on Takano's case was Yasuhisa Tanaka. Tanaka had been a member of the Young Jurists League, a group loosely affiliated with the Communist Party. The District Court duly found in Takano's favor, and the High Court affirmed.[3] True, Takano had lied about his political activities, but only because Mitsubishi Plastics had asked about them. Given that the Constitution protected freedom of political beliefs, wrote the lower courts, he could properly

---

[2] Rodo kijun ho [Labor Standards Act], Law No. 49 of 1947, as translated in http://www.ilo.org/dyn/natlex/docs/WEBTEXT/27776/64846/E95JPN01.htm#a001.

[3] Takano v. Mitsubishi jushi, K.K., (Tokyo D. Ct. July 17, 1967), at www.cc.kyoto-su.ac.jp/~suga/hanrei/8-1.html, affirmed, Takano v. Mitsubishi jushi, K.K. shiso undo kenkyu sho, ed., Osorubeki Saiban [Fearsome Trials](Tokyo: Zenbo sha, 1969)., (Tokyo High Ct. June 12, 1968), at www.cc.kyoto-su.ac.jp/~suga/hanrei/8-2.html.

lie.

The lower court judges went out of their way to sec-ond-guess the employees Mitsubishi Plastics needed. The High Court explained: [4]

> An employee's thoughts and beliefs will not injure a firm's performance. To require an applicant to report his po-litical thoughts and beliefs on his hiring examination violates the public order and good morals [of Civil Code, Sec. 90].

Indeed, continued the court, in lying Takano did nothing fraudulent: [5]

> The facts which he hid and about which he filed his false report were facts about his political thoughts and be-liefs. Employees may properly hide these facts when taking a firm's hiring examination. They do not act fraudulently in hiding them or in filing falses report about them.

Sitting en banc, the Supreme Court unanimously reversed. Much as a U.S. court would have done, it explained that the Consti-tution only regulated the relations between citizens and the state. It does not govern relations between private parties. Given that this dispute involved only a private firm and a private applicant, the Con-stitution did not apply.

Takano and Mitsubishi Plastics settled out of court in 1976. As part of that deal, the firm hired him for one of its smaller subsid-iaries. The firm had already won at the Supreme Court. Why it now offered him a job in a subsidiary illustrates the character of the New Left groups in 1970s Japan.

In 1962, part of the Zengakuren would split off as the Chuka-

---

[4] Takano v. Mitsubishi jushi, K.K., Tokyo High Ct. June 12, 1968), at www.cc.kyo-to-su.ac.jp/~suga/hanrei/8-2.html.

[5] Takano v. Mitsubishi jushi, K.K., Tokyo High Ct. June 12, 1968), at www.cc.kyo-to-su.ac.jp/~suga/hanrei/8-2.html.

ku-ha (the Revolutionary Communist League). Their rivals in the Zenga-kuren would split off as the Kakumaru-ha (the Japanese Revolutionary Communist League Revolutionary Marxist faction). Both were virulently violent Trotskyite groups, and by the 1970s were locked in a murderous feud. In 1970, police recorded 175 clashes among fringe-left groups. The pitched battles left 527 people injured and 2 dead. By 1975, police counted 229 clashes that left 543 people injured and 20 dead. Of those 20, 16 had died in the war between the Chukaku-ha and the Kakumaru-ha.[6] The Japanese Red Army hijacked a JAL plane to North Korea in 1970. In 1972, it took over a mountain lodge, executed 12 of its own members, and ended the seige only with a shootout that killed two police and a community member.

According to one investigative firm, after losing at the Supreme Court Takano's "supporters" began organizing demonstrations. They ran these demonstrations outside the homes of the board members of Mitsubishi Plastics' parent corporation Mitsubishi Chemical.[7] The firm does not detail what sort of supporters these might have been. Given Takano's background in the Chukaku-ha, however, it would not be unreasonable to think the demonstrations might have left the board members uneasy. To convince these men and women to leave them alone, the directors apparently —— in 1976 —— offered Takano a job after all.

2 The reasoning

Obviously, the Supreme Court's decision was massively

---

[6] J. Mark Ramseyer & Minoru Nakazato, Japanese Law 160 (Chicago: University of Chicago Press, 1999).

[7] Nomura Yasuhiro konin kaikeishi, Mitsubishi jushi jiken to ha [Regarding the Mitsubishi Plastics Case]. Available at http://www.fuseichosa.jp/2014/02/17.

over-determined. Takano lied about his political activities —— both on the application forms and at the hiring interview. Honesty matters. Quite reasonably, firms care whether the people they hire tell the truth. Takano did not tell the truth —— and Mitsubishi Plastics did not want to employ him.

Second, Takano had led a hyper-violent New Left group. The Zengakuren was not a public charity. It was not a get-out-the-vote campaign or a university legal aid clinic. It was a New Left student group. During the very time that Takano worked on the Central Committee, the Tohoku University Zengakuren had transformed itself into the Chukaku-ha terrorist group.

At stake is the principle of freedom of choice in private markets. Firms value talent and ability, but they also value fit. They want people who will share the firm's goals, who will sacrifice to help accomplish them, and who will help build cohesive group dynamics among their co-workers. Firms do not necessarily care about politics in their own right. But they do care about politics if a worker's preferences correlate with other attributes that matter directly.

"[V]oluntary sorting can reduce the costs of making and enforcing group decisions," explains Richard Epstein.[8] If firms can choose the workers they want, and workers can choose the firms they want, then workers and firms will sort themselves in ways that benefit both. Workers and firms may sort themselves along characteristics that strike outsiders as dubious —— but not necessarily because of any bias. They sort along those lines because the characteristics correlate with other attributes that contribute to the requisite group dynamics. The sorting can take "place on racial, ethnic, religious, or sexual lines," notes Epstein:

---

[8] Richard A. Epstein, Forbidden Grounds: The Case Against Employment Discrimination Laws 67-68 (Cambridge: Harvard University Press, 1992).

[P]ersons who are 'the same' in some fundamental way are more likley to bring similar preferences to the workplace. … Workers may prefer to sort themselves out by language. It is easier and cheaper for everyone if Spanish-speaking workers work with Spanish-speaking workers and Polish-speaking workers with Polish-speaking workers, all other things held constant. … The commonality of preferences may extend beyond language to other features of collective life: the music played in the workplace, the food that is brought in for lunch, the holidays on which the business is to be closed down, the banter around the coffeepot, the places chosen for firm outings, and a thousand other small details that contribute to the efficiency of the firm.

Ultimately, this is the value —— freedom of choice and association in private markets —— that the Supreme Court affirmed in *Mitsubishi Plastics*.

解 説　COMMENT　**憲法の基本権条項は私人間に適用されるか**

　本件判決は，憲法の基本権条項が私人間の紛争について，どのように「適用」されるか（されないか）に関して，間接適用説を採用したものだと理解されている。基本権条項は私人間の紛争に直接には適用されない。ただし，民法90条や709条を典型とする私法上の一般的・概括的条項の解釈にあたって基本権条項の趣旨が勘案されることがある。私人間の紛争に適用されるのは，あくまで私法上の条項である。その意味内容を理解するにあたって，基本権条項の趣旨が勘案されるにとどまる。この立場が「間接適用説」と言われる。

　基本権条項は実際に「適用」されてはいない。むしろ無効力と言うべきではないかと言われることもある（高橋和之「『憲法上の人権』の効力は私人間に及ばない」ジュリスト1245号137頁）。ただ，基本権条項が「適用」されているか否

20

かは，肝心な問題ではない。そもそも，基本権条項が「適用」される典型的な場面である公権力と私人との紛争においても，基本権条項の果たす役割は，通常の法令の役割とはきわめて異なっているからである。

現代の代表的な法哲学者であるジョゼフ・ラズの議論が，この点で参照に値する（簡単な紹介として，長谷部恭男『法とは何か』〔増補改訂版〕〔河出書房新社，2015〕1章および8章参照）。人はどのように生きるか，どう行動するかにあたって，理由 (reason) に照らして自分で考え，自分で判断する。法もそうした理由の一種であるが，しかし民事法や刑事法など，通常の法令は，特殊な理由として働く。こうした法令は「自分で判断するな，私の言う通りにしろ，その方が，あなたが本来とるべき行動をよりよくとることができるから」と主張する。法令は「権威 authority」であると主張するわけである。多くの場合，人々はそうした法令の主張を尊重し，法令に沿って行動する。

ところが，法令に沿って行動することが道理に合わないこと，本来とるべき行動をとることにならないことも，例外的にはある。そうしたときに出番が来るのが，基本権条項である。「表現の自由を尊重せよ」「人はみな平等だ」と宣言する基本権条項は，「自分で判断するな，私の言う通りにしろ」と言っているわけではない。「人はみな平等だ」と言われても，どう行動すればいいか具体的には見当がつかない。基本権条項は，人々の判断を遮断しその行動を枠付ける通常の法令とは異なる役割を果たしている。基本権条項は，法令の権威主張を脇に置いて，そもそもの出発点であったはずの，自分で考え自分で判断する地平，つまり実践理性一般の地平に戻れ，と言っている。そう呼びかけられているのは直接には裁判官である。裁判官も人間であるから，究極的には，どのように紛争を解決するかを自分の良心に照らして，つまり理由に照らして自分で考えるしかない。

通常の法令とは異なる役割を果たすこうした条項は，民事法や刑事法の中にもある。民法90条や709条，刑法35条などがそれである。こうした条項を具体の事件に適用するにあたっては，やはり，実践理性一般の地平に立ち戻る必要がある場合が少なくない。これらの条項の意味内容を理解するにあたって，基本権条項が「間接適用」されているか，それとも適用されていないかは，したがって本質的な問題ではない。「実践理性一般の地平に立ち戻れ」という声に，必要に応じて耳を傾けることができるか否かが問題である。

営利企業が労働者の雇い入れに際して，思想信条を調査しようとするの
は，労働力の品質が思想信条と関連していると営利企業が信じているからであ
る。労働力の品質は何年も働かせてみないと本当にはわからない。そこで，こ
の隠された品質を示すと企業の側が信じている別のわかりやすい指標（出身大
学，所属したクラブ，場合によっては人種や性別等）をもとに雇い入れるか否か
を決することになる。企業にとっての情報費用は主観的には低下する。問題は，
企業が信じている関連性が，実際に存在するか否かである。一般論として，思
想信条が労働力の品質と関連することが，どれほどあるだろうか。

　最高裁は，こうした裏付けの不確かな関連性に関する想定（偏見）に基づい
て雇い入れの可否を決することも，企業の契約の自由の一環であると認めたこ
とになる。もっとも，そうした自由を法令によって制約することが違憲だとま
で言っているわけではない。

Kurokawa v. Chiba ken senkyo kanri iinkai

30 Saihan minshu 223 (Sup. Ct. Apr. 14, 1976).

衆議院議員定数配分規定違憲訴訟
(最大判昭和 51 年 4 月 14 日民集 30 巻 3 号 223 頁)

1 The facts

The dispute concerned the December 1972 election to the lower house. In the election, voters each held one non-transferrable vote, but together selected several representatives (with one exception, 3 to 5 members) from each district. At the time of the last reapportionment in 1964, the least-represented district had held twice the population per legislator as the most-represented district. As people moved steadily from rural prefectures to the metropolitan centers, that ratio climbed from 2 : 1 to 5 : 1.

A voter from Chiba in suburban Tokyo challenged the 1972 election on the grounds that it violated the principle in Article 14 of the Constitution that all people be "equal under the law."

2 The decision

The Supreme Court held the unequal apportionment unconstitutional. Were it to void the election, however, it would leave the legislature without the representatives necessary to reapportion the districts. To avoid the resulting quandary, it declined to do so.

3 Discussion

a. The history Legislative districts need not turn unconstitutional suddenly, noted the Supreme Court. Instead, as people move from district to district, the inequality increases gradually. Eventually, it may reach the point where the disproportionate legislative representation becomes impermissible. Charged by the Constitution with drawing district lines, the legislature will need to redraw the districts. Because this takes time, districts become unconstitutional only if the legislature does not correct the electoral inequality within a reasonable amount of time.

The Supreme Court had faced a challenge to legislative districts in 1964. At the time, the difference in representation between the least- and most-represented districts had been 4 : 1. That inequality the Court had held constitutional.[1]

Consequently, the 1976 opinion represented the first time that the Supreme Court held an apportionment scheme unconstitutional. Since then, it has held disproportionate representation unconstitutional several times. Already in 1975 (before the Court issued this opinion), the legislature had redrawn district lines to reduce the disproportionate representation to 2.92 : 1. The migration to the cities continued, however, and by 1980 that ratio had climbed to 3.94 : 1. When voters sued, the Supreme Court declared the apportionment unacceptable. However, it reasoned that the legislature had not yet had time to draw new districts, and declined to hold it unconstitutional yet.[2] By 1983 the ratio of representation at the least- to most-represented districts had climbed to 4.4 : 1. The Court now held it unconstitutional (though it

---

[1] Koshiyama v. Tokyo to senkyo kanri iinkai, 18 Saihan minshu 270 (Sup. Ct. Feb. 5, 1964).

[2] [No Parties given], 37 Saihan minshu 1243 (Sup. Ct. Nov. 7, 1983).

again opted not to void the election).[3]

In 1986, the legislature redrew the districts. It lowered the least- to most-represented ratio to 2.99 : 1, and the Supreme Court held the apportionment scheme constitutional.[4] When the ratio again hit 3.18 : 1 in the 1990 election, the Supreme Court held it unacceptable. On the grounds that the legislature had not yet had time to revise the districts, it once more declined to hold them unconstitutional.[5] The legislature redrew the lines, brought the ratio back to 2.82 : 1, and the Supreme Court held the new districts constitutional in 1992.[6]

b. The U.S. comparison American readers of these Japanese cases routinely feign outrage. They declare it strange that a Court would hold a 2 : 1 ratio constitutional. They pronounce it stranger still that it would hold a 5 : 1 ratio unconstitutional but refuse to void the elections.

"The lady doth protest too much," as Shakespeare put it. U.S. courts do hold districts for the House of Representative to exacting standards.[7] But American readers forget that California and Wyoming both elect two Senators. California has a population of 37.7 million, and Wyoming of 580,000. The relevant ratio for the U.S. Senate is 65 : 1.

c. The politics The more intriguing question concerns Jap-

---

[3] Kanao v. Hiroshima ken senkyo kanri iinkai, 39 Saihan minshu 1100 (Sup. Ct. July 17, 1985).

[4] Miyakawa v. Chiba senkyo iinkai, 42 Saihan minshu 644 (Sup. Ct. Oct. 21, 1988).

[5] Kawahara v. Tokyo to senkyo kanri iinkai, 47 Saihan minshu 67 (Sup. Ct. Jan. 20, 1993).

[6] Kasuga v. Tokyo to senkyo kanri iinkai, 49 Saihan minshu 1443 (Sup. Ct. June 8, 1995).

[7] Subject to a variety of caveats, discussed in, e.g., Sanford Levinson, One Person, One Vote: A Mantra in Need of Meaning, 80 N.C. L. Rev. 1269 (2002).

Table 1 Fastest and Slowest Growing Prefectures,1960-1990, in Thousands

	1960	1970	1980	1990	Growth, 1960–80
Japan	93,419	103,720	117,060	123,611	0.25
Saitama-ken	2,431	3,866	5,420	6,405	1.23
Chiba-ken	2,306	3,367	4,735	5,555	1.05
Kanagawa-ken	3,443	5,472	6,924	7,980	1.01
Nara-ken	781	930	1,209	1,375	0.55
Osaka-fu	5,505	7,620	8,473	8,735	0.54
Aichi-ken	4,206	5,386	6,222	6,691	0.48
Hyogo-ken	3,906	4,668	5,145	5,405	0.32
Shiga-ken	843	890	1,080	1,222	0.28
Kyoto-fu	1,993	2,250	2,527	2,602	0.27
Hiroshima-ken	2,184	2,436	2,739	2,850	0.25
Iwate-ken	1,449	1,371	1,422	1,417	−0.02
Tokushima-ken	847	791	825	832	−0.03
Kochi-ken	855	787	831	825	−0.03
Kumamoto-ken	1,856	1,700	1,790	1,840	−0.04
Yamagata-ken	1,321	1,226	1,252	1,258	−0.05
Akita-ken	1,336	1,241	1,257	1,227	−0.06
Saga-ken	943	838	866	878	−0.08
Kagoshima-ken	1,963	1,729	1,785	1,798	−0.09
Nagasaki-ken	1,760	1,570	1,591	1,563	−0.10
Shimane-ken	889	774	785	781	−0.12

anese politics. After all, as noted in connection with the *Sunagawa* case (Case 1), the ruling Liberal Democratic Party (LDP) exercises indirect but strong control over the courts. Through the 1960s and early 1970s, the party catered to the farm vote. That worked as long as Japan remained rural, but these were years of massive internal migration. From 1960 to 1980, the population in three prefectures adjoining Tokyo (Saitama, Chiba, and Kanagawa) more than doubled (Table 1) . The population in rural prefectures in Kyushu and the northeast declined.

The migration split the LDP. Representatives from solidly LDP districts in the rural areas fought to keep their places in the legislature. The party leadership, however, increasingly saw this strategy as unsustainable. Rather than rely on the dwindling farm vote, they sought to reposition the LDP as a party of the urban consumer. They recognized that this strategy would cost them loyal representatives from rural districts, but reasoned that it would work to the party's advantage long-term.

The courts followed the LDP leadership. At the time of the 1964 challenge, the party still relied on the rural vote, and the Supreme Court held the inequality constitutional. By 1976, however, the party was locked in an internal battle: its leaders wanted to shift the party toward the urban consumer, while individual politicians sought to keep their rural seats.

In *Kurokawa*, the Supreme Court followed the party leaders. Through the case, it forced the LDP to redraw district lines. Effectively, it forced it to shift its base from the farms to the cities.

Return, then, to the study of lower court judicial careers introduced in the context of the *Sunagawa* case (Case1). By the late 20th century, the lower courts had published 69 opinions on electoral apportionment claims. Take these cases, hold constant a variety of proxies for judicial ability, and ask whether a decision holding electoral districts unconstitutional affected a judge's career.

Before the lower court opinion in *Kurokawa*, an opinion finding the districts unconstitutional did indeed hurt a judge's career. A judge who held the districts unconstitutional before 1974 spent a larger fraction of the decade after the opinion in branch offices, and less time in prestigious administrative posts. After 1974, that effect disappeared. The Supreme Court had signalled that it supported the LDP leadership in shifting the party away from the rural vote. After it did so, a judge who held electoral districts unconstitutional no longer risked his career.[8]

解説 COMMENT　投票価値の較差

　投票価値の較差に関する訴訟は，公職選挙法上の選挙無効訴訟の形式を借りて提起されているが，選挙無効訴訟は，そもそも選挙区割りや定数配分自体の違憲性を理由に提起されることを予定していないこともあって，いくつかの論点につき，最高裁による創造的判断が求められることになった。

　第一に，選挙無効訴訟は選挙区ごとの選挙の有効性を争うものであるため，当該選挙区の投票価値と全国の平均値との較差のみを争うことができるのか，それとも当該選挙区にとどまらず配分規定全体の最大較差をも違憲の理由として主張できるのかという論点が生ずる。この点につき最高裁は，議員定数の配分は議員総数と関連させながら，相互に有機的な関連をもって行われ，不可分の一体をなすものであるから，原告は配分規定全体の最大較差の違憲性を主張し得るし，また，違憲の瑕疵も配分規定全体に及ぶとした。

　第二に最高裁は，投票価値の不平等が国会の裁量権の行使として合理性を是認し得ない状態に達することで直ちに配分規定の違憲性が帰結するわけではなく，違憲との判断は，国会が憲法上要求される合理的な期間内にその是正を行わなかった場合にはじめて下されるとした（合理的期間論）。これは，投票価値の不平等が人口の変動などにより変化するものであることから，国会にある程度の猶予期間を与えようとの考慮に基づくものである。

---

[8] We include the detailed statistical results in J. Mark Ramseyer & Eric B. Rasmusen, Why Are Japanese Judges so Conservative in Politically Charged Cases?, 95 Am. Pol. Sci. Rev. 331 (2001).

第三に，投票価値の不平等が国会の合理的裁量を超え，かつ，是正に必要な合理的期間を徒過した場合，配分規定は全体として違憲の瑕疵を帯びることとなり，それに基づく当該選挙区の選挙も違法と判断されることになるが，その帰結として，当該選挙区の選挙が無効とされるべきかという問題がある。本件大法廷判決は，選挙を無効とすれば当該選挙区の議員がいなくなるだけであり，また全国で同様の訴訟が提起されれば，大多数の議員がいなくなってしまう等の憲法の所期しない不当な結果が生ずることを指摘して，行政事件訴訟法31条1項の定める事情判決制度の背景にある法の基本原則に基づき，選挙が違法であることを主文で宣言するが，選挙を無効とする請求は棄却すべきであるとした。

　もっとも，憲法の所期しない結果が生ずる可能性があることを理由につねに事情判決の法理に基づき選挙を無効とする請求を棄却し続けるならば，国会が投票価値の較差を是正しようとしなくなるという，やはり憲法の所期しない結果がもたらされる危険がある。その後の投票価値の較差にかかわるいくつかの大法廷判決には，いったん事情判決の法理に基づいて違憲性が指摘された選挙区割りについて，国会による是正がなされず，そのまま次の選挙が行われた場合には，選挙を無効とせざるを得ない場合もある旨を指摘する個別意見が付されている（最大判昭和60・7・17民集39巻5号1100頁，最大判平成24・10・17民集66巻10号3357頁等）。

Isa v. Kono

48 Saihan minshu 149 (Sup. Ct. Feb. 8, 1994).

ノンフィクション「逆転」事件
(最判平成 6 年 2 月 8 日民集 48 巻 2 号 149 頁)

1 The facts

It was three in the morning on an August night in subtropical Okinawa, 1964. Two American marines and four young Japanese men met on the street. They had been drinking. They brawled. And when they finished, one of the Americans lay in the street, dead.[1]

Okinawa was under American control at the time, and the U.S. government prosecuted the four men for battery and the Japanese crime of bodily injury leading to death (similar to manslaughter). The four faced a U.S.-style 12-member jury trial. Eleven of the twelve argued for conviction, and one for acquittal. After long deliberation, the twelve compromised and convicted the four only of battery. The judge then sentenced three of the men to three-year prison terms.

The juror who argued for acquital was one Chihiro Isa. The U.S. government had used its bases on Okinawa to stage its increasingly unpopular war in Vietnam. Like many Okinawans (and like many

---

[1] Background facts can be seen at, e.g., Tadayasu Ozaki, Shohyo [Book Review], 56 Aichi kyoiku daigaku kenkyu hokoku 169 (2007); Gyakuten, gyakuten, mata gyakuten [Reversed, Reversed, and Reversed Again], available at http://ishigurokenji.com/report/report_159.html.

Japanese on the mainland), Isa thought the American presence on the island an outrage. He also thought the trial of the four a travesty. And the three-year sentence for battery he interpreted as a judicial end-run around independent jurors. The jury had acquitted the four of the serious crime (at Isa's urging), and Isa reasoned that the American judge had imposed the sentence he wanted to impose for the serious crime on the lighter crime instead. About it all, he wrote a book.

Envisioning his book as non-fiction, Isa decided to use the four men's real names. After all, he wanted to exonerate them of the reputational harm caused by unfair U.S. policy. From three of the four, he obtained consent to use their names. He tried to find the fourth as well, but could not locate him. He published the book with the names of all four, acquired considerable fame, and won a book prize.

In fact, the fourth man had left the island to escape his notoriety. After serving his prison sentence, he had moved to Tokyo and hidden his past. He hid his conviction on his job application, and found employment driving a bus. He hid it from prospective wives, and married a co-worker. Now, the national television network planned a documentary based on Isa's book. Determined to interview all four men, the network found the fourth and asked him to appear on the program.

The man panicked. Should news of his conviction surface, he feared that his employer would fire him. He feared that his wife would divorce him. He sued to enjoin the network, and settled for its agreement not to use his real name.

The man then sued Isa for using his name in the book and disclosing his past. He did not argue that Isa had said anything untrue. Given that Isa had fought to acquit him of the serious crime, Isa was not even unsympathetic. In fact, when the man's past hit the news on the mainland, the bus company did not fire him anyway, and neither did his wife leave him. But the man had wanted his past kept secret, and Isa had documented it. For this, he demanded compensation.

The district court awarded the man 500,000 yen, and the high court affirmed.[2] He had had a legally protected interest in keeping his past to himself, it reasoned. Isa had no compelling reason to disclose his name. By telling the world about the man's past, he committed a tort.

The Supreme Court affirmed. Criminal convictions and prison time go to honor and trust, it reasoned. For a man struggling to rehabilitate himself, its disclosure can have serious consequences. In order to encourage ex-convicts to rehabilitate themselves, the courts should protect their interest in living peaceably without fear of disclosure.

At stake, the Court continued, was a balancing test. The outcome might be different if a crime involved historical or social significance. It might be different if the person concerned were a prominent member of society or running for public office. But here the man (a simple bus driver) was a private individual, the crime (a drunken brawl) involved no significance, and the event was now long past (twelve years). The man's interest in keeping the information private outweighed any public interest in its disclosure.

2 The U.S. comparison

The ex-convict trying to live a quiet life in Tokyo would not have recovered "at common law." The outcome in this case is not the judgment a U.S. court would have issued in the 19th century. At com-

---

[2] Kono v. Isa, 1987 WLJPCA 11201051, (Tokyo D. Ct. Nov. 20, 1987), aff'd, 1323 Hanrei jiho 37 (Tokyo High Ct. Sept. 5, 1989).

mon law, courts let a person recover for statements about his private life only if they were false. If false, he could sue for defamation —— slander if spoken, libel if written. When true, he lost —— for truth was always an absolute defense.[3]

As the Second Restatement of Torts put it, a plaintiff could sue on a statement only if "false and defamatory" (Sec. 558). Conversely:

> One who publishes a defamatory statement of fact is not subject to liability for defamation if the statement is true.

The Restatement (2d) of Torts, Sec. 581A. The official Comment (a) to the section continued:

> To create liability for defamation there must be publication of matter that is both defamatory and false. ... There can be no recovery in defamation for a statement of fact that is true, [even if] the statement is made for no good purpose and is inspired by ill will toward the person about whom it is published and is made solely for the purpose of harming him.

Faced with an ex-convict who sought to start life anew in a distant city, a 19th-century U.S. judge would not have done what Supreme Court did here. He would not have balanced the convict's interest in rehabilitation against the author's (or the public's) interest in documenting the past. He would simply have asked whether the author's account were true. If it were, the ex-convict lost.

The law has changed in the U.S. Often, scholars attribute the change to Samuel Warren and Louis Brandeis.[4] Writing in 1890, the two urged judges to adopt a "right to be let alone." Newspapers were

---

[3] See W. Page Keeton, Defamation and Freedom of the Press, 54 Tex. L. Rev. 1221 (1976).

[4] Samuel D. Warren & Louis D. Brandeis, The Right to Privacy, 4 Harv. L. Rev. 193 (1890).

publishing gossip. They were not necessarily saying anything false, but they were bothering the people discussed, and providing (claimed Warren and Brandeis) no public benefit. "The press is overstepping in every direction the obvious bounds of propriety and of decency,"[5] they declared. The courts should protect the public from that press.

Many courts now let people recover for publications even when true. Often, they explain that they protect a "right to privacy." In many ways, they take a position much like that of the Japanese Supreme Court. Perhaps the principal difference concerns their approach to public documents like criminal records.[6] After all, they have voided as unconstitutional some statutes designed to stop the press from publishing the names of people prosecuted. As the Supreme Court put it in 1977:[7]

> [T]he First and Fourteenth Amendments will not permit a state court to prohibit the publication of widely disseminated information obtained at court proceedings which were in fact open to the public.

A recent variation on this right to privacy appears as the European "right to be forgotten."[8] The *Isa* case dates from the days before the internet, of course, while the modern right to be forgotten directly targets internet searches. But the logic behind the two approaches track each other. The European right lets people demand that Google and its competitors remove old material that is personal even when true. Here, for example, is how the European Commission

---

[5] Id. at 196.

[6] See generally Erwin Chemerinsky, Rediscovering Brandeis's Right to Privacy, 45 Brandeis L.J. 643 (2006).

[7] Oklahoma Publishing Co. v. District Court, 430 U.S. 308, 310 (1977); see also Smith v. Daily Mail Publishing Co., 443 U.S. 97 (1979); Cox Broadcasting Corp. v. Cohn, 420 U.S. 469 (1975).

[8] European Commission, Factsheet on the "Right to be forgotten" ruling.

described a recent case involving the new right:

> In 2010 a Spanish citizen lodged a complaint against a Spanish newspaper ... and ... Google Inc. The citizen complained that an auction notice of his repossessed home on Google's search results infringed his privacy rights because the proceedings concerning him had been fully resolved for a number of years and hence the reference to these was entirely irrelevant. He requested ... [that] Google Inc. be required to remove the personal data relating to him ....

The European Union Court held, on May 13, 2014:

> Individuals have the right - under certain conditions - to ask search engines to remove links with personal information about them. This applies where the information is ... irrelevant or excessive for the purposes of data processing .... The ... Court explicitly clarified that the right to be forgotten is not absolute but will always need to be balanced against other fundamental rights, such as the freedom of expression and of the media .... A case-by-case assessment is needed considering the type of information in question, its sensitivity for the individual's private life and the interest of the public in having access to that information.

Whether Google searches or Isa's book, the logic is the same. Private citizens have an interest in keeping their past to themselves. Even when information about that past is true, they may want to keep it private. Whether they can stop others (Google, nonfiction authors) from publicizing it depends on the balance between the public's interest in disclosure and the individual's interest in privacy.

3 Protecting fraud?

Perhaps the oddest dimension to this case involves the plaintiff's damages. He sued to enjoin the broadcasting station from using his name, and sued Isa for disclosing his name in the book. To explain his claim, he gave two reasons:

(a) He had hidden his past when he applied for his job as a bus driver. Should his employer learn of the conviction, it might fire him for lying on his job application.

(b) He had hidden his past from his wife. Should she learn of the conviction, she might divorce him for lying to her about his past.

By awarding damages for this claim, the court effectively announced that it will help men deceive their employers and wives.

Members of the public may have an interest in helping ex-convicts start their lives afresh, but they do not have an interest in helping ex-convicts do it by lying about their crimes. The court declares that if an ex-convict can hide his past for twenty years, then it will help him keep it hidden for the rest of his life. This sends exactly the wrong message. Given the public interest in helping ex-convicts start new lives *honestly*, the right message is to tell ex-convicts: lie about your past, and you will live the rest of your life in fear of exposure.

The character of the defendant turns this case particularly perverse. Isa was not negligent. Neither was he malicious. Instead, he made a good faith effort to find the fourth man and obtain his consent; he failed to find him only because the man had deliberately hidden himself. He published what he did to exonerate the fourth man; he thought the U.S. government had mistreated him, and sought to demonstrate that fact.

In the U.S. context, the well-known University of Chicago law professor, Harry Kalven, Jr., nicely captured the problem with suits like this.[9] By starting the courts down this path, he explained, Warren and Brandeis started them toward a mistake:

Although privacy is for me a great and important value, tort law's effort to protect the right of privacy seems to me a mistake.

At root, the tort was simply too nebulous. Virtually any publication could generate a claim. The rules were so vague that no journalist (or author) was necessarily safe —— and journalists cannot write if every article potentially generates a claim:

> We do not know what constitutes a prima facie case, we do not know on what basis damages are to be measured, we do not know whether the basis of liability is limited to intentional invasions or includes also negligent invasions and even strict liability.

The problem, as he put it, was that the tort had no boundaries:

> The conduct, I take it, will involve some reference to the plaintiff in the mass media without his consent, which reference must involve the use of his name, his likeness, or some recognizable personal detail of his personality or bigraphy. And, ... the reference will be an accurate one. The problem of definition then is to state what less than every such unconsented-to reference is prima facie tortious.

The *Isa* decision does not differ qualitatively from similar cases in the U.S., but it is more extreme. Ask what article about a past crime, after this case, is *not* potentially tortious. When will an author know he can publish a person's name? Isa had been accurate. He had been sympathetic. He had used public information. The only loss to the plaintiff involved a job and a marriage that he had obtained through deception.

If Isa's book is tortious, when can an author safely write

▼9 Harry Kalven, Jr., Privacy in Tort Law —— Were Warren and Brandeis Wrong?, 31 L. & Cont. Prob. 326 (1966).

about any criminal case?

解説 COMMENT　プライバシーは何を守るのか

　本件判決はプライバシーという概念を使用していないが，結論を導く上で総合的な利益衡量のアプローチが用いられるべきだとされた点も含め，現在ではプライバシーに関する権威ある先例として扱われている（最判平成15・3・14民集57巻3号229頁〔長良川事件報道訴訟〕等）。プライバシーという概念の下で，何が守られようとしているのかについては，見解の対立がある。実際には，いくつかの異なる性質の利益が問題となっている。

　このことは，表現の自由についても言えることであろう。表現の自由を守ることがなぜ重要なのかという問いに対しては，①公共的な利益に関する多様で豊かな情報空間を形成することで，民主的な政治過程を維持することに役立つ，②多様な情報や見解に触れることで，各自が自律的に人格を形成し，発展させることに役立つ，③商品やサービスに関する多様で豊かな情報を流通させることで，消費者の賢い選択や経済活動の振興に役立つ等，さまざまな答を提示することができる。そのうち，一つだけが正解で他は誤っているというわけではないであろう。表現の自由を保障することは，さまざまな利益の実現に貢献する。

　プライバシーもさまざまな利益の実現に役立つ。①他人の批判の目から自由な領域を確保することで個人が自律的に各々の能力・性向を発展させる場を保障する。②私的な場面での政治的討論や結集の機会を保障することで，民主的政治過程の維持と発展に貢献する。③気兼ねのないスムーズなコミュニケーションを保護することで，自由な経済活動の振興に役立つ。④自分の選ぶ相手と，自分の選ぶ程度の親密さのある人間関係を構築することができる。本件判決は，前科等をみだりに公表されないことで，犯罪者が更生し社会復帰を果たす利益もプライバシーの保護する利益として認めていることになる。

　他方で，表現の自由にもプライバシーにも，人々の利益を阻害する側面がある。所狭しとけばけばしい看板や広告を掲げれば，街の美観は損なわれる。過激なことばや知りたくもない情報で情緒を傷つけられる人も少なくないであろ

う。怪しげな宗教宣伝にひっかかって大金を失う人もいるかもしれない。プライバシーについても，本人に関する正確な情報を他人の目から隠すことになり，正確な情報を入手する費用を高めることになって社会全体の利益を損なうという指摘もある。

　本件では，表現の自由とプライバシーとが対立している。本当のことなのだから世間一般に公表しても構わないではないか，というのは一つの割り切り方である。しかし，人間は本当のことであっても，世間一般には知らせていないことが沢山ある。その中には，家族や勤め先にも知らせていないことが少なからずあるだろう。なぜ知らせていないか。その理由は，上述の通り，いくつもあるはずである。葬ったつもりの過去に囚われて生き続ける人もいるだろう。それはその人自身の問題である。他人がとやかく言うことではない。

　本件で問題とされたノンフィクション作品は，社会に貢献する情報を含んだすぐれた作品である。沖縄の現状や陪審裁判のありようを世の中に広く知らせる意義がある。しかし，そうした貢献をする上で，原告の実名を使用することが必要だったのか。最高裁は，具体的状況に即した利益衡量の末，その必要性を否定している。

CASE 5

[Unnamed Parties]

67 Saihan minshu 1320 (Sup. Ct. Sept. 4, 2013).

●

非嫡出子法定相続分違憲訴訟

(最大決平成 25 年 9 月 4 日民集 67 巻 6 号 1320 頁)

1 The facts

Take one of the two disputes behind this Supreme Court opinion. Husband H married wife W, we are told. They bore two children, the "legitimate" children L_1 and L_2. In time, H began an affair with a girl friend and bore another two children, the "illegitimate" children I_1 and I_2.

If H now died intestate, his estate would have gone to five heirs: W and his four children. By Sec. 900 (a) of the Civil Code, 1/2 of his estate would have gone to W. The other 1/2 would have gone to his children.

In fact, however, W died before H. As a result, when H died intestate, his entire estate went to his four children. By Secs. 900 (a) and (d), the two illegitimate children took half the portions of his two legitimate children. Let s represent an legitimate child's share. That child would take s/(s + s + s/2 + s/2), or 1/3. In turn, each illegitimate child would take 1/6. The two 1/3 shares and two 1/6 shares obviously total 1.

The four children fought over the estate in family court. I_1 and I_2 argued that the Sec. 900 (d) provision giving them half the amounts granted L_1 and L_2 violated Article 14 of the Constitution:

40

[T]here shall be no discrimination in political, economic or social relations because of race, creed, sex, social status or family origin.

As recently as 1995, the Supreme Court had said that Sec. 900(d) did not violate the Constitution.[1] Following that precedent, in the litigation below both the family court and the appellate court had rejected I1 and I2's claim. The two illegitimate children then appealed.

2 The decision

The Supreme Court held the legitimacy-based distinction in Sec. 900(d) unconstitutional. According to established jurisprudence, Article 14 bans only "unreasonable" discrimination. By precedent, this qualification grants the legislature considerable flexibility. And at one time, the Court explained, the legitimacy-based distinction was indeed reasonable.

But no more, held the Court. Public attitudes toward family relations have changed. Given modern attitudes, Sec. 900(d) no longer passes the "reasonableness" test. Instead, it straightforwardly violates Article 14. Because of the need for repose in legal relations, however, the Court added that the opinion did not apply retroactively.

To justify its holding, the Court pointed to a wide variety of social changes, both domestically and internationally. Within Japan, it explained, people increasingly bear children outside of marriage. They hold a wide range of opinions about the phenomenon. They no longer ascribe to the family the central role that they once assigned it. They increasingly see Sec. 900(d) as problematic, and politicians have

---

[1] Kono v. Otsuno, 1540 Hanrei jiho 3 (Sup. Ct. July 5, 1995). The issues in this chapter are explored more fully in J. Mark Ramseyer, the sins of their Fathers, in S. Levmore & F. Fagan, eds., The Timing of Lawmaking (2016).

convened multiple study sessions to amend it.

Other wealthy societies have seen changes even more extreme. In the West, people bear children outside of marriage at much higher rates. They have abandoned their earlier religious objections to illegitimacy. And they no longer maintain the distinction seen in Sec. 900 (d).

According to the Court, modern Japanese now share a consensus on the need to protect children. More specifically, they have reached a consensus on the need to protect children as individuals, and to recognize that as individuals they hold rights. Children should not stand at a disadvantage because of a decision over which they had no control. Whether their parents chose to marry represents exactly such a decision. As a result, how much they inherit from those parents should not turn on whether their parents chose to marry.

∃ Discussion

a. The facts The antiseptic Supreme Court opinion in this dispute excises virtually all the facts. For the most part, legal scholars and mainstream journalists have flooded the press with sympathy for illegitimate children and praise for the Court. A few accounts, however, add some of the missing details to one of the two cases on appeal.[2] They suggest the equities are less clear than legal scholars and mainstream journalists contend.

Apparently, H (born 1929) and W ran a restaurant together in Wakayama. They both worked at the place, and over time W bore

---

[2] Hideji Yagi, Hichakushutsushi no isan sozoku hanketsu ni okina gimon [Major Doubts about the Opinion on the Inheritance of Illegitimate Children] (Oct. 15, 2013), available at: http://seiron-sankei.com/2529; Fujiko Goto, "Sozoku sabetsu" to iu keredo [It's Called "Inheritance Discrimination," but Still] (July 2013), available at http://www.midori-lo.com/column_lawyer_77.html.

H two children. Given Japanese custom (I surmise here), H probably owned the restaurant in his own name. Further, he probably did not pay W a wage for her work. In turn, she probably did not care because her imputed wages were part of the restaurant's profits. Formally, H would have earned those profits in his own name, but substantively W would have been able to spend them for household expenses.

In time, W became ill —— according to one account, because of the long hours she spent at the restaurant.[3]   To work in her place, in 1966 H hired student L. Eventually, H and L began an affair. H then evicted W and their two children (now aged 11 and 6) from their home. He installed L in their stead, and bore another two children with her.

Presumably, H could evict his wife and children because he (given Japanese custom; I again surmise) owned the house in his own name. Yet recall that W probably received no wages for her work in the restaurant. Certainly, she received no wages for her work in the home. As a result, H would have bought and maintained this house with assets that resulted from their joint efforts. He did not buy and maintain it only with the yield from his work at the restaurant. Instead, he drew on the yield from W's work in the restaurant and her work in their home.

W continued to toil in the restaurant even after the marriage collapsed. Probably (the news accounts do not say), she now demanded explicit wages. But about the labor that she had earlier invested in the restaurant and their home, her daughter claimed she relied on the terms of the Civil Code.

"My late mother had talked to a lawyer," the daughter ex-

▼**3**   Yagi, supra note 2.

plained. "She always promised me that 'the law will protect you.' She lived in hell for more than 40 years, but she counted on the Civil Code to take her revenge on the lover and her children."[4] Of the claims of her two half-sisters, she had no sympathy. "The family peace was destroyed. We were chased out of our house. We lived with this psychological pain for 40 years. And before my father died, he transferred to the illegitimate children substantial assets. So where's the inequality?"[5]

W died before H. H himself died in 2001.

b. The rules of inheritance For all the celebration it inspired among scholars and mainstream journalists, the opinion accomplished very little. Sec. 900(d) disadvantaged illegitimate children less than those writers complained. The opinion now protects those children less than they proclaimed.

To understand why the opinion accomplishes so little, begin with the distinction between "intestacy rules" (hotei sozoku bun; Civil Code Sec. 900) and "elective shares" (iryu bun; Sec. 902, 1028). The husband in this case died without a will (died "intestate"). Social commentators routinely claim that Japanese do not write wills because writing wills is not the Japanese way of doing things. Maybe so —— though maybe not. Most stereotypes about Japanese law-related behavior are flatly false. But if this claim about Japanese cultural norms be true, perhaps H never wrote a will because he conformed with social norms (though he hardly conformed on other dimensions). On the other hand, perhaps, he never wrote a will because he simply liked the rules the courts would apply if he died intestate. Or perhaps (unfortunately, the hypothesis seems to fit these facts well) he merely skipped a will be-

---

[4] Yagi, supra note 2.
[5] Goto, supra note 2.

cause he was an irresponsible lout.

When people die without a will, the courts distribute their estate according to the legal system's intestacy rules. Because people can avoid these rules by writing a will, the rules constitute "default terms." The rules, in other words, apply "by default" when people elect not to avoid them.

The concept of "default terms" is fundamental to contract law. After all, provided contracting parties bring the requisite sophistication they can freely negotiate a broad range of terms. Yet if they had to negotiate terms to cover every possible contingency, they would spend massive resources. To help them economize on those costs, the law provides terms that apply when they do not specify terms otherwise. If the parties do not like those terms, they can negotiate terms to the contrary. But if those default terms do what they want, they can draft a shorter contract and trust the courts to apply the terms to the contingencies they did not negotiate.

The intestacy rules represent an example of a default term. Take an uncomplicated family —— a father, a mother (married to the father) and several children. If the father dies before the mother, under the Civil Code the mother takes half his assets and the children take equal parts of the remainder. The Code does this for a simple reason: it approximates the arrangement that most uncomplicated families would choose. Given that they would choose this arrangement anyway, the Code provides it as a default.

Elective shares refer to a very different concept: a mandatory minimum share of an estate. Perhaps a government has decided that wives should always inherit at least a given share of their husband's estate. Perhaps it has decided that children should always inherit at least a given share. Put otherwise, perhaps a government has decided that men should not be able entirely to disinherit their wives and children. The minimum amounts that spouses and children may

CASE
5

非嫡出子法定相続分違憲訴訟
[Unnamed Parties]

claim from a decedent represent their elective share.

Under the Civil Code, an heir's elective share is determined by multiplying his or her intestate share by half of the decedent's estate. For example, because a wife's intestate share is 1/2, her elective share is $1/2*1/2 = 1/4$. Even if her husband tries to disinherit her entirely, she may claim 1/4 of his estate. If a father dies with no wife and four legitimate children, each child has an elective share of $1/4*1/2 = 1/8$.

Return to the case at hand. H died intestate with two legitimate and two illegitimate children. Under the earlier Civil Code (as explained above), his legitimate children each took 1/3 of his estate and his illegitimate children received 1/6. On the logic that this was unfair, the court announced that all four children should receive 1/4.

Yet the old Sec. 900(d) did not prevent H from leaving his children 1/4 each; neither does the court's opinion now stop him from leaving his legitimate children twice what he leaves the other two. Suppose H had wanted to leave the children equal shares under the old code. He could accomplish this by any of three simple methods.

First, H could have written a will that left each 1/4. Recall that the intestate share of the legitimate children was 1/3 and of the illegitimate children 1/6. Since each child had an elective share equal to 1/2 the estate times that intestate share, the legitimate children had an elective share of $1/3*1/2 = 1/6$ and the illegitimate children $1/6*1/2 = 1/12$. Because the 1/4 share that they each receive under the will is larger than their elective shares, no child can block H's preferred allocation by claiming an elective share.

Second, H could have increased the amount he left his illegitimate children through "inter vivos gifts": by giving them assets before he died. According to newspaper accounts (quoted above), his legitimate children claimed he did exactly that. If the court then awarded each child 1/4 of the estate that remained after those gifts, it effectively gave the illegitimate children more than it gave the others.

Alternatively, suppose that despite this opinion (and of the Civil Code revision implementing the opinion) H wanted to leave his legitimate children twice his illegitimate children's shares. He has two equally simple ways of doing so.

First, H can give his legitimate children assets inter vivos. Given that many philandering fathers probably live with their wives rather than their lovers, they probably do this routinely.

Second, H can leave each of his legitimate children 1/3 of his estate by will, and each of his illegitimate children 1/6. Because each of the four children now has an intestate share of 1/4, each has an elective share of $1/4 * 1/2 = 1/8$. Since 1/3 and 1/6 exceed 1/8, no child can block H's preferred allocation by claiming an elective share.

In short, the old Sec. 900(d) did not stop fathers from leaving their legitimate and illegitimate children equal amounts. The court's opinion (and the new Sec. 900) does not stop fathers from giving their legitimate children twice as much as they give their illegitimate children. For all the celebration about individuality and human rights, the opinion changes nothing of substance.

c. A counter-majoritarian corrective? One of the oddest aspects of the opinion concerns the Court's claims about social consensus. Japanese once believed that parents should always raise their children within a family, the Court explains. They no longer share that belief. Instead, they countenance a wide variety of family relations. Sec. 900 (d) fit the earlier consensus about traditional family structure, but it no longer suits public opinion. Given that the statute does not fit any consensus, it violates the constitution.

This approach takes a fundamentally opposite tack from classic American jurisprudence. Scholars and judges in the U.S. justify judicial review by the need to protect people from hostile majorities.

A group with majority support can use its voting power to control the executive and legislative branches. Through that control, it can then use the government to transfer wealth and other perquisites to itself.

Under the U.S. approach, judges do not review statutes to ensure that they follow majority preferences. After all, groups with majority support can pass whatever statutes they want. Judges review statutes to ensure that the majority does not oppress the minority.

The Supreme Court took the opposite tack. It did not void Sec. 900 (d) to protect a minority group (illegitimate children). After all, illegitimate children had received half the shares of other children for decades. As long as most Japanese supported that distinction, explained the Court, the discrimination was "reasonable" and fine. The discrimination was now "unreasonable" only because the majority no longer supported it.

The Court's logic is particularly troubling in a judicial system as closely controlled by the ruling party as in Japan. As discussed in **Case1** [commentary on *Sunagawa* case], the Japanese ruling party indirectly —— but strongly —— controls the careers of sitting judges. The Japanese judiciary functions well, but it does not function independently. In the case at hand, the Court claimed only to implement majority preferences. Given the ruling party's control over judicial careers, a theory of judicial review that merely implements majority preferences does nothing to confine the power of that majority.

Perhaps, however, the Court is simply disingenuous. As a median voter party, the ruling Liberal Democratic Party (LDP) generally enacts the statutes that the voting majority wants. It does not always do so, to be sure. Like any majority party, it sometimes caters to minority blocks with intensely held preferences and ignores the majority preferences. Yet on the distinction between legitimate and illegitimate children, no minority block exists that would stop the LDP from implementing a majority preference (if there were such a preference) for equal inheritance shares.

More plausibly, the majority of Japanese voters did not want equal inheritance shares. The Court notes the multiple study groups that explored revisions to Sec. 900(d). Yet despite the groups, the legislature never revised the statute. Probably, it did not revise it because a majority of Japanese did not want it revised. And that is exactly what public opinion surveys suggest. According to one 2012 survey, for example, 35.6 percent of the respondents opposed giving illegitimate children the same inheritance share. Only 25.8 percent supported such a change.[6]

d. Illegitimacy and social structure In hesitating to dismantle legal structures that encouraged people to bear their children within marriage, the Japanese public had good reason. Given the politicization of family relations in the West, the concept of "illegitimacy" has itself become problematic, of course. Many scholars avoid the word entirely. Yet illegitimacy correlates with a wide range of dysfunctional behavior. Causation is hard to show, of course, but the correlation is clear.

Take one survey of the massive U.S.-based body of scholarship. The authors conclude:[7]

> Children born to unmarried mothers are more likely to be poor, to grow up in a single-parent family, and to experience

---

[6] Sakurai Yoshiko, Nihon shakai ni au no ka, Saikosai handan [Does it Suit Japanese Society, this Supreme Court Opinion] (Sept. 19, 2013), available at http://yoshiko-sakurai.jp/2013/09/19/4903.

[7] Kristin Anderson Moore, Susan M. Jekielek, & Carol Emig, Marriage from a Child's Perspective: How Does Family Structure Affect Children, and What Can We Do about It?, Trends in Child Research Brief (June 2002), at pp. 1-2. One of the many studies reaching a similar conclusion include Daniel T. Lichter, Christie D. Batson & J. Brian Brown, Welfare Reform and Marriage Promotion: The Marital Expectations and Desires of Single and Cohabiting Mothers, 78 Soc. Serv. Rev. 2 (2004).

multiple living arrangements during childhood. These factors, in turn, are associated with lower educational attainment and a higher risk of teen and nonmarital childbearing. ... [I]t is not simply the presence of two parents, as some have assumed, but the presence of *two biological parents* that seems to support children's development.

As another sociologist summarized the literature, children of unmarried parents "fall short in significant developmental domains," including "education, behavior problems, and emotional well-being."[8] He continued:[9]

[The social science survey] clearly reveals that children appear most apt to succeed well as adults —— on multiple counts and across a variety of domains —— when they spend their entire childhood with their married mother and father, and especially when the parents remain married to the present day.

Nor is there much reason to expect different results in Japan. Currently, the rate of illegitimacy is much lower in Japan than comparable wealthy societies. In Japan, couples bear 2 percent of children outside of marriage (2 percent in South Korea; 4 percent in Taiwan). In the U.S., couples bear 41 percent outside of marriage (among African Americans, the rate climbs to 70 percent). And in Europe, the rates range from 18 percent in Italy to 55 percent in Sweden.[10]

Yet even though the illegitimacy rate in the U.S. is 20 times the rate in Japan, many of the same associations appear in Japanese data.[11] For example, take the 2010 prefecture-level illegitimacy rate.

---

[8] Mark Regerus, How Different Are the Adult Children of Parents Who Have Same-sex Relationships? Findings from the New Family Structures Study, 41 Soc. Sci. Res. 752, 752 (2012).

[9] Id., at 766.

[10] Social Trends Institute, The Sustainable Demographic Dividend 32 tab. 2 (2011).

The numbers correlate at the prefectural level positively with the rate of divorce (statistically significant at the 1 percent level), negatively with the rate of advance to high school (10 percent level), negatively with the rate of advance to university (1 percent level), negatively with per capita income (1 percent level), negatively with performance on standardized tests (*zenkoku gakuryoku tesuto*; 1 percent level), and negatively with the voter turnout at the 2003 election (1 percent level).[12]

解 説　COMMENT　**非嫡出子の法定相続分**

　本件決定は，民法 900 条 4 号ただし書きを違憲とする理由として，日本における婚姻や家族の実態の変化およびそのあり方に対する国民の意識の変化の他にもいくつかの点を挙げている。①現在，嫡出性の有無によって相続分に差異を設けている国は欧米諸国にはないこと。②国際人権 B 規約や児童の権利条約に関係する委員会から本件規定について，懸念の表明や是正を求める勧告を受けていること。③国籍法違憲判決（最大判平成 20・6・4 民集 62 巻 6 号 1367 頁）等の最近の判例や法制の動き。④本件規定を合憲とする平成 7 年大法廷決定以来の先例に，本件規定の合理性がもはや失われつつあるとの個別意見が繰り返し付されてきたこと等である。

　本件大法廷決定は，「その中のいずれか一つを捉えて，本件規定による法定相続分の区別を不合理とすべき決定的な理由とし得るものではない」としつつ，

---

[11]　I give the sources for these variables in J. Mark Ramseyer, Social Capital and the Formal Legal System: Evidence from Prefecture-Level Data in Japan, Harvard Law School, John M. Olin Center for Law, Economics & Organization, Discussion Paper 767, http://papers.ssrn.com/sol3/papers.cfm?abstract_id=2425763.

[12]　Indeed, the rate seems to capture something strongly structural. Suppose we take the 1925 illegitimacy rate. The numbers correlate positively with the 2010 illegitimacy rate (1 percent level), and even with the 2010 divorce rate (5 percent level) and current per capita income (1 percent level).

「総合的に考察すれば，……父母が婚姻関係になかったという，子にとっては自ら選択ないし修正する余地のない事柄を理由としてその子に不利益を及ぼすことは許されず，子を個人として尊重し，その権利を保障すべきであるという考え方が確立されてきている」として，本件規定は，被相続人が死亡した平成13（2001）年7月当時には，憲法14条1項に違反していたと結論づけた。

子は自分が生まれてくる家族を選ぶことはできない。その意味では，相続という制度自体，子の選ぶことのできない事由によって，経済的地位の格差をもたらすもので，本来，平等の理念と親和的な制度とは言い難い（宮沢俊義『憲法Ⅱ〔新版〕』〔有斐閣，1971〕324-25頁）。本件決定は，その相続制度の一構成要素である法定相続分という，遺言のない場合の補充的規定について，子は本来みな平等に尊重されるべきだという原則に反するとし，民法900条4号ただし書きの規定を違憲とした。そうすることが，個別具体の子の経済的福祉に関して実質的正義（具体的衡平）を実現するか否かという点よりは，この規定が果たす象徴的意義――婚外子に嫡出子と同等の地位は認められないという意義――に着目した判断と見ることも許されよう。

本件決定は，最高裁の憲法判断に「事実上の拘束性」があることを正面から認めた上で，本件規定の違憲判断につき，その拘束性の遡及を限定した点にも特徴がある。すでに解決済みの遺産分割等の効力を事後的に覆すことがもたらす重大な影響を考慮したものである。判例には遡及効のあることが原則だが，立法は遡及効のないことが原則である。確立した判例を信頼した多数の当事者の行為が過去に蓄積している場合，裁判所は立法による事態の解決を期待して，先例を変更することに慎重な態度をとる。平成7年の大法廷決定以降，最高裁が立法による問題の解決が望ましい旨のメッセージを発し続けてきたのも，そのためである（この点については，長谷部恭男「判例の遡及効の限定について」同『憲法の論理』〔有斐閣，2017〕第12章参照）。

PART 2

行政法

CASE	
6	武蔵野市長給水拒否事件
7	強制予防接種事件

CASE 6

Kuni v. Goto

1328 Hanrei jiho 16 (Sup. Ct. Nov. 8, 1989).[1]

●

武蔵野市長給水拒否事件
（最決平成元年 11 月 8 日判例時報 1328 号 16 頁）

1 Introduction

How the world has changed.

It is bit hard to believe, but it was not that long ago that thoughtful, prominent scholars (especially my colleagues in the West) declared that bureaucrats ran the Japanese economy. The bureaucrats had the brains. They thought long and hard. They issued orders. And firms and citizens complied. The bureaucrats had no legal authority to order what they did, but courts refused to review their instructions. Firms and citizens just did what they said.

Bureaucrats, scholars continued, planned which firms should invest what, where, and when. They told people what to buy, and what not to build. The Diet had passed no law that might have given them the power to issue these orders. But when bureaucrats told firms and citizens what to do, they issued their instructions as informal "administrative guidance" (*gyosei shido*). Firms and citizens rarely

---

[1] Aff'g 1166 Hanrei jiho 41 (Tokyo High Ct. Aug. 30, 1985), aff'g 1114 Hanrei jiho 10 (Tokyo D. Ct. Hachioji Br. Off. Feb. 24, 1984). This chapter is based heavily on J. Mark Ramseyer, Rethinking Administrative Guidance, in Masahiko Aoki & Gary R. Saxonhouse, Finance, Governance, and Competitiveness in Japan 199 (Oxford: Oxford University Press, 2000).

questioned the guidance, and even had they questioned it the courts would not have helped them.

Were someone to have contested a Japanese bureaucrat's instruction in court, explained scholars (again, particularly those in the West), judges would have refused to review it. They simply did not question informal administrative activity. As necessary, bureaucrats could punish the rare non-compliant firm through unrelated powers. They could take Edo's revenge in Nagasaki, as the classic aphorism put it. They might control access to foreign exchange, for example, or crucial imported resources. They could use those controls to punish firms that refused to do as they said. If they did, courts would never stop them.

According to Harvard sociologist Ezra Vogel, for instance, Japanese bureaucrats "boldly tr[ied] to restructure industry, concentrating resources in areas where they think Japan will be competitive internationally in the future."[2] British scholar Ronald Dore claimed that "control over the long-term growth and structure of the economy has been highly concentrated in a single ministry, MITI."[3] Hitotsubashi and Harvard economists Kazushi Ohkawa and Henry Rosovsky described Japan as "the only capitalist country in the world in which the Government decides how many firms should be in a given industry, and sets about to arrange the desired number."[4]

Firms and citizens apparently obeyed bureaucrats out of cultural pressure, according to these scholars. Japanese writers (many of them highly-respected intellectuals) published the cultural stereotypes as *Nihonjin ron*, and foreign scholars repeated them as gospel. One

---

[2] Ezra Vogel, Japan as Number One 65, 71 (Cambridge: Harvard University Press, 1979).

[3] Ronald Dore, Felxible Rigidities 25 (Stanford: Stanford University Press, 1986).

[4] Kazushi Ohkawa & Henry Rosovsky, Japanese Economic Growth 223 (Stanford: Stanford University Press, 1973).

German scholar managed to hit all the principal cultural stereotypes in a single article.[5] "More than half of the activity of administrative agencies in Japan" involves administrative guidance, he wrote.[6] The guidance "has deep roots in the sociocultural foundations of Japanese society."[7] Japanese citizens realize the need for "harmony with governmental agencies."[8] They defer to bureaucrats out of what the scholar saw as a sense of "*giri*" (he cited Ruth Benedict), the "vertical" character of Japanese society (citing Chie Nakane), and widespread focus on the importance of "*amae*" (citing Takeo Doi).[9] Ohkawa and Rosovsky explained that "no Japanese would dare ask" a MITI official what legal grounds he had for his order.[10] And Nobel laureate Paul Krugman simply found Japan to be "a fuzzy kind of society." Firms complied, he wrote, out of "habits of deference to central authority" rather than "the hard-edged legalisms that Americans ... expect."[11]

2 Classic examples

Several Western scholars motivated these accounts through two examples. First, in the early 1970s, the Ministry of International Trade & Industry (MITI; now the Ministry of Economy, Trade & Industry) tried to allocate production cuts among petroleum refineries. When OPEC called a boycott of Japan, economic output had fallen sharply. MITI responded, the U.S. scholars explained, by organizing a cartel. Rather than rely directly on a statute, the ministry organized

---

[5] Wolfgang Pape, Gyōsei shidō and the Antimonopoly Law, 15 L. Japan 12 (1982).

[6] Id., at 12.

[7] Id., at 13.

[8] Id., at 14-15.

[9] Id., at 14-15.

[10] Ohkawa & Rosovsky, supra note 4, at 223.

[11] Paul Krugman, The Age of Diminishing Expectations 139-40 (3d ed., 1997).

it through administrative guidance. Second, in the mid-1960s, MITI enforced a cartel in the steel industry. Sumitomo Metals tried to fight the cartel, but MITI used its power over imported coking coal to force it to follow the industry's terms.

In fact, neither of these examples demonstrates government power. In the oil cartel dispute, prosecutors brought criminal charges against firms and executives in the refining industry for organizing the cartels. The Tokyo High Court convicted the defendants, and the Supreme Court affirmed most of the convictions. MITI's administrative guidance in the petroleum industry was simply illegal. I discuss the case at length in **Case 24**, and will not elaborate further here.

In the steel cartel, MITI —— not Sumitomo Metals —— backed down.[12] The six major steel firms had met for several years to discuss their collective production capacity. In early 1965, they agreed to cut production, but could not agree on how to allocate the cuts. More specifically, Sumitomo wanted to produce more than the others would allow.

The five firms other than Sumitomo asked MITI to enforce their cartel, and the ministry agreed. Sumitomo refused to cooperate. Should MITI try to punish it for producing more than its rivals allowed —— it announced —— it planned "immediately to file suit."[13] Never mind Ohkawa & Rosovsky's 1973 claim that "no Japanese would dare ask" MITI what legal basis it had. Sumitomo straightforwardly declared it would take MITI to court.

---

[12] The discussion is based on Yoshiro Miwa & J. Mark Ramseyer, Sangyo seisaku ron no gokai [Misunderstandings of Industrial Policy] ch. 9 (Tokyo: Toyo keizai shinpo sha, 2002); Yoshiro Miwa & J. Mark Ramseyer, The Fable of the Keiretsu 122-26 (Chicago: University of Chicago Press, 2006); Yoshiro Miwa & J. Mark Ramseyer, Capitalist Politicians, Socialist Bureaucrats? Legends of Government Planning from Japan, 48 Antitrust Bull. 595 (2003).

[13] Quoted in Nikkei, Nov. 28, 1965.

And Sumitomo obtained what it wanted. The firm had exported more than its rivals, and wanted the industry to exclude exports from the cartel. In the end, MITI enforced a cartel that excluded exactly what Sumitomo exported.

By the middle of 1966, Sumitomo announced that it wanted all production restraints repealed. Its rivals complained, but Sumitomo declared that it would ignore the cartel. "Even if the industry decides to continue the crude steel adjustments into October," the president announced, "we have no intention of complying." Given Sumitomo's refusal to obey, MITI repealed the production restraints in mid-1966.

Sumitomo had reason to threaten litigation. Already in 1969, the Tokyo District Court would declare it illegal for MITI to use its control over foreign exchange to enforce unrelated policy. That year, a group of firms applied to take militarily sensitive equipment to a Chinese trade fair. Citing American opposition, MITI used its foreign exchange controls to block them from doing so. The firms sued, and the court reviewed the legal basis for MITI's instructions, and declared them illegal.[14]

3 Municipal administrative guidance

a. Musashino It took the litigation over the informal restrictions on suburban housing development to show how strictly —— even brutally —— Japanese courts review informal government instructions. Even as Japanese voters nationally continued to reelect politicians from the conservative Liberal Democratic Party (LDP), urban voters elected politicians from the fringe-left. In 1967, Tokyo vot-

---

[14] 1969 nen Hokkyo jokai Nihon kogyo tenran kai v. Kuni, 560 Hanrei jiho 6 (Tokyo D. Ct. July 8, 1969).

ers elected Ryokichi Minobe governor. Son of the iconoclastic pre-war constitutional law scholar Tatsukichi Minobe, the younger Minobe had taught Marxist economics at several universities. He ran on the joint endorsement of the Socialist and Communist Parties.[15]

Tokyo had taken a hard left turn. Already in 1963 the suburban city of Musashino had elected Socialist Party candidate Kihachiro Goto. In 1971, Goto set new limits on large developers. Should a firm want to build a large apartment complex, Goto announced, it would need to do two things. First, it needed to donate land or funds (he specified the amounts) to the city. The new apartments increased the burden on the schools, he argued, and the developers should compensate the town for it. Second, it needed to obtain the agreement of all its neighbors. Apartment buildings can block air and sunlight, he explained. Developers should arrange their projects in ways to which other residents do not object. If a developer tried to build apartments without complying with these two requirements, warned Goto, he would refuse to provide water or sewage services.

In doing this, Goto straightforwardly redistributed wealth from developers to local voters. He had no legal authority for his program. Instead, he had instituted it as a variation on administrative guidance, one that would become known as "outline guidance" (*shido yoko*). The electoral appeal was straightforward, of course. The first requirement transferred funds to the local fisc. Threatening to withhold services unless a firm makes a legally-not-required payment is simple extortion, of course, but voters will notice that it reduces their own liability to fund the government. The second requirement gives

---

[15] Indeed, by 1975 less than 15 percent of the mayors and governors in power had run exclusively on an LDP endorsement. See J. Mark Ramseyer & Frances McCall Rosenbluth, Japan's Political Marketplace 48 (Cambridge: Harvard University Press, 1993).

each neighbor a chance to halt the project. In effect, it lets everyone "hold up" the project until the developer pays the desired amount. Voters like it because it transfers funds directly to them. "A government with the policy to rob Peter to pay Paul," noted G.B. Shaw, "can be assured of the support of Paul."

Almost immediately after he announced his new system, Goto encountered Kiharu Yamada. Yamada ran the local Yamaki Construction firm. When he learned of the requirements, he stormed into Goto's office:[16]

> You've made something that's not a statute or a regulation. And you're forcing it on us. That violates the separation of powers, it does. You've got a problem? Fight it out in court.

Aggressively building a series of condominium complexes, Yamada appears to have had no intention of meeting Goto's extra-legal demands. He only occasionally contributed to the Musashino government. He only occasionally made peace with his neighbors. Instead, he proceeded apace, and litigated when people tried to stop him.

Goto tried to stop Yamada. When the developer ignored the city's demands, Goto refused to supply water and sewage services. Yamada responded by suing, and in 1975 the Tokyo District Court held in his favor. The city could not refuse the services.[17] Yamada's neighbors tried too. Angry residents tried to block access to his construction site. Yamada sued them too, and won.[18] When he finally finished his projects, he sued the city again. Through its opposition, the city had raised Yamada's costs. It now owed him damages.[19]

---

[16] Kuni v. Goto, 1114 Hanrei jiho at 13 (as translated in Ramseyer, supra note 1).

[17] Yamaki kensetsu, K.K. v. Musashino shi, 803 Hanrei jiho 18 (Tokyo D. Ct. Dec. 8, 1975).

[18] Yamaki kensetsu, K.K. v. Suzuki, 1151 Hanrei jiho 24 (Tokyo High Ct. Mar. 26, 1985).

Crucially, prosecutors decided to stop Goto. The law obligated the city to provide water and sewage services to applicants meeting statutorily specified requirements. Yamada met those requirements, but Goto had wanted more. He had wanted Yamada to transfer more money to the city government and his neighbors besides.

To the prosecutors, Goto's attempts to use withholding water and sewage services to extract additional amounts from Yamada violated the law, and in 1978 they filed criminal charges against the mayor. By 1984, the Tokyo District Court convicted him, and in time the Tokyo High Court and Supreme Court affirmed.[20] Wrote the High Court:[21]

> The premise behind administrative guidance is that the recipient acts "voluntarily." When there is a chance that a recipient might agree to the administrative guidance, the guidance may be acceptable. Yet if a recipient firmly indicates that he will not comply and allows no possibility that he might change his mind, then ... any refusal to act on the recipient's application is illegal.

In this case, wrote the Supreme Court:[22]

> By the time the defendants denied the water application from condominium builder Yamaki Construction and its buyers, Yamaki had unambiguously indicated its intent not to comply with Musashino city's outline guidance relat-

---

[19] Yamaki kensetsu, K.K. v. Musashino shi, 1465 Hanrei jiho 106 (Tokyo D. Ct. Hachioji Br. Off. Dec. 9, 1992).

[20] Kuni v. Goto, 1328 Hanrei jiho 16 (Sup. Ct. Nov. 8, 1989), aff'g 1166 Hanrei jiho 41 (Tokyo High Ct. Aug. 30, 1985), aff'g 1114 Hanrei jiho 10 (Tokyo D. Ct. Hachioji Br. Off. Feb. 24, 1984).

[21] Kuni v. Goto, 1166 Hanrei jiho at 43 (as translated in Ramseyer, supra note 1).

[22] Kuni v. Goto, 1328 Hanrei jiho at 18 (as translated in Ramseyer, supra note 1).

ing to residential development. ... Once this point had been reached, ... it was illegal to refuse to act on application for a water contract.

Yamada did not let matters lie. When prosecuted for refusing Yamada his water and sewage, Goto had incurred legal fees. Given that he had incurred the fees for actions he took in his capacity as mayor, Goto charged them to the city. Yamada then sued as a Musashino resident for reimbursement. Goto, he argued, could not charge the city for the cost of his criminal defense. Instead, he should reimburse his legal fees to the city. The District Court agreed, and ordered Goto to pay the city. He appealed, but the High Court and Supreme Court affirmed.[23]

Once the courts made clear the illegality of the informal municipal guidance, developers sued to recover the "donations" they had "voluntarily" made to city governments. In 1993, one Musashino developer (not Yamada) reached the Supreme Court. The justices ordered the city to refund his donations:[24]

> The outline guidance is not based on law. It is, for the appellee [Musashino city], simply a set of internal standards that describe the administrative guidance to be given entrepreneurs. Because of measures like the refusal to provide water service contracts, however, entrepreneurs effectively have no choice but to comply. ... [Given that the

---

[23] Goto v. Yamada, 1354 Hanrei jiho 62 (Sup. Ct. Mar. 23, 1990), affirming 1186 Hanrei jiho 46 (Tokyo High Ct. Mar. 26, 1986), affirming 1010 Hanrei jiho 40 (Tokyo D. Ct. May 27, 1983). After the mayor of suburban Tokyo Tanashi city withheld water from a developer who refused to follow his guidance, the city paid the developer compensation. Citizens similarly sued the mayor on behalf of the city, and in 1983 the court ordered him personally to reimburse it. Y.G. Seron nyusha v. Tanashi shicho, 504 Hanrei taimuzu 128 (Tokyo D. Ct. May 11, 1983).

[24] Takahashi v. Musashino shi, 1506 Hanrei jiho 106 (Sup. Ct. Feb. 18, 1993) (as translated in Ramseyer, supra note 1).

amounts of the contributions are standardized as well,] it is hard to conclude that the entrepreneurs paid the amounts voluntarily. ...

Granted, the administrative guidance under the outline guidance was designed to protect the living environment of Musashino citizens from uncontrolled development. Granted, too, the administrative guidance enjoyed broad support from Musashino citizens. Nonetheless, the conduct above went beyond the limits of acceptable administrative guidance —— the solicitation of voluntary contributions. Accordingly, it was an illegal exercise of public power.

b. Other cities Firms did not just challenge the Musashino government. Mayors and governors had adopted the informal strategy widely, and developers challenged local governments the country over. In 1972, for example, a developer applied for a construction permit from Minobe's Tokyo government. When the developer refused to take the steps necessary to obtain his neighbor's consent, the government stalled his application. He sued over the delay, and in 1979 the Tokyo High Court awarded him damages.[25] In 1985, the Supreme Court duly affirmed.[26] Another developer planned a pair of condominium complexes in Tokyo. He too refused to placate his neighbors, and the government again stalled. In 1982, the Tokyo District Court awarded compensation.[27]

Developers did not all win, but enough won that a list even of the published cases can turn tedious. A Kyoto developer planned

---

[25] G.G. Nakaya honten v. Tokyo to, 955 Hanrei jiho 73 (Tokyo High Ct. Dec. 24, 1979), reversing 928 Hanrei jiho 79 (Tokyo D. Ct. July 31, 1978).

[26] G.G. Nakaya honten v. Tokyo to, 1168 Hanrei jiho 45, 47 (Sup. Ct. July 16, 1985).

[27] Fujisawa kensetsu, K.K. v. Tokyo to, 1074 Hanrei jiho 80 (Tokyo D. Ct. Nov. 12, 1982).

a hotel. The prefecture told him to obtain his neighbors' permission. He sued for his permit instead, and in 1984 won.[28] A Tochigi firm planned an industrial waste disposal plant. When the prefecture refused to issue a permit until it obtained the consent of the local residents, it sued. In 1991, the court ordered the government to act.[29] When Yamanashi prefecture told a developer planning a vacation condominium complex to comply with its administrative guidance, this developer sued too. In 1992, the court told the prefecture to act on the application.[30] A Kyushu city government told a condominium developer that it would not supply water unless he reduced the size of his planned building. The developer refused, sued, and the court told the government to accept the application (1992).[31] The Chiba prefectural government told a golf-course developer to follow its administrative guidance. He refused, sued, and the court again told the government to accept the application (1992).[32]

Nor were these cases a temporary aberration. Developers continue to challenge local governments that try to force them to accept terms without a legal basis, and developers continue to win. When a Miyagi developer tried to build a large-scale industrial waste facility without following the informal prefectural guidance, the government stalled his application. He sued, and the court in 1998 ordered the government to proceed with his application.[33] An Okayama developer tried the same strategy, and this prefectural gov-

---

[28] Sankei kanko, Y.G. v. Kyoto fu, 1116 Hanrei jiho 56 (Kyoto D. Ct. Jan. 19, 1984).

[29] Shiroyama kankyo joka, Y.G. v. Tochigi ken chiji, 1385 Hanrei jiho 42 (Utsunomiya D. Ct. Feb. 28, 1991).

[30] Arakawa kensetsu kogyo, K.K. v. Yamanashi ken kenchiku shuji, 1457 Hanrei jiho 85 (Kofu D. Ct. Feb. 24, 1992).

[31] Higashimine jutaku sangyo, K.K. v. Shime machi, 1438 Hanrei jiho 118 (Fukuoka D. Ct. Feb. 13, 1992).

[32] K.K. Yoka ichiba kanko kaihatsu v. Chiba ken chiji, 1471 Hanrei jiho 84 (Chiba D. Ct. Oct. 28, 1992).

ernment stalled as well. Here too, the court (in 2000) declared the delay illegal.[34] Gunma prefecture cited their guidance to block a vacation condominium complex on the grounds that the developer did not do enough either to protect the environment or to appease local opposition. In 2002, the Tokyo High Court awarded the developer damages.[35] The Itami city government refused to cooperate with a condominium developer who would not contribute land to the city. Again in 2002, the court awarded the developer damages.[36] Once more in the same year, a court awarded a chicken-farm developer damages when a local government cited informal guidance to deny him a permit.[37] And in 2014, the Osaka High Court faced another application for an industrial waste facility. The prefecture had stalled the developer's permit until he made peace with its neighbors. The tactic was illegal, and the court ordered the prefecture to pay the developer damages.[38]

*　　*　　*

The lessons for comparisons between the U.S. and Japan are obvious enough —— the only real puzzle is why they were not obvious 30 years ago. Japanese firms do indeed contest instructions from bureaucrats. They refuse to comply. As necessary, they sue. In the resulting litigation, courts review what bureaucrats order. And

---

[33] K.K. Minami zao ebakuriin v. Miyagi ken chiji, 1676 Hanrei Jiho 43 (Sendai D. Ct. Jan. 27, 1998).

[34] Ishii v. [No name given], 214 Hanrei chiho jichi 70 (Hiroshima High Ct. Okayama Br. Off. Apr. 27, 2000).

[35] K.K. Taisei kikaku v. Gunma ken, 1757 Hanrei jiho 81 (Tokyo High Ct. July 16, 2001).

[36] [No names given], 2002 WLJPCA 06189006 (Kobe D. Ct. June 18, 2002).

[37] Shimoyama kogen nojo v. Shimoyama mura, 240 Hanrei chiho jichi 102 (Nagoya D. Ct. Mar 20, 2002).

[38] Taiyo sangyo, K.K. v. Shiga ken, 1901 Hanrei jiho 28 (Osaka High Ct. May 28, 2014).

when those bureaucrats act without legal authority, the courts declare the action illegal.

解説 COMMENT　　日本における行政指導をめぐる状況の変遷

　かつて，欧米の日本研究者の間では，日本は官僚国家であり，法的根拠なしに行政指導により自己の政策を実現することが可能であり，日本の企業も国民も，行政指導に法的根拠がないことを指摘して争うことはせず服従するというステレオタイプが有力であった。経済的には先進国でありながら，「法の支配」ではなく，行政指導に基づく官僚支配が行われているという日本観を基にして，その特殊性の原因をさまざまな観点から説明する文献が少なからず著されたのである（官尊民卑やパターナリズム，争訟回避等の文化的・社会的観点からの説明も少なくないが，John O. Haley, "Sheathing the Sword of Justice in Japan: An Essay on Law Without Sanctions", 8 J. Japanese Stud. 125〔1980〕のように，日本における行政指導の多用の要因を日本の行政機関がフォーマルな法執行権限をほとんど有しないことに求めるものもある）。このような日本観には，全く根拠がなかったわけではなく，それを裏付ける事例も存在した（たとえば，Frank K. Upham, " The Man Who Would Import: A Cautionary Tale About Backing the System in Japan," 17 J. Japanese Stud. 323〔1991〕参照）。しかし，日本の企業や国民がすべからく行政指導に無批判に服従するというのは神話であり，行政指導に従わず，訴訟で法的解決を求めようとする例も存在する。ラムザイヤー教授の「解説」で紹介されている住友金属事件（▶ 2 ）では，住友金属が，旧通商産業省の行政指導を批判し，訴訟で争う意思を明確に表明したため，社会的な注目を集めた。

　行政手続法・行政手続条例が制定される前は，申請や契約の申込みを受理せず，受理前に申請内容の変更を求めたり，指導要綱の遵守を求める行政指導を行うことが稀でなかったが（要綱行政の背景と要綱行政をめぐる訴訟について詳しくは，宇賀克也『行政手続法の理論』〔東京大学出版会，1995〕93頁以下参照），行政指導に従わない旨の真摯かつ明確な拒絶の意思表示がなされた後は，行政

指導の継続を理由として，許認可等や契約締結を留保することは，原則として
違法とするのが判例の立場であった。宅地開発指導要綱を遵守しない山基建設
に対する給水拒否が行われた武蔵野マンション事件は，要綱行政の法的限界を
如実に示したといえよう。また，行政指導に従わない業者に対する許認可等の
留保を違法と判示した裁判例も枚挙に暇がない。行政手続法・行政手続条例の
制定（行政手続法における行政指導の規定について，宇賀克也『行政手続三法の
解説〔第 2 次改訂版〕』〔学陽書房，2016〕158 頁以下参照，行政手続条例における
行政指導の多様な規定について，同『自治体行政手続の改革』〔ぎょうせい，1996〕
147 頁以下参照）や行政指導の法的拘束力の欠如を指摘する一連の裁判例により，
行政指導が相手方の任意の協力を求めるものであり，行政指導に従わないこと
を理由とする不利益な措置を講ずることができないという認識は，公務員の間
でも一般的になっているといえよう。しかし，このことは，わが国で行政指導
の利用が減少したことを意味するわけでは必ずしもなく，相変わらず，行政指
導は多用されているといってよいと思われる。しかし，上記の武蔵野マンショ
ン事件で問題になったような行政指導への不服従を理由とするあからさまな制
裁は過去のものになったといえよう。

CASE

7

Yoshihara v. Kuni

1445 Hanrei jiho 3 (Tokyo High Ct. Dec. 18, 1992).

●

強制予防接種事件
（東京高判平成 4 年 12 月 18 日判例時報 1445 号 3 頁）

1 The facts [1]

Over the course of 1972-1981, 160 people sued the Japanese government for injuries they claimed to have sustained from its public vaccination campaigns. One set of parents sued on behalf of 26 children who died after receiving the vaccines. Another set of parents and 36 children sued for damages stemming from disabilities they claimed the children suffered.

Between 1952 and 1974, the government had vaccinated the children for influenza, small pox, polio, pertussis (whooping cough), Japanese encephalitis, typhoid fever, or paratyphoid fever. Physicians had given the vaccines through mass programs run either by the national government directly or by local governments working under national programs. Facing time pressures imposed by the programs, they had screened the children only cursorily if at all. The plaintiffs blamed the side effects on the government's failure to exclude children

---

[1] See generally commentary preceding the opinion at 807 Hanrei taimuzu 78 (1993); Katsuya Uga, Case Comment, Jurisuto-gyosei ho 7: 54; Junko Obata, Case Comment, 151 Hogaku kyoshitsu 110 (1993). The sources give modestly conflicting numbers for the children killed, children disabled, and total plaintiffs.

68

in groups potentially at high risk.

The plaintiffs brought two legal claims. First, they sued under the National Compensation Act. The Japanese equivalent of the Federal Torts Claims Act, the Act lets people sue the government for negligence: [2]

> If in the course of employment a national government employee ... injures a person either intentionally or through negligence, the nation ... must pay compensation.

Second, the plaintiffs sued directly under the Constitution. Article 29(c) requires the government to pay "just compensation" if it takes "private property ... for public use." Article 13 requires it to keep the "right to life, liberty, and the pursuit of happiness ... the supreme consideration in legislation"; Article 14(a) provides that "all of the people are equal under the law"; and Article 25 both promises the "right to maintain the minimum standards of wholesome and cultured living," and obligates the government to "use its endeavors for the promotion and extension of ... public health." All this together, argued the plaintiffs, entitled them to compensation for injuries from the vaccination campaigns.

2 The decision [3]

a. The disposition The Tokyo High Court let the plaintiffs (other than those barred by the statute of limitations) collect under the National Compensation Act. It did not find that the individual physicians had acted negligently. Too many doctors had participated

---

[2] Kokka baisho ho [National Compensation Act], Law No. 125 of 1947, Sec 1(a).

[3] Yoshihara v. Kuni, 1118 Hanrei jiho 28 (Tokyo D. Ct. May 18, 1984), rev'd, 1445 Hanrei jiho 3 (Tokyo High Ct. Dec. 18, 1992), aff'd sub nom. Furukawa v. Kuni, 1644 Hanrei jiho 42 (Sup. Ct. June 12, 1998).

and too many years had passed for any such decision of the sort. Instead, it held the government itself negligent for failing to exclude high-risk children. In effect, it held (a) that the government should have excluded all children at high-risk (however defined), (b) that the plaintiffs had been in such high-risk groups, and (c) that the government had failed to exclude them because it used non-specialist physicians, had not adequately trained the doctors it did use, and had rushed them so badly that they could not have screened high-risk children had they wanted.

Conversely, the High Court rejected the plaintiffs' constitutional claims. It noted that Article 29 promises compensation if the government takes property, but observed that the government had not taken the plaintiffs' property. It had caused bodily harm. The Tokyo District Court had held that Articles 13, 14, 25 and 29 together gave the plaintiffs a direct right of action for that bodily harm, but the High Court reversed. The Constitution gave no such right.[4]

b. The reasoning The Tokyo High Court did not require the plaintiffs to show that they had been part of high-risk groups that the government had negligently failed to identify. Instead, it simply held the government liable for failure to screen. Vaccines can cause dangerous side effects, it noted. The government knew those risks. To avoid unnecessary harm, it had a duty to identify and exclude those children most likely to suffer adverse side effects.

That screening the government largely did not do, continued the court. It focused instead on vaccinating as many children as it

---

[4] On appeal, the Supreme Court did not address the substantive constitutional or statutory claims. Instead, it merely affirmed those claims that the lower court had dismissed on statute-of-limitations grounds. See Furukawa v. Kuni, 1644 Hanrei jiho 42 (Sup. Ct. June 12, 1998).

could. When it learned of side effects, it hid the information. To maximize the number of children it vaccinated, it hired non-specialist doctors on temporary terms. It gave them minimal training. It required them to vaccinate as many as 150 children per hour.

To let the plaintiffs collect damages without proving that they had been in a high-risk group, Tokyo High Court cited a 1991 Supreme Court case:[5]

> Suppose a claimant suffers these serious disabilities as a result of a vaccine. The reasonable presumption is that he was a member of a high-risk group that should not have been vaccinated unless: either （i）a court finds that [the defendant or an agent of the defendant conducted] an examination appropriate to determine whether the claimant was a member of such a group and found no reason to think he was such a member, or （ii）a court finds that the claimant had individual characteristics making him unusually susceptible to the disabilities [caused by the vaccine].

In effect, given the plaintiffs' symptoms the Tokyo High Court simply presumed that they had been high-risk.

Neither did the Tokyo High Court require anyone to prove that the vaccines had caused the harm the child suffered. The district court had found the requisite causation by focusing (according to the government) on the absence of any other conceivable explanation. This, reasoned the government, amounted to switching the burden of proof. The appellate court denied that it switched any burden, and simply affirmed. It was an odd denial. The government had failed to identify any alternative explanation for the harm, it explained, so the plaintiffs won.

---

[5] Ohashi v. Kuni, 1386 Hanrei jiho 35 (Sup. Ct. Apr. 19, 1991).

3 Infectious disease and vaccines

Infectious diseases plagued people everywhere through the first half of the 20th century, and they plagued Japan too. Even as recently as 1947, tuberculosis killed more Japanese —— 146,000 —— than any other cause. Pneumonia and bronchitis killed another 136,000, and gastroenteritis (viral, bacterial, and parasitic) killed 106,000.[6]

Japan was sick: in 1946, 88,000 Japanese contracted dysentery. Another 44,000 caught typhoid fever, 9,000 caught paratyphoid fever, 32,000 caught epidemic typhus. About 49,800 caught diphtheria. And most brutally, perhaps, 17,900 came down with small pox.[7] Polio came and went, but in 1961 5,000 people suffered the debilitating disease.[8]

And Japan was poor: even as late as 1957, per capita income in then-current prices stood at $249. By 1970 it had trebled to $794, but still only approached French and German levels.[9] Because it was poor, nutrition was primitive —— and infectious diseases took a more devastating toll than in Japan's wealthier peers. A disease with only a "morbidity" effect in a wealthy community, noted *Nature*, has a "mortality" effect among the poor. When a country is rich, a disease may sicken. When it is poor, the same disease will kill.[10] Indeed,

---

[6] See generally data available at http://www.mhlw.go.jp/toukei/saikin/hw/jinkou/suii09/deth7.html.

[7] See generally data on Hotei densen byo kanja su [Number of Patients of Designated Contagious Diseases], available at www.e-stat.go.jp.

[8] Nihon no porio 1962-1995 [Polio in Japan, 1962-1995], 18 IASR No. 1, available at http://idsc.nih.go.jp/iasr/18/203/tpc203-j.html.

[9] Kondo, shotoku baizo keikaku to shakai hosho [The Income Doubling Plan and Social Insurance], at http://www.jili.or.jp/research/search/pdf/B_7_2.pdf.

[10] Roy M. Anderson & Robert M. May, Vaccination and Herd Immunity to Infectious Diseases, 318 Nature 323, 327 (1985).

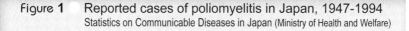

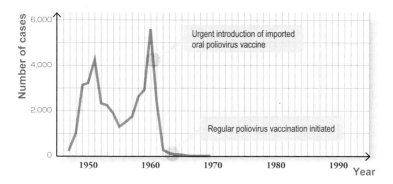

Sources: Poliomyelitis, Japan, 1962-1995, IASR Vol. 18 No. 1 (Jan. 1997), available at http://idsc.nih.go.jp/iasr/18/203/tpc203.html.

pertussis still slaughters 200,000 to 400,000 people a year —— but almost all are children in the developing world. In Japan, it barely kills 10 anymore.

Faced with regular epidemic scourges, in 1948 the Japanese government launched the first of many mass vaccination campaigns.[11] As with any mass project anywhere, the programs had their problems. When U.S. scientists developed a new small pox vaccine, they inadvertently gave the disease to 200 children and killed several. When in 1948 a Japanese pharmaceutical company mishandled its diphtheria vaccine, it killed 84.[12]

But over time the vaccines worked. Year after year they saved lives, thousands of lives. During the polio epidemic of 1960-

---

[11] Under the Yobo sesshu ho [Preventive Vaccination Act], Law No. 68 of 1948.

[12] Kurihara, 1948 kyoto shimane jifuteria yobo sesshu ka jiken (sono 1) [Diptheria Vaccine Injury Case: 1948 Kyoto, Shimane], 36 Atarashii yakugaku wo mezashite 47 (2007).

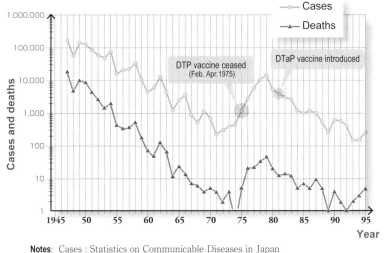

Figure 2 Reported cases of and deaths from pertussis in Japan, 1947-1995 (Ministry of Health and Welfare)

Notes: Cases : Statistics on Communicable Diseases in Japan
Deaths : Vital Statistics of Japan
Sources: Pertussis, Japan, 1982-1996, IASR, Vol. 18 No. 5 (May 1997). Available at http://idsc.nih.go.jp/iasr/18/207/tpc207.html.

61, the government turned to the new Sabin vaccine and the number infected plummeted (Figure 1). By 1965 the disease had largely disappeared.[13] Much the same thing happened with the other mid-century killers. Barely 2,100 die of tuberculosis anymore.[14] In 1994, 1200 people caught dysentery, 81 caught typhoid fever, 32 paratyphoid, no one caught epidemic typhus, and fewer than 10 caught diphtheria (Figure 2 for pertussis figures). The last Japanese to come down with small pox caught it in 1973 and 1974, and the disease then

---

[13] Poliomyelitis, Japan, 1962-1995, IASR Vol. 18 No. 1 (Jan. 1997), available at http://idsc.nih.go.jp/iasr/18/203/tpc203.html.

[14] See data available at http://www.mhlw.go.jp/bunya/kenkou/kekkaku-kansenshou03/12.html.

disappeared.[15]

4   Vaccine externalities

a. **Herd immunity** Vaccines "work" by benefiting not just the child inoculated, but others with whom he has contact as well. A child who receives a vaccine does not just lower his own health risks. By lowering the odds that the disease will spread, he lowers the health risks to everyone. He generates for his community a "positive externality."

Scholars in public health call it "herd immunity." As explained by the Philadelphia College of Physicians:[16]

> When a large percentage of the population is vaccinated, the spread of disease is limited. This indirectly protects unimmunized individuals ... This is the principle of herd immunity. ... As the number of those vaccinated increases, the protective effect of herd immunity increases. ... [D]epending on the contagiousness of the disease, vaccination rates may need to be as high as 80%-95%.

Or as Roy Anderson and Robert May put it in the journal *Nature:*[17]

---

[15]   See Densen byo tokei [Statistics on Contagious Diseases], available at http://www.e-stat.go.jp/SG1/estat/GL08020101.do?_toGL08020101_&tstatCode=000001024039&requestSender=dsearch.

[16]   The College of Physicians of Philadelphia, "Herd immunity." Available at: www.historyofvaccines.org. See also, e.g., Mark Fischetti, The Danger of Opting out, 308 Scientific American 96 (June 2013) ("When vaccinations drop below the herd immunity threshold —— the proportion of immune individuals needed to prevent widespread transmission —— outbreaks rise"); Editorial, Modern Heroes, 473 Nature 420 (2011): ("Some people think that [measles] is poised to surge again in the developing world .... Europe has already seen outbreaks, in part because vaccination rates dipped after the combined measles, mumps and rubella (MMR) vaccine was falsely linked to autism.").

[17]   See Anderson & May, supra note 10.

The persistence of infectious disease within a population requires the density of susceptible individuals to exceed a critical value such that, on average, each primary case of infection generates at least one secondary case. For example, continue Anderson and May, by vaccinating 92-96 percent of the children a society will eliminate measles and pertussis. For those diseases, that level constitutes the critical "herd immunity" threshold.

b. Side effects and the disease environment The side-effect risks from a vaccine do not depend on the disease environment, but the private and public benefits do. Where a disease is endemic, a child has a large risk of catching it —— and earns a correspondingly large benefit from the vaccine. Because others also bear that risk, the positive externality to the vaccine is large as well. Once a society crosses the critical herd immunity level, the infection risk largely disappears. As it does, so does the private benefit that the child earns from the vaccine, and the positive externality it generates.[18]

Consequently, when the risk of disease is high, the benefits from the vaccine will usually outweigh the side-effect risks; as the disease risk falls, the risk of side effects may (especially for those in high-risk groups) begin to exceed the benefits. In Anderson and May's words:

[V]accination almost invariably carries some risk (usually extremely small) to the individual. At the start of a mass-immunization programme, the probability of serious disease arising from vaccination is usually orders of

---

[18] See, e.g., Roberta Kwok, Vaccines: The Real Issues in Vaccine Safety, 473 Nature 436 (2011): "Even if immunization does prove risky for certain children, withholding the vaccine could pose a greater threat."

magnitude smaller than the risk of serious disease arising from natural infection. As the point of eradication is approached, the relative magnitude of these two probabilities must inevitably be reversed.

Unfortunately, this calculus will cause people to opt out of vaccination before society reaches herd immunity. The inefficient result occurs because a child vaccinated bears all the cost of the vaccination (the risk of side-effects), but does not capture all the benefits. Because he weighs only his private gain against the side-effect risk, he will tend to reject the vaccination program before the total costs and benefits of the campaign have equalized.

    c. **Age at vaccination and the disease environment** The plaintiffs also complained that the government vaccinated children at too young an age. For some vaccines, the side-effect risks decline with age: all else equal, parents will want to wait to vaccinate their children until those risks fall. The longer they wait, however, the greater the risk that the child will contract the disease.

As a result, the optimal age to vaccinate a child depends on the disease environment. If a society has already reached herd immunity, a young child bears no risk in waiting to vaccinate, and society incurs no cost in letting him do so. The disease will not spread —— and society can safely let him defer the vaccine. If the society has not yet reached that level, however, each additional child vaccinated reduces the odds of an epidemic, and generates a positive externality. The longer society waits before vaccinating children, the higher the odds that each child will become infected, and the the larger the risk of that epidemic.

Note that the socially optimal vaccination age will also depend on the community's age composition. If only a small fraction of the population is young, the society will not appreciably raise the odds of an epidemic by waiting to vaccinate its children. If a large cohort is young, then every year it waits to vaccinate raises that epidemic risk.

5 Government negligence and the disease environment

Given this discussion, perhaps the most troubling aspect of the High Court opinion lies in its failure to situate the vaccination programs in history: in the early post-war years. Whether in Japan or in the U.S., negligence turns on the balance between (i) the benefits generated by a precaution and (ii) the costs incurred. Over time, the benefits to screening high-risk patients (the side-effects avoided) stayed largely unchanged. The costs (the epidemic risks) fell dramatically.

In 1960 (much less 1950), Japan was far from the critical herd immunity level. The population was young, it was unvaccinated, and it was sick. Given the high odds of contracting a disease, the private benefits to vaccination (and early vaccination) were very high; given the long distance from herd immunity, the positive externalities were high as well. Every patient the government vaccinated lowered the odds of an epidemic. So too did every year earlier it vaccinated a child.

By ignoring the disease environment, the court implicitly biased the analysis toward finding negligence. By the time it decided the case in 1992, Japan had comfortably crossed the herd immunity threshold. Epidemics were a thing of the past. A child who opted not to receive a vaccine would not contract the disease, and neither would he increase the odds of an epidemic. If the government failed to screen and exclude high-risk children, it imposed high costs and earned very little benefit. The probability that it met the negligence threshold was high indeed.

In the Japan of 1950 and 1960, the side effect risks paled next to the risks of an epidemic. The failure to screen higher-risk patients that constituted legal negligence in 1992 would not necessarily have constituted negligence in the disease environment of 1950. As one scholar put it:[19]

> Vaccines face a tougher safety standard than most pharmaceutical products because they are given to healthy people, often children. What they stave off is unseen, and many of the diseases are now rare, with their effects forgotten. So only the risks of vaccines, low as they may be, loom in the public imagination.

Unfortunately, the Tokyo High Court blithely ignored the change in the vaccination programs' disease environment.

6 Government negligence and the state of knowledge

Legal negligence also turns on the knowledge available. It turns on cost-benefit analysis to be sure, but on an analysis that uses the information available at the time. In this case, it turns on the knowledge about side effects available in the 1950s and 1960s.

In the early post-war years, most vaccines were new. To be sure, Edward Jenner famously developed the small pox vaccine in 1798, and physicians had access to the typhoid fever vaccine by the early 20th century. But the other medicines arrived much later. Scientists did not develop the influenza and pertussis vaccines until the 1930s. They did not invent the Japanese encephalitis vaccine until the 1950s. Jonas Salk did not discover the polio vaccine until 1952.

When the government began these vaccination campaigns, much of the information about side effects simply was not available. Epidemics were rampant, and killed thousands. Against them,

---

[19] Roberta Kwok, Vaccines: The Real Issues in Vaccine Safety, 473 Nature 436 (2011).

the new vaccines saved massive numbers of lives. Ironically, the government lacked information about side effects precisely because the vaccines were so safe. So low was the probability of a side effect that physicians could learn about it only after they had given the vaccines to hundreds of thousands of children. As Edward Belongia and Allison Naleway explained:[20]

> Although vaccines must undergo stringent safety tests before distribution, the trials typically don't enroll enough people to catch risks on the order of one case per 10,000–100,000 people .... The only way to find such side effects is to deploy the vaccine in the population and watch.

So safe were the vaccines, in other words, that the government did not —— and logically could not —— obtain information about side effects.

7 Incentive effects

a. Vaccines Unlike most tort disputes, this case leaves incentives largely unchanged. Typically, scholars locate the benefits to tort liability in the incentives it gives actors to take efficient levels of care. Applied correctly, both negligence (the regime at stake) and strict liability (the regime under the current compensation program for vaccine side effects) give actors incentives to undertake all cost-justified precautions, but only cost-justified precautions. Applied correctly, tort law encourages people to undertake their activities at efficient levels.[21]

For the most part, however, this case does not affect

---

[20] Edward A. Belongia & Allison L. Naleway, Smallpox Vaccine: The Good, the Bad, and the Ugly, 1 Clinical Med Res. 87 (2003).

[21] See, e.g., Richard A. Posner, The Economic Analysis of Law, 9th ed. Ch. 6 (New York: Wolters Kluwer, 2014).

anyone's incentives. Voters elect politicians, monitor them, and replace them if someone else offers better performance. Politicians appoint bureaucrats and do the same.[22] Yet the liability here leaves voters with mostly the same incentives. Suppose the court holds the government (as it did here) liable for its negligence. Because the government will pay damages and citizens fund the public fisc, ex ante all citizens (as taxpayers) will bear the expected cost of a vaccination program. Suppose (by contrast) the court holds the government immune from liability. Because the side effects appear randomly, ex ante all citizens (as patients in the vaccination programs) will bear the same expected cost of the vaccination program.

Liability changes voter incentives only to the extent that people bearing the largest share of tax liability differ from the people with the highest odds of suffering side effects. Suppose the government only vaccinates children. Childless taxpayers bear the cost of court-imposed compensation but not the risk of vaccination side effects. Low-income parents of young children bear the risk of side effects but not the cost of compensation.

Beyond these misalignments, however, voter incentives under either legal regime are largely the same. In one, they bear their proportionate share of the tax liability necessary to pay the required compensation. In the other, they bear their proportionate share of the risk of side effects. Because the total compensation will equal (other than administrative costs) the cost of the side effects, under either regime the total burden will remain largely unchanged.

Put another way, the voters do have an incentive to adopt cost-justified precautions —— but not because of the liability. Given

---

[22] On the relation between politicians and bureaucrats in Japan, see J. Mark Ramseyer & Frances McCall Rosenbluth, Japan's Political Marketplace (Cambridge: Harvard University Press, 1993).

that the government is liable to pay compensation (under this opinion), voters have an incentive to urge it to adopt cost-justified precautions. By contrast, suppose the government is not liable. As patients of the vaccination programs, voters still bear the cost of any failure to adopt cost-justified precautions. Necessarily, they still have an incentive to urge the government to adopt such precautions.

b. Article 29 That all citizens bear the risk of vaccine side effects distinguishes the case from the risks targeted by the Constitution's Article 29:

Private property may be taken for public use upon just compensation therefor.

By the terms of the Article, the government may confiscate a citizen's property, but only if it pays him the value of the property.

In part, the article exists to stop one group of citizens from using the government to redistribute another group's property to themselves. To be sure, from time to time, the government will find that it can promote the general good by taking someone's property. Perhaps it needs land for a new highway. Perhaps it needs it for an airport or a hydroelectric dam. Were transactions costs 0, it could negotiate a purchase from the owner, but transaction costs are not always 0. When the owner refuses even a market price offer, Article 29 lets the government promote the efficient outcome.

From time to time the government may try to promote the greater good —— but only from time to time. Other times, one identifiable electorally powerful group of citizens may manipulate the government to redistribute wealth from another identifiable but electorally less powerful group. Take the post-war land reform program. Tenant farmers vastly outnumbered landowners, and under electoral democracy numbers matter. The program did not raise productivity,[23] but it did redistribute wealth from the economically rich but (relatively scarce and) politically weak landowners to the economically poor but (relatively numerous and) politically strong tenants. By requiring the government to compensate the landowners, Article 29 might lower the incentive for tenants to demand such measures. Unfortunately, the government paid the landowners only a trivial amount, and the Supreme Court upheld the price —— and effectively gutted the clause.[24]

The vaccination campaigns did not raise this risk of redistribution. Ex ante, everyone vaccinated bore a risk of side effects. Rather than one identifiable group targeting another identifiable group, the campaign imposed on everyone the risk of random bad luck. Compensate everyone or compensate no one —— the ex ante cost to each voter remained the same. Hence the irrelevance of Article 29.

解 説 COMMENT   **強制予防接種の被害者の救済**

わが国では、かつて、児童に対して強制予防接種が行われていた。予防接種は、被接種児童が感染症に罹患する危険を軽減させることも目的としているものの、それのみでは、接種を義務付ける根拠としては薄弱である。予防接種を受けないことにより感染症に罹患する危険と、予防接種により副作用が生ずる危険を比較衡量し、予防接種を受けるか否かを自己決定する権利が保障されるべきであるからである。したがって、強制予防接種を正当化する根拠は、予防接種の公益性に求められることになる。すなわち、社会の相当部分が予防接種により免疫を有するようになれば、社会全体が感染症の危険を免れるという"herd

---

[23] See J. Mark Ramseyer, The Fable of Land Reform, Journal Econ. & Mgmt. Strategy (forthcoming 2015).

[24] Hoshina v. Kuni, 7 Saihan minshu 1523 (S. Ct. Dec. 23, 1953) (en banc).

83

immunity" の理論こそ，予防接種を強制する根拠であったのである。したがって，予防接種の強制は，社会防衛も目的としていたのであり，強制予防接種の対象とされたのが学童であったことから，「学童防波堤論」と呼ばれることもある（なお，1994年の予防接種法改正により，強制接種制度は廃止されたが，勧奨接種は現在でも行われている）。東京地判昭和59・5・18判時1118号28頁，大阪地判昭和62・9・30判時1255号45頁，福岡地判平成元・4・18判時1313号17頁が，憲法29条3項の規定を類推適用または勿論解釈をして損失補償の法理により救済を行った背景には，強制予防接種（および事実上強制と受け取られていた勧奨接種）が社会防衛のために行われ，その結果，少数の者が「悪魔の籤」を引き特別の犠牲を被ったという認識が存在する。これに対し，東京高判平成4・12・18判時1445号3頁は，生命・健康の収用は，日本国憲法の下で認められないという理由で損失補償の法理による救済を否定する一方，国の予防接種行政についての組織的過失を認めて，国家賠償請求を認容した。集団予防接種禍訴訟において，被害者全員について，損害賠償の法理により救済される可能性は，過失の認定の困難さゆえに極めて低いと考えられていたにもかかわらず，前掲東京高判平成4・12・18が除斥期間の経過により救済が否定された1名を除き，原告全員について損害賠償請求を認容できたのは，2つの最高裁判決が存在したからである（秋山幹男＝河野敬＝小町谷育子編『予防接種被害の救済』〔信山社，2007〕参照）。すなわち，最判平成3・4・19民集45巻4号367頁は，予防接種により重篤な健康被害が生じた場合，禁忌者を識別するために必要な予診を尽くしたが禁忌者に該当する事由を発見できなかったこと，被接種者が後遺障害を発生しやすい個人的素因を有していたことなどの特段の事情のない限り，被接種者は禁忌者に該当していたものと推定すべきであるとした。さらに，最判昭和51・9・30民集30巻8号816頁は，接種を実施する医師が接種対象者につき禁忌者を識別するための適切な問診を尽くさなかったため，その識別を誤って接種をした場合に，その異常な副反応により対象者が死亡または罹病したときは，当該医師はその結果を予見し得たのに過誤により予見しなかったものと推定すべきであると判示した。したがって，十分な問診を尽くさず，誤って禁忌者に接種した場合には，過失が推定されることになる。このように，この2つの最高裁判決を組み合わせることにより，前掲東京高判平成4・12・18は，損害賠償の法理による救済を図ることができたのである。もっとも，この

ことは，損失補償の法理による救済方法の検討が不要になったことを必ずしも意味しない。禁忌者を識別するための十分な問診体制が整備され，それに従って接種がなされたにもかかわらず，重篤な副作用が発生した場合，過失の推定は行われず，損害賠償の法理による救済は困難になる。その場合のバックアップのために，損失補償の法理による救済の可能性を残す解釈論が意味を持ち得ると思われる（宇賀克也『行政法概説Ⅱ〔第6版〕』〔有斐閣, 2018〕536頁以下参照）。

CASE
7

強制予防接種事件
Yoshihara v. Kuni

PART 3

租 税 法

CASE	
8	サラリーマン税金訴訟（大島訴訟）大法廷判決
9	興銀税務訴訟

CASE 8

Oshima v. Sakyo zeimusho cho

1149 Hanrei jiho 30 (Sup. Ct. Mar. 27, 1985).

サラリーマン税金訴訟（大島訴訟）大法廷判決
（最大判昭和 60 年 3 月 27 日民集 39 巻 2 号 247 頁）

1 The facts

His colleagues thought him something of a Don Quixote.[1] Tadashi Oshima had taught Spanish literature and language at Doshisha University. In 1964, he failed to file a tax return. The Sakyo tax office in Kyoto took his wage income, subtracted the standard deduction of 135,000 yen, and estimated his net taxable income at 1.6 million yen.

Oshima claimed the assessment violated Article 14 (a) of the Constitution:

> All of the people are equal under the law and there shall be no discrimination in political, economic or social relations because of race, creed, sex, social status or family origin.

It was discrimination against wage earners, he argued, apparently by "social status."

Oshima claimed that the tax law discriminated against wage earners in three separate ways. First, it did not let them deduct their

---

[1] See the discussion at http://www.alt-invest.com/aic/about/tax14.html..

88

necessary expenses from their wage income. Under its "schedular" approach, the Japanese tax law catalogued all income into 10 categories, and separately levied a tax on each. It let taxpayers deduct actual expenses against their business or investment income, but not against wage income. They could take a standard deduction, but one that Oshima claimed fell far short of his real expenses. The standard deduction gave him 135,000 yen. He claimed 387,900 —— including clothing, dry-cleaning, haircuts, and commuting expenses.

U.S. tax law takes a "global" rather than schedular approach, and aggregates income "from whatever source derived" (I.R.C. Sec. 61). Within that global formula, however, it varies the deductions it allows by the type of income. In practice, this may not differ that substantially from the Japanese schedular approach. Much of what Oshima wanted to deduct against his wage income, for example, U.S. law would disallow under Sec. 262.

Second, because employers withhold tax from wage income at source, wage earners complied with the law at higher rates than taxpayers with other income. Given their lower rates of evasion, they faced higher effective tax rates. 9-6-4, went a popular adage: wage-earners paid tax on 90 percent of their income, small business owners on 60 percent, and farmers on 40 percent. 10-5-3-1, went another: wage-earners paid tax on 100 percent of their income, business owners on 50 percent, farmers on 30 percent, and politicians on 10 percent. Whatever the real numbers, given their greater compliance wage earners faced higher effective tax rates.

Third, wage earners had few legal shelters available to them. Business owners could shelter income with a wide range of statutory devices. Wage earners had many fewer. Again, because they reported a higher fraction of their income, they faced higher effective rates.

The lower courts dismissed Oshima's claims. The Supreme Court affirmed their dismissal.

2 Discrimination

Article 14 does not ban all discrimination. Rather, it bans discrimination by "race, creed, sex, social status or family origin." It does so to prevent politically powerful groups from manipulating the institutional process against the more vulnerable.

Politicians maximize votes. The point follows by definition, since candidates who do not maximize votes tend to lose elections to candidates who do. Necessarily, this gives groups who can deliver votes the ability to enshrine their preferences in statute. The traditional concern for African-Americans in U.S. constitutional law goes exactly to this concern: that whites, who outnumber blacks, might manipulate the legislative process to their private benefit.

Upper-middle-class salaried workers —— like professors of Spanish literature —— are not the typical political victim. Instead, they usually rank among those most able to manipulate the political process. Indeed, the graduated income tax itself epitomizes this political influence: although the rich control large amounts of wealth, the middle-class out-number the rich and use their resulting political power to redistribute wealth from the rich to themselves. Politicians maximize votes, in other words, by moving weath from the (small numbers of) rich taxpayers to the much larger number of middle-class (or lower class) taxpayers.

University of Chicago economist George Stigler called it "Director's Law," after his college Aaron Director who first proposed it: at least in the U.S., redistributive politics generally favors the middle class. As formulated by Stigler: [2]

Public expenditures are made for the primary ben-

---

[2] George J. Stigler, Director's Law of Public Income Redistribution, 13 J.L. & Econ. 1, 1 (1970).

efit of the middle classes, and financed with taxes which are borne in considerable part by the poor and the rich.

Other economists extend it to modern parliamentary democracies as well: [3]

> [P]arliamentary democracies with a low degree of de facto fiscal decentralization will be particularly vulnerable to redistributive politics being made according to Director's Law.

Economist Gary Becker echoes Stigler's point, and notes that "the *net* redistribution to the poor appears to be modest, at least in the United States ...."[4]

> Hence the point: upper-middle-class wage earners like Oshima do not constitute a politically vulnerable group. They claim a disadvantage —— but it is a disingenuous claim. They do not suffer in the electoral competition. Instead, they win —— they constitute the group most likely to control the electoral process.

3 Tax incidence

Oshima argued that the Constitution required the tax system to treat everyone equally. In the process, he avoided the question of what "equally" might mean. For example, the government could impose a "head tax." Each citizen would pay the same amount. The tax is obviously equal, but just as obviously not what anyone realistically proposes.

Alternatively, the government could impose a "flat tax."

---

[3] Lars P. Feld & Jan Schnellenbach, Still a Director's Law? On the Political Economy of Income Redistribution, IREF Europe. Available at: http://www.irefeurope.org/sites/default/files/DirectorsLaw-IREF_Final+-+copie.pdf.

[4] Gary S. Becker, Public Policies, Pressure Groups, and Dead Weight Costs, 28 J. Pub. Econ. 329, 343 (1985).

Each taxpayer would pay the same fraction of income as a tax. This tax is "equal" too —— yet it generates a very different incidence than the head tax. Under both regimes, taxpayers pay "equal" taxes —— but in one they pay equal amounts, and in the other they pay equal rates.

The government could also raise revenue through taxes on measures other than income. Oshima does not seem to think the income tax constitutionally required. These non-income taxes could be "equal" as well, even if once again differently equal. For instance, the government could finance itself though Henry George's famous land tax. It would assess a tax using equal rates per land value. The tax incidence would again differ. Or the government could finance itself through a consumption or value-added tax. Again, the tax could be equal, but differently equal once more.

Governments tax income at different rates because income varies in its tax elasticity. Wage income, for instance, has low elasticity: the amount of income recognized does not much vary with the tax rate. If the government raises its tax rate, taxpayers will work less and enjoy more leisure —— but only slightly. They work because they need to eat, after all, and they need to eat whether the tax rate is high or low. By contrast, capital gain income has high elasticity. Taxpayers can choose when to pay the capital gains tax by choosing when to sell their appreciated assets. If the government raises the rate, many will choose to hold their assets. Much the same holds true of business income. A firm will earn a profit when times are good, but it enjoys considerable flexibility in what to do with its earnings. If rates are low it may recognize its earnings as taxable income, but if the government raises its rates the firm may reinvest them in new productive assets.

Given this differential elasticity, higher tax rates do not generate the same amounts of revenue in all sectors. In sectors where elasticity is low (e.g., wages), a government that raises rates will tend to earn correspondingly higher revenue. In sectors where elasticity is high (e.g., capital gains), a government that raises rates may find its revenues only modestly higher. In the extreme, it may even find its revenues actually lower.

Governments tax different kinds of income differently be-cause of this differential elasticity. How taxpayers respond to a rate change depends on the kind of income involved. To demand —— as Oshima demands —— that the government treat all incomes equally would render fiscal planning perverse in the extreme.

4 Deviations from economic income

As Director's Law implies, salaried professionals are hardly the tax victims Oshima implied. The standard definition of income for tax purposes is the "Haig-Simons" formula, but the tax law includes plenty of deviations from that formula that benefit the upper-mid-dle-class. As Henry Simons put it, personal income is the:[5]

> algebraic sum of (1) the market value of rights exercised in consumption and (2) the change in the value of the store of property rights between the beginning and the end of the pe-riod in question.

Salaried professionals enjoy a wide range of deviations from this Haig-Simons formula that fall in their favor. Many such workers receive pensions or lump-sum payments when they retire. They do not pay tax on the value of these retirement payments as compensa-tion when they earn them. Instead, they defer the tax until they even-tually retire. Many enjoy the use of a well-stocked company cafeteria, a comfortable company vacation resort, or even a company car. They

---

[5] Henry C. Simons, Personal Income Taxation 50 (1938).

receive these perquisites as compensation for their work, yet they do not pay tax on them.

For most workers, perhaps the largest violation of Haig-Simons is the exclusion of the imputed value of owner-occupied housing and non-market household services.[6] Salaried professionals often own their own home. When they do, the right to live in the house is a return to the money they invested in buying the home. Although it is income under the Haig-Simons definition, it is not taxed. To understand this concept, take the discussion given by Richard Posner:[7]

> A man gives his two sons, A and B, $10,000 each. A puts his $10,000 in a savings bank that pays 5 percent annual interest, which he uses to pay the rent on the apartment that he leases. Because he is in the 20 percent federal income tax bracket, he pays $100 of the interest he receives each year to the government. B, who is in the same tax bracket as A, uses his $10,000 to purchase an apartment that has the same rental value as the apartment rented by A. B pays no income tax although he has put the same amount of money to the identical use as A.

Similarly, many married couples have one spouse (generally the husband) work in the labor market while the other provides house-keeping and child-rearing services.[8] They might both have chosen to work in the labor market and to purchase house-keeping and child-rearing services on the market. In that case, they would have paid taxes on both of their earnings. If instead one of them (gen-

---

[6] The non-taxed imputed income from owner-occupied assets and from household production is discussed in Hiroshi Kaneko, Sozeiho [Tax Law] 188 (Tokyo: Kobundo, 22nd ed., 2017).

[7] Richard A. Posner, Economic Analysis of Law, Third Edition 465 (Boston: Little, Brown & Co., 1986).

[8] Posner, supra note 7, at 464-65.

erally the wife) works directly for the family, they do not pay taxes on the value of her work. Marvin Chirelstein explains the logic: [9]

> [Consider] the housewife's uncompensated labor as nurse and homemaker. The value of those services, though in some instances a significant fraction of the family's economic income, is obviously not treated as [taxable] "income" .... By contrast, the working wife who uses some or all of her earnings to pay for equivalent domestic help gets no compensating deduction for the amounts expended.

Again, this violates Haig-Simons. Again, it widely benefits upper-middle-class salaried families.

5 Administrative costs

To an American observer, the Oshima dispute seems to miss the most intriguing aspect of the Japanese tax system: the almost trivial burden it imposes on taxpayers. The court focuses on the constitutional challenge, and rejects it. To an American observer, it very sensibly rejects it. U.S. taxpayers routinely challenge the constitutionality of the U.S. tax system too, and the courts just-as-routinely reject their challenges. Indeed, the Treasury routinely fines them frivolous-challenge penalties (I.R.C. Sec. 6702) as well.

Oshima decries the standardization in the Japanese tax system, but that very standardization generates enormous social savings. By eliminating individualized deductions to wage-earners, the system makes it unnecessary for most taxpayers to file returns. In the U.S., by contrast, nearly everyone who works must file a return.

The administrative costs are substantial. In the U.S., on a

---

[9] Marvin A. Chirelstein, Federal Income Taxation 24 (Westbury: Foundation, 7th ed., 1994).

population of 316 million, 136 million people file tax returns. Given that married couples file a joint return, these returns represent the claims of substantially more than 136 million taxpayers.[10] Estimates of the cost of complying with the requirement range from \$168 billion to \$431 billion.[11] By contrast, on a population of 127 million, only 14.5 million Japanese file any returns at all.[12]

解 説　COMMENT　**大法廷判決に見る租税政策論と法律学**

　本判決は大法廷判決であり，日本の租税法において，もっとも重要なものの一つであるといえよう（金子宏・判例評論 322 号 2 頁，同・租税判例百選〔第 3 版，第 4 版，第 5 版〕第 1 事件，泉德治・最高裁判所判例解説（民事）昭和 60 年度 74 頁，水野正一・ジュリスト 837 号 31 頁，中里実・税務事例 400 号 12 頁）。事件の内容それ自体が重要というよりも，判決の中で，租税の定義，納税義務の本質，租税法律主義の意義，租税の機能，租税法律の定立に関する立法裁量，租税公平主義と給与所得控除・所得捕捉率・租税特別措置の関係，等々の重要な理論的論点についてきわめて詳細に記述されており，かつ，それが現在の租税法理論の通説である金子宏名誉教授の考え方をほぼそのまま反映したものとなっている点が注目される。最高裁判所が，ここまで一人の研究者の学説を忠実に記述したことは，きわめてまれなのではなかろうか。

---

[10] See data given at http://taxfoundation.org/article/summary-latest-federal-income-tax-data-0.

[11] Compare estimates given at http://www.washingtonpost.com/blogs/fact-checker/post/claims-about-the-cost-and-time-it-takes-to-file-taxes/2013/04/13/858a97fc-a455-11e2-9c03-6952ff305f35_blog.html (\$168 billion estimate), with http://www.laffercenter.com/wp-content/uploads/2011/06/2011-Laffer-TaxCodeComplexity.pdf (\$431 billion estimate).

[12] 21.9 million Japanese taxpayers file returns. See data available at http://www.nta.go.jp/kohyo/katsudou/report/2012/02_4.htm. Of these, however, 7.4 million are businesses. http://www.cao.go.jp/zeicho/tosin/zeichof/z2013.html.

また，かつて，租税関係の訴訟に関しては，納税者が，自らの政策的・政治的な主張を行うための一つの手段として訴訟を利用する場合もなくはなかった。実情は必ずしもよくはわからないが，本件も，そのようなものの一つとして位置付けることができるかもしれない。そのような訴訟の利用に関する評価はさまざまあろうが，結果として，一人の研究者（すなわち，本件訴訟を提起した大島教授）の信念と，それを引き継いだ遺族の訴訟により，このような大法廷判決が下されたことの意義は大きいといえよう。

　具体的な争点は，租税公平主義との関連における，所得類型ごとの所得捕捉率の差異と，給与所得控除の是非ということになるのであろうが，いずれの点についても，憲法適合性の観点に関してのみいうならば，立法府の政策的判断が重要な意味を有するものとして尊重されるべきであることはまちがいなかろう。しかし，租税法を学ぶ際には，本件で合憲とされたとはいえ，果たして，政策論として，給与所得と事業所得の扱いの差異は現状のままでいいのかというような立法論に踏み込んだ議論をしてみると，より勉強になると思われる。結局，租税法の領域においては，そのような税制改革に絡む租税政策論が，法律学の世界においても，かなりの重要性を有すると考えられるからである。

　租税制度のあり方，就中，個人所得税制度のあり方は，社会経済の実情を反映して，国により，また時代により，かなりの差異がある。そのようなさまざまな制度のあり方の中で，どのようなものが望ましいのかという点について考えてみることは，立法論・政策論に触れる機会の少ない法律学の世界において，貴重な機会となるであろう。

　なお，日本の給与所得控除に直接対応する制度のないアメリカにおいては，本件のような問題は生じないものと思われる点に留意されたい。

CASE 9

K.K. Nihon kogyo ginko sosho shokeinin v. Kojimachi zeimusho cho

58 Saihan minshu 2637 (Sup. Ct. Dec. 24, 2004).[1]

興銀税務訴訟

(最判平成 16 年 12 月 24 日民集 58 巻 9 号 2637 頁)

1 The facts

The Industrial Bank of Japan (IBJ; now part of the Mizuho Bank) owned a minority stake in Japan Housing Loan, K.K. (JHL). As of early 1996, the JHL owed it 376 billion yen. The JHL had lent that money to home owners and commercial real estate developers, and many of those borrowers had defaulted. It had little (if any) hope of retrieving much of that money from them, and the IBJ had little hope of retrieving much money from the JHL.

Under pressure from the government, the IBJ agreed in March 1996 to abandon all claims against JHL. That still left other claimants against the JHL. They had no legal claims against the IBJ (at least no straightforward legal claims), but some of them held substantial political power. The IBJ insisted that the government clarify the extent of the IBJ's exposure, and spend its own funds to help resolve the problem. The IBJ would, it explained, abandon its claims only if the government passed a statute clarifying the responsibilities of the

---

[1] Reversing 1783 Hanrei jiho 52 (Tokyo High Ct. Mar. 14, 2002), reversing Kojimachi Tax Office v. K.K. Nihon kogyo ginko, 1783 Hanrei jiho 52 (Tokyo High Ct. Mar. 14, 2002).

parties involved. The Diet pased the statute in June 1996, the IBJ abandoned its claims, and the JHL filed for liquidation.

IBJ reported its loss from the JHL debt on its return for the taxable year ending March 1996. Sec. 22(c)(iii) of the Corporate Tax Act allows firms to deduct "the amount of loss during the firm's relevant taxable year, other than that accruing from a capital transaction."[2] IBJ argued that the bad-debt write-off constituted just such a loss.

The tax office replied that the debt (if deductible at all) was deductible in 1996-97, not 1995-96. The IBJ had promised to abandon its claims only if the Diet passed a statute, and the Diet did not pass it until June. At the close of the 1995-96 year in March, the IBJ's claims against the the JHL were not yet completely worthless. As a result, the IBJ could deduct the loss only during the succeeding year (if at all).

Timing was crucial, for the IBJ had recognized a large tax gain in anticipation of the debt write-down. Having decided to acquiesce to the government and abandon its claims against the JHL, the IBJ had sold a large block of appreciated stock. It now badly needed the taxable loss from the write-down, and needed it in 1995-96.[3]

The District Court held for the IBJ:[4]

> Even where some recovery might still be possible if the taxpayer made use of legal measures, if the use of those

---

[2] Hojinzei ho [Corporate Tax Act], Law No. 34 of 1965. The U.S. tax code (IRC, Sec. 166(a)(i)) provides: "There shall be allowed as a deduction any debt which becomes worthless within the taxable year."

[3] See Hiroyoshi Obuchi, Zeiho kaishaku ni okeru sozei horitsu shugi to sozei kohei shugi to no sokoku [The Conflict Between the Principles of Statutory Basis for Taxation and Equality in Taxation], at 47, available at http://www.tkc.jp/tkcnf/news/docs/taxforum2014report_slc03.pdf; Tatsuo Aoyagi, Kashidaore saiken no sonkin keijo jiki (jo) [The Timing of Bad Debt Losses], 54 Yamaguchi keizaigaku zasshi 705 (nd).

[4] K.K. Nihon kogyo ginko v. Kojimachi zeimu shocho, 1742 Hanrei jiho 25 (Tokyo D. Ct. Mar. 2, 2001) (Westlaw op. at 79-80).

measures would be harmful or unprofitable, and economically unreasonable, the claim is economically worthless. By the common sense of society, the loan is unrecoverable.

Whether a loan falls within that category depends on a variety of considerations: the assets and liabilities of the debtor, the nature of the debtor's business, the relationship between the debtor and creditor, the creditor's economic circumstances, whether the debt is of the sort that is amenable to judicial enforcement; if not amenable then whether the debtor admits the debt, such that the debt can even be identified, and the costs and time involved in that identification; the possibility and extent of judicial enforcement; the risks of the reaction and likely opposition of the parties associated with the debtor to such legal measures.

The tax office appealed, and the Tokyo High Court reversed.[5] As of March 1996, it explained, the IBJ's debt was not completely worthless. IBJ appealed, and the Supreme Court reversed again. It reasoned: [6]

For a bad-debt loss to fall within a given firm year as "the amount of loss during the firm's relevant taxable year" under Sec. 22(c) (iii) of the Corporate Tax Act, the amount of the financial claim must be unrecoverable. Indeed, it must be objectively clear that the entire amount of the claim is unrecoverable. That decision, however, must follow social common sense. It must take into account: the asset situation of the debtor, the debtor's ability to pay, the effort

---

[5] Kojimachi zeimu shocho v. K.K. Nihon kogyo ginko, 1783 Hanrei jiho 52 (Tokyo High Ct. Mar. 14, 2002).

[6] K.K. Nihon kogyo ginko, 1883 Hanrei jiho 31 (Sup. Ct. Dec. 24, 2004) (Westlaw opinion at 9-10).

necessary to recover the claim, a comparison of the amount of the claim and the cost of recovery, the bad will (and business loss) created among other creditors by any attempt judicially to recover the claim.

The resulting legal doctrine follows straightforwardly. A firm may deduct a debt in the year it abandons the debt as worthless. That worthlessness should turn not on whether the firm has a legal claim against the debtor, but on whether it can realistically collect on the debt. By the end of the 1995-96 year, it was clear that the IBJ could not realistically collect. Accordingly, the IBJ could deduct.

2 Why did the government do this?

The story is as bizarre as it sounds: the government pressured a bank to forgive a loan; the bank complied; and the government then refused to let it deduct the loss on its tax return. What could it have been thinking? ▼7

a. **Housing subsidies** The story begins in the 1970s, and combines implicit housing subsidies with partisan turmoil. Voters like to own their homes. Most lack the money to buy them, of course, and need loans from banks. Yet many who want to own their homes lack the resources necessary to convince banks to lend them that money. Banks can make money lending funds, but they do not make money lending to people who default. People who would borrow need to convince banks that they will repay the loans, and to do so they need savings and income. Many who want to own their own homes lack those

---

▼7 A point nicely made by Minoru Nakazato, Kogin jiken ni miru sozeiho to shakai tsunen [Tax Law and Social Common Sense in the IBJ Decision], 43-5 Zeimu jirei 38 (2011).

101

savings and incomes.

Facing voter demand for loans, Japanese politicians began pressuring banks to lend. More precisely, they began pressuring banks to make loans they would not otherwise have chosen to make. Given that banks will happily lend to people who will safely repay principal and interest, politicians began pressuring banks to lend to voters presenting higher odds of default.

U.S. politicians did exactly the same thing during the years before 2008, of course. Voters wanted to own their homes. Many lacked the income and savings they needed to convince a bank to lend them the necessary funds. They pressured politicians to force the banks to lend them the money. Being heavily regulated institutions, banks complied. When the economy shifted, the borrowers (being high-risk to begin with) defaulted en masse. And the crisis of 2008 ensued.[8]

Seventeen years earlier, much the same phenomena had happened in Japan. To induce profit-maximizing banks to make loans they otherwise considered too high-risk, politicians pressed them to organize eight retail mortgage firms (*jusen*). The banks were to lend mortgage firms money. And the firms were to make retail mortgage loans that the banks thought too risky.[9]

Under this government pressure, the IBJ joined four other financial institutions and organized JHL. The five firms lent it funds. In turn, the JHL re-lent the money to consumers for home mortgages.

---

[8] See, e.g., John B. Taylor, Causes of the Financial Crisis and the Slow Recovery, in Martin Neil Baily & John B. Taylor, Across the Great Divide: New Perspectives on the Financial Crisis 51, at 55 (Stanford: Hoover Press, 2014); Patric H. Hendershott & Kevin Villani, What Made the Financial Crisis Systemic?, Policy Analysis, Mar. 6, 2012; Peter J. Wallison, Government Housing Policy and the Financial Crisis, Cato J., 30(2)(2010).

[9] Curtis J. Milhaupt & Geoffrey P. Miller, Cooperation, Conflict, and Convergence in Japanese Finance: Evidence from the "Jusen" Problem, 29 L. & Pol'y Int'l Bus. 1, 24 (1997-98).

Over the course of the 1980s, it diversified into commercial real estate as well.[10]

After rising spectacularly in the 1980s, however, land prices plummeted (see **Figure** on page 145). Borrowers found themselves unable (or at least unwilling) to repay the loans. Recall that these were borrowers that the banks had thought too risky, and who had received loans only after the government forced the banks to organize the mortgage firms. They now defaulted on their loans to these mortgage firms in massive numbers, and the mortgage firms defaulted on their loans to the banks.[11]

For politicians subject to competitive electoral markets, this phenomenon presents a problem. Politicians do not want banks using the legal system. Sensible lenders take legally enforceable security interests to protect themselves against exactly these situations. If a borrower defaults, they turn to these legal rights. They may repossess assets. They may throw borrowers into bankruptcy. They may evict borrowers from their homes, or shutter local employers. Politicians do not want any of this.

To prevent banks from using the legal devices they create, politicians exploit a deeply rooted hostility toward bankers. That hostility runs deep, both in the West and in Japan. The top American college graduates may have volunteered for Goldman Sachs in the early 2000s,[12] and the top Japanese graduates may have marched to the big banks in the 1980s. But voters in both countries carry a prejudice against money-lenders with a long cultural tradition. Shakespeare famously captured the occidental hostility in the Merchant of Venice.

---

[10] Milhaupt & Miller, supra note 9, at 3, 25, 28-29; K.K. Nihon kogyo ginko, 1742 Hanrei jiho 25 (Tokyo D. Ct. Mar. 2, 2001).

[11] See the general discussion Milhaupt & Miller, supra note 9, at 46; K.K. Nihon kogyo ginko, 1742 Hanrei jiho 25 (Tokyo D. Ct. Mar. 2, 2001).

Tokugawa-era playwrights reflected the traditional Japanese skeptism in kabuki and joruri.

But populist politicians do not just pander to voters generally; they protect their most loyal supporters against gambles they lose. When General Motors failed after the 2008 debacle, the labor unions would have lost badly. Rather than let them do so, the Obama administration routed them funds the law did not allow them.[13] When the real estate market collapsed in 1991 Japan, the agricultural cooperatives (*nokyo*) stood to lose badly. The cooperatives sometimes played a pivotal role in helping the conservative Liberal Democratic Party (LDP) collect votes in rural communities.[14] As Curtis Milhaupt and Geoffrey Miller put it, the "political power of the cooperatives derives from the importance of agricultural policy in Japan and the vote-gathering capacity of the system for the LDP."[15] Farmers had deposited their savings in the cooperatives, and the cooperatives had lent heavily to the mortgage firms. When the mortgage firms collapsed, the cooperatives —— and their farmer depositors —— now stood to lose massively.

Indeed, the cooperatives had lent the mortgage firms more than had the financial firms that had created them (like the IBJ). By

---

[12] Amy J. Binder, Why Are Harvard Grads Still Flocking to Wall Street?, Washington Monthly, Sept.-Oct. 2014, at: http://www.washingtonmonthly.com/magazine/septemberoctober_2014/features/why_are_harvard_grads_still_fl051758.php?page=all (claiming that "In 2007, just before the global financial meltdown, almost 50 percent of Harvard seniors (58 percent of the men, 43 percent of the women) took jobs on Wall Street.").

[13] J. Mark Ramseyer & Eric Rasmusen, Can the Treasury Exempt its Own Companies from Tax? The $45 Billion GM NOL Carryforward, 1 Cato Papers Pub. Pol. 1 (2011).

[14] Milhaupt & Miller, supra note 9, at 29-38.

[15] Curtis J. Milhaupt & Geoffrey P. Miller, Regulatory Failure and the Collapse of Japan's Home Mortgage Lending Industry: A Legal and Economic Analysis, 22 L. & Pol. 245, 263 (2000).

the time of the crisis, the founding financial firms had lent the mortgage firms 3.5 trillion yen. Other banks had lent them 3.8 trillion And the agricultural cooperatives had lent 5.5 trillion.[16] Were the banks to throw the firms into bankruptcy, they would lose amounts that reflected the relative legal priority of those claims. In general, however, they would probably lose amounts roughly proportional to their relative exposure. The creditors that stood to lose the most: the agricultural cooperatives.

  b. Partisan turmoil But in 1996 Japan, it was not politics as usual.

  In 1993 —— for the first time since 1955 —— the LDP lost power. The renegade ex-LDP politician Morihiro Hosokawa formed the first post-LDP cabinet in 1993. Fellow renegade Tsutomu Hata followed him briefly in 1994. Then, however, socialist Tomiichi Murayama took power and ruled until 1996. During Murayama's tenure, other powerful LDP politicians bolted the party. The most successful would form the New Frontier Party (NFP; Shinshinto). The party would collapse in 1997, but during the time of the IBJ-JHL-agricultural-cooperative dispute, it posed a strong populist threat to the LDP. In the lower house elections of late 1996, it took 156 seats to the LDP's 239.

  Toward the banks, NFP politicians played hardline demogogues. Banks (like the IBJ) had organized the mortgage firms (like the JHL) out of greed, they insisted. They dominated them. They pushed them toward high-risk strategies, and those strategies had now caused the predictable debacles. They should not just abandon their claims. They should compensate the other claimants to the mortgage firms for their losses. Certainly, taxpayers should pay nothing more.[17]

---

[16] Milhaupt & Miller, supra note 15, at 270, tab 1 (from Shoji homu, 1996).

In effect, NFP politicians argued that principles of "lender liability" should apply.[18] Under U.S. law, if a creditor dominates the affairs of a debtor, he may be liable for the debtor's obligations. In dealing with third parties, the debtor has acted on his "behalf." As principal to the debtor as agent, the creditor is now liable for the debts the debtor incurs. Courts apply the doctrine only rarely in the U.S., and it remains exceedingly controverial. It is, however, what NFP politicians argued should control this case.

To push the founding banks to accept their demands, the NFP politicians threatened criminal prosecution.[19] Quite what crime the banks might have committed is unclear. Losing money is not criminal, after all. But NFP politicians threatened prosecution should the founding banks refuse to pay the debts of the insolvent mortgage firms.

Consider the position of the IBJ. Under government pressure, it had formed and invested in a firm (JHL) that would extend the mortgage loans that it (the IBJ) thought imprudent. That mortgage firm had made loans secured by real estate, and when prices collapsed had defaulted on its debts. When the bank had embarked on this project, the government had been under the control of the conservative LDP. Now, power had shifted to a socialist. Incendiary politicians were demanding that it make good the JHL's debts, and threatening criminal prosecution if it refused.

IBJ and the other founding banks still thought the law was on their side. Throughout these negotiations with the government, they repeatedly threatened to take the case to court. They threatened to throw the mortgage firms into bankruptcy proceedings. If they did,

---

[17] Nihon kogyo ginko, 1742 Hanrei jiho 25 (Tokyo D. Ct. Mar. 2, 2001) (Westlaw op, at 68-69).

[18] J. Mark Ramseyer, Business Organizations 6-7 (New York: Wolters Kluwer, 2012).

[19] Nihon kogyo ginko, 1742 Hanrei jiho 25 (Tokyo D. Ct. Mar. 2, 2001).

they might have been able to recover some of the money that the mortgage firms owed them. The agricultural cooperatives would have borne a large share of the losses. But even politicians not insisting on lender liability wanted the founding banks to abandon their claims and let the cooperatives recover their funds. Before the founding banks agreed to this, they wanted some assurance that they would not also be liable for the full scope of the mortgage firm's outstanding debts. Toward that end, they needed the statute that eventually passed in June 1996.[20]

解説 COMMENT **興銀税務訴訟が租税訴訟に与えた影響**

本件は，納税者の政策的・政治的な主張の表現としてではなく，納税者である大手企業が，もっぱらビジネス上の理由から国税当局を相手取って真剣に訴訟を行ったほぼ最初の事例であり，これ以降，日本の租税訴訟のあり方が，以下のように大きく変わったという点で，日本の租税法において重要な意義を有するものであるということができる。すなわち，

① **企業による租税訴訟提起の増加**

伝統的に，日本の大企業が国税当局を相手取って訴訟を起こすということはほとんどなかった。それが，本件が先例となったためか，本件の訴訟提起以降，企業が租税訴訟（しかも，高額なもの）を提起する例が増加した。

② **高額な租税訴訟の一般化**

本件最高裁判決の結果として，約 1500 億円の課税処分が取り消され，約 1000 億円の還付加算金が納税者に支払われた他，地方税に関しても支払税額と還付加算金を合わせて約 700 億円が支払われた。その後，本件がきっかけとなったためか，租税訴訟においては，課税処分 100 億円を超える事件が数多く納税

---

[20] Obuchi, supra note 3, at 47; Aoyagi, supra note 3, at 709-10; Hiroyoshi Obuchi opinion, as reproduced at: http://www.torikai.gr.jp/tax/3264.

者勝訴のかたちで決着している他，1000億円を超えるような事件も，いくつか納税者勝訴のかたちで決着している。

③　司法国家化の進展

本件以降，一流企業が課税処分の内容について，裁判所という「出るところ」に出て正々堂々と課税庁と議論するという，法治国家においてきわめて健全な法的紛争解決形態が一般化した点は，大いに評価することができよう。このことにより，結果として，租税行政も進歩することになるからである。

④　企業経営への影響

他方，企業の方も，課税処分が違法である場合に放置しておくと，代表訴訟等を通じて経営者が責任を問われる場合が生じてきている。これは，租税制度が，コーポレート・ガバナンスの充実に貢献している例としてとらえることができよう。

本件に関して，理論的な観点から見て重要なのは事実認定と社会通念である（これらについては，以下を参照〔中里実『デフレ下の法人課税改革』（有斐閣，2003）第3章，同「借用概念と事実認定——租税法における社会通念」税経通信64巻14号（886号）17頁，同「興銀事件に見る租税法と社会通念」税務事例43巻5号38頁〕）。第一に，租税訴訟において事実認定の有する意味はきわめて大きい。複雑怪奇な租税法規の解釈に立ち入る前に，詳細な事実認定を前提として問題を解決することができれば，司法による問題解決の有用性が明らかになる。そして，本件では，貸付債権が貸し倒れているか否かという点が正面から争われ，その結果として，納税者勝訴の判断となったのである。

第二に，そのような事実認定を行うに際して，社会通念の果たす役割が大きいことを，本判決は明示している。社会通念に基づいて判断を行うということは，結局は，裁判所の役割を重視することであり，法治国家において望ましいことであるといえよう。

PART 4

刑事法

CASE

| 10 | 光市母子殺害事件第二次上告審判決 |
| 11 | 狭山事件 |

CASE 10

[No names given]

2167 Hanrei jiho 118 (Sup. Ct. Feb. 20, 2012).

●

光市母子殺害事件第二次上告審判決
（最判平成 24 年 2 月 20 日判例時報 2167 号 118 頁）

1 The facts

On April 14, 1999, a young man decided that he wanted to have sex. At age eighteen he was still a virgin, but he decided to end that status.

Upon graduating from high school, the young man had taken a job. Quickly alienated from his employer, he stopped going to work, but left the house every morning anyway to deflect his parents' suspicions. Some days, he played video games. Other days, he spent with his friends.

On April 14, the young man left his house as always, but determined this time to find a young woman alone. He tried several apartments within his local complex. At about 2:30 p.m., he arrived at the apartment of 23-year-old woman. When she came to the door, he explained that he had come from the local sewage company to inspect the equipment. He went to her lavatory, and pretended to check her toilet.

Upon exiting the bathroom, the young man grabbed her from behind. She fought back, and he grabbed her by the neck. She struggled to escape, but he squeezed her neck harder, choked her —— and killed her. He then raped her corpse. For no obvious reason (he would

110

later explain that he worried she might come back to life), he sealed her nostrils with adhesive tape. When her 11-month-old daughter started crying, the young man smashed her head on the floor. He then stuffed the two corpses in the closet, took the mother's wallet, and left. He used the stolen money to play at the local video parlor for the rest of the day.

The trial court convicted the young man and sentenced him to life in prison.[1] Seeing some chance that he might reform, the appellate court affirmed.[2] The Supreme Court vacated the sentence. Absent some unusual reason, it explained, a crime this vicious left no room for prison. It told the court below to explore whether the crime raised any such special reason, and —— if not —— to sentence him to death.[3] The high court duly imposed the death penalty, and on re-appeal the Supreme Court affirmed.[4]

2 The reasoning

In 1983, the Supreme Court had outlined the factors it wanted lower court judges to consider in deciding whether to sentence defendants to death:[5]

> The death penalty is appropriate when a defendant's criminal responsibility is truly large, and the sentence is necessary to maintain balance among the various criminal penalties or to preserve general deterrence. This necessity, in turn, depends the nature of the crime, the defendant's mo-

---

[1] [No name given], Hanrei taikei 28175279 (Yamaguchi D. Ct. Mar. 22, 2000).

[2] [No name given], 1941 Hanrei jiho 45 (Hiroshima High Ct. Mar. 14, 2002).

[3] [No name given], 1941 Hanrei jiho 38 (Sup. Ct. June 20, 2006).

[4] [No name given], 2167 Hanrei jiho 122 (Hiroshima High Ct. Apr. 22, 2008); [No names given], 2167 Hanrei jiho 118 (Sup. Ct. Feb. 20, 2012).

[5] Kuni v. Nagayama, 1099 Hanrei jiho 148, 150 (Sup. Ct. July 8, 1983).

tive, the specific situation (in particular, the ... brutality of the murder), the magnitude of the result (particularly, the number of victims), the emotional damage to the survivors, the social impact, and the suspect's age, prior criminal history, and post-crime circumstances.

This list of factors may make sense for a trial court that hears evidence. It makes less sense for a Supreme Court to use (as it purported to do here) in deciding whether to vacate a life sentence and require the death penalty instead. After all, Supreme Court justices do not hear witnesses or take testimony. They simply examine the lower court record. About most of these factors, they will know only what the lower court chooses to tell them.

For instance, the list includes the "brutality" of a murder: the more brutal the murder, the more inclined a judge should be to execute the defendant. This, however, is something the Supreme Court will know only by examining the record, and the lower court will have constructed that record to avoid reversal. If the Supreme Court requires the death penalty for "brutal" murders, then judges who want to hang a defendant will describe his crime "brutally." Those who want to give him a life sentence will describe it more ambiguously.

Much the same holds true for a defendant's "motive," and most of the other factors the Court includes. Human beings are complex beasts. They do what they do for a host of contradictory motives, few of which are ever clear. The lower court judges take testimony about those motives, but the Supreme Court does not. The lower court judge in this case wrote that the young man left his house determined to rape a young woman. But his lawyers had introduced evidence to the contrary. They had added that his mother had killed herself when he was in middle school, that his father had abused him, that he had the emotional maturity of a 12-year-old, even that he thought he might be reincarnated as victim's husband.

Nonetheless, the Supreme Court summarized the lower court's findings and declared them insufficient to warrant life in prison:

> The factors weighed in determining the punishment (both by the opinion below and by the trial court it affirmed), whether considered independently or collectively, do not justify the decision not to apply the death penalty.

The question, in short, was not whether the court below found reason to impose the death penalty. Instead, it was whether the court below found reason to avoid it. The Supreme Court said no, and remanded the case to determine whether any other factors justified skirting the death penalty. The High Court understood the obvious implication, and sentenced the young man to death.

3 The number of victims

The Supreme Court may be signalling something close to a mandatory death penalty for multiple-murder cases. Japanese courts have long keyed penalties to the number of victims involved. In 2012, for example, I examined all 200 murder opinions published since 1980, and sorted them by the number of victims. Where a defendant killed one victim, the courts imposed a death penalty in 4.1 percent of the cases. Where he killed two, it sentenced him to death in 54.3 percent. And where he killed 3 or more, it sentenced him to death in 75.8 percent of the cases.[6]

Under this practice, this case was not an obvious one for the death penalty. If a defendant killed two people, the courts had sentenced him to die only half the time. Even had the court considered

---

[6] J. Mark Ramseyer, Who Hangs Whom for What? The Death Penalty in Japan, 4 J. Legal Anal. 365, 385 tab. 3 (2012).

rape the equivalent of a murder (it did not say whether it did), it still would only have executed him 3/4 of the time.

Given this background, perhaps the Supreme Court wanted to change practice. Effective 2009, the lower courts began using juries (saiban-in) to help decide capital cases. According to some commentators, perhaps the Supreme Court wanted to introduce a clear standard. Rather than leave jurors with the heavily discretionary and largely indeterminate 1983 standards, perhaps it wanted a simple rule: if a defendant killed more than one person, hang him.[7]

In turn, however, the new clear rule (if such is what it is) introduces a serious "marginal deterrence" problem. Suppose A breaks into a house to steal the owner's jewels. He thought the house was empty, but it was not. He encounters the owner and his wife. If the penalty for burglary is 10 years in prison, he will pause before killing the owner and his wife. Killing them may raise the odds that he can escape safely, but it also raises the penalty he suffers if ultimately caught. Out of rational self-interest, he may decide to spare their lives.

When a criminal faces a mandatory death penalty, he no longer has reason to avoid further crimes. Suppose he decides to kill the couple, and suppose the courts always hang defendants who kill two people. If the criminal is caught, he faces a mandatory death penalty. No matter what else he may do, his penalty will not change. In essence, the penalty he suffers for any additional crimes is now zero. If he has already killed two people, he no longer has any reason not to kill a third.

This marginal deterrence problem particularly endangers

---

[7] Hikari shi jiken bengodan, Hikari shi jiken: bengodan ha naniwo rissho shita no ka [The Hikari City Case: What did the Lawyers Prove] 44 (Tokyo: Inpakuto shuppan, 2008).

police officers —— who must chase and try to capture dangerous killers. A killer who thought he still could avoid the death penalty might
be careful what he did. A killer already subject to a mandatory death
penalty has little reason not to kill any pursuing officer. A mandatory
death penalty for multiple-victim murders might seem to fit the crime
—— but it dramatically raises the risks to police.

4 The politics

a. Victim rights This case raised at least two prominent but
(here) conflicting political pressures. The late victim's husband, made
the case a platform for victim's rights —— and a particularly vindic-
tive platform at that. On the day of the murder, he had returned from
work and found his wife's body: stripped, gagged, raped, and strangled. He had called the police, and they found his murdered daughter
as well. They then declared him the prime suspect and interrogated
him all through the night.[8]

A few days later, the police located the young man who confessed to the crime. Given his age, however, they sent him to family
court, where he had no access to any information about the proceedings. Only after the family court sent the case to the prosecutors' office did he learn anything about the young man.

He then launched what seems almost a private prosecution campaign. He attended the young man's court proceedings. He
brought his wife's and daughter's photographs to the court gallery.[9]
He published his and his wife's love letters as a book. He let others

---

[8] Kaoru Inoue, Saibankan ga mita Hikarishi boshi satsugai jiken [A Judge's
Perspective on the Hikari City Mother-Daughter Murder Case] 26 (Tokyo: Bungei
shunju, 2009).

[9] Inoue, supra note 8, at 40.

make the book into a movie. And when the trial court sentenced the young man to life in prison, he held a press conference:[10]

> I've lost hope in the court system. I don't want an appeal to the High Court or the Supreme Court. Just send the guy back into society, but near where I can reach him. I'll kill him with my own hands.

Victim's rights, he seemed to declare, required the courts to cater to his own vindictiveness.

b. The death penalty The case also galvanized opposition to the death penalty. To be sure, Japanese government surveys show strong public support (over 80 percent) for the death penalty.[11] Obviously, the numbers will turn on the actual wording of the questions, but U.S. surveys typically show support only in the 60-70 percent range.[12] But the Japanese bar association stands to the left of the public on many years, and it strongly opposes the death penalty.[13] Other activists do as well. In this case, 21 lawyers joined in handling the young man's appeals.[14]

Yet opponents to the death penalty face a hard moral prob-

---

[10] Inoue, supra note 8, at 58-59.

[11] Naikakufu, Kihon teki hoseido ni kansuru seron chosa [Opinion Survey Relating to Basic Legal System] (2016). Available at: http://survey.gov-online.go.jp/h26/h26-houseido/index.html.

[12] Gallup Historical Trends: Death Penalty (2015). Available at: http://www.gallup.com/poll/1606/death-penalty.aspx.

[13] Nihon bengoshi rengo kai, Shikei seido ni kansuru seifu no seron chosa ni taisuru ikensho [Opinion Regarding the Government Opinion Survey on the Death Penalty] (2013). Available at: http://www.nichibenren.or.jp/activity/document/opinion/year/2013/131122_4.html. The American Bar Association has shown similar (though not as strong) skepticism toward the death penalty. See http://www.americanbar.org/groups/individual_rights/projects/death_penalty_due_process_review_project/policy.html.

[14] Hikari shi jiken bengodan, supra note 7.

lem. Apparently, the death penalty deters crime. This impact is hard to measure in Japan, because the country maintains only one national criminal justice system. In the U.S., however, each state runs its own criminal law regime. Some states impose the death penalty, some do not, and many states change the practices they impose over time.

Scholars can use this state-level variation to study the death penalty's deterrent effect. Take two otherwise similar states A and B. Suppose both states have imposed the death penalty for murder for years. Now suppose that the Supreme Court in state A abolishes the penalty on moral grounds. By comparing the crime rates in A and B before and after this decision, the scholar can begin to estimate the effect that the death penalty has on criminal behavior.

Most empirical scholars find that the death penalty has a substantial deterrent effect. They are not unanimous. Some insist that the evidence does not show a deterrent impact. But several scholars find that each execution deters multiple murders. The estimated number deterred varies —— but generally ranges from 5 to 24.[15] For each murderer executed, in other words, the number of murder victims falls by 5 to 24.

If each execution deters 5 to 24 murders, then the moral case against it becomes profoundly troubling. Those inclined to an ontolog-

---

[15] H. Naci Mocan & R. Kaj Gittings, Getting Off Death Row: Commuted Sentences and the Deterrent Effect of Capital Punishment, 46 J. L. & Econ. 453 (2003) (each execution deters 5 murders); Hashem Dezhbakhsh, Paul Rubin, & Joanna M. Shepherd, Does Capital Punishment Have a Deterrent Effect? New Evidence form Postmoratorium Panel Data. Am Econ Rev., 5: 344 (2003) (each execution deters 18 murders); Isaac Ehrlich, Capital Punishment and Deterrence: Some Further thoughts and Additional Evidence, 85 J. Pol. Eco., 741 (1977) (each execution deters 20-24 murders). See also Isaac Ehrlich & Zhiqiang Liu. Sensitivity Analyses of the Deterrence Hypothesis: Let's keep the Econ in Econometrics. J. L. & Econ. 42: 455 (1999) (death penalty deters crime); Lawrence Katz, Steven D. Levitt & Ellen Shustorovich, Prison Conditions, Capital Punishment, and Deterrence. 5 Am. L. & Econ. Rev. 318 (2003) (harsh prison conditions deter crime).

ical approach will continue to insist that executions are simply *wrong*
——deterrence or no deterrence, killing anyone is morally wrong.
Yet those willing to consider the net social welfare must now weigh
relative costs. On the one hand, they have the convicted murderer
who will or will not be executed. On the other hand, they have the 5
to 24 other people whose lives will be saved by the execution because
the *threat* of execution will deter *other* criminals from murder. Indeed, for exactly this reason, two prominent scholars argued recently
that morality may actually *require* the death penalty.[16]

5 How mandatory is mandatory?

A focus on the Supreme Court case law can miss what happens in practice. According to the Supreme Court, unless the lower
court could find additional extenuating circumstances (which it could
not), it needed to apply the death penalty. If anyone rapes a mother
and kills her and her daughter, the Court seemed to say, he must die.

But to interpret the opinion in this way misses what happens
in Japan. Defendants sentenced to death do not necessarily die. Instead, the Minister of Justice controls the decision to execute, and he
does not execute everyone sentenced to death.

From 1980 to 2010, the Minister of Justice actually executed
fewer than half of the people sentenced to death. During that period,
trial courts sentenced 240 defendants to death. The courts imposed final death orders (at the close of the appeals) on 209 defendants. During
the same period, however, only 99 defendants actually died. Over the
31 years, the number of executions was only 41 percent of the number
of people sentenced to death.[17]

---

[16] Cass R. Sunstein & Adrian Vermeule, Is Capital Punishment Morally Required?
Acts, Omissions, and Life-Life Tradeoffs, 58 Stan. L. Rev. 703 (2005).

Even since 2000, the government carries out fewer than half of the the death sentences. Perhaps reflecting the effect of court opinions like the one here, courts impose more such penalties. Actual executions, however, remain a minority. From 2000 to 2010, the trial courts ordered 127 defendants executed. The courts issued final orders for 121. And the Minister of Justice executed 48.[18]

解 説　COMMENT　死刑の選択基準

　本件は，犯行時に18歳と30日であった被告人が，主婦を強姦目的で殺害したうえ姦淫するとともに，その場で生後11か月の幼児をも殺害し，さらに被害者の財布を窃取したという事件である。第1審および控訴審が，被告人に無期懲役を言い渡したのに対し，最高裁は，著しい量刑不当を理由にそれを破棄した。最高裁が，量刑不当により原判決を破棄すること自体が異例であるうえに，本件は，被告人が18歳になって間もない少年であったことや，犯行に計画性がなかった点などから，それまでの先例からすると無期懲役が相当ともみえる事案であったため，最高裁が，本判決によって死刑選択の基準を実質的に変更したのではないかという意見も示されることになった。

　最高裁による死刑選択の基準は，1983年の永山事件判決（最判昭和58・7・8刑集37巻6号609頁）で示されたものであり，一般に，永山基準と呼ばれる。それは，「犯行の罪質，動機，態様ことに殺害の手段方法の執拗性・残虐性，結果の重大性ことに殺害された被害者の数，遺族の被害感情，社会的影響，犯人の年齢，前科，犯行後の情状等各般の情状を併せ考察したとき，その罪責が誠に重大であつて，罪刑の均衡の見地からも一般予防の見地からも極刑がやむをえないと認められる場合には，死刑の選択も許される」とするものである。そこでは，裁判所が死刑を選択するか否かの判断にあたって考慮すべき要素が挙

CASE
10
光市母子殺害事件第二次上告審判決
[No names given]

---

[17]　Ramseyer, supra note 6, at 371 tab. 1.
[18]　Ramseyer, supra note 6.

げられているとはいえ，それぞれの要素の重要度は何も示されていないし，そこで挙げられていない要素の考慮が否定されるものでもない。その意味で，死刑選択の基準が示されたとはいっても，その適用にあたっては，個別の事件ごとの裁判所の判断に委ねられる部分が大きいのである。

それを踏まえて，ラムザイヤー教授の「解説」では，本判決は，裁判員制度の導入を契機に，最高裁が，殺害された被害者が複数の場合には死刑を選択すべきであるという，裁判員にも判断が容易にできる明確な死刑選択基準を示そうとしたものではないかという解釈が示されている。しかし，本判決以後も，被害者が複数の事件において，死刑ではなく無期懲役を言い渡した原判決を，最高裁が維持したものが少なからずあるし，逆に，被害者が1人の事件で死刑判決が維持されたものもある。したがって，その後の最高裁は，本判決は，「解説」が示唆するような強いメッセージを込めたものではないと理解していることになろう。いずれにしても，それが充足されれば，事実上必ず死刑が選択されるといった基準は未だ存在していない。

他方で，アメリカにおいては，州ごとに規定は異なるものの，法律上，一定の犯罪について，一定の加重事由が存在する場合に限って，死刑を選択できるというかたちで，裁判所の裁量に枠をはめている例が数多くみられる。

また，本件は，被害者の夫であり父であった遺族が，公の場で，第1審および控訴審の無期懲役の判断に強い不満を表明し，結果として，上告審でそれが覆ったために，永山判決において死刑選択にあたっての考慮要素の1つとされている遺族の被害感情の位置づけについても議論を呼び起こすことになった。もっとも，量刑実務上は，被害者遺族の被害感情が死刑選択にあたって決定的な意味を持つことはないとされており，本件においても，被害者遺族の死刑を求める声が強かったがゆえに最高裁が原判決を破棄したわけではないとする理解が一般的である。

他方，アメリカでは，そもそも，死刑事件の量刑手続において，被害者の遺族が，犯罪が与えた影響を陳述することが許されるかどうかが問題とされ，連邦最高裁は，当初，それは許されないという立場をとっていたが，1991年の判決（Payne v. Tennessee, 501 U.S. 808）において，それを認めるに至ったという経緯がある。

最後に，本件もそうであったように，死刑か無期懲役かが争われる事件の背

後には，死刑制度の当否についての対立が伏在している。この問題は，わが国でもアメリカでも，長く議論がなされてきており，「解説」で紹介されているように，アメリカでは，死刑存廃論の争点の 1 つである。死刑が特別な威嚇力，犯罪抑止力を持つか否かという点につき，死刑を存置している州とそれを廃止した州の犯罪発生率を比較する等の手法による実証的研究も数多くなされている。ちなみに，アメリカでは，2019 年 6 月末現在で，連邦と 29 の州が死刑を存置，21 州とコロンビア特別区が廃止している。また，存置州のうち 4 州では，州知事により死刑の執行が停止されている。

CASE
10

光市母子殺害事件第二次上告審判決
[No names given]

CASE 11

Kuni v. Ishikawa

864 Hanrei jiho 22 (Sup. Ct. Aug. 9, 1977). [1]

狭山事件
(最決昭和 52 年 8 月 9 日判例時報 864 号 22 頁)

1 The facts

It rained in Sayama on the afternoon of May 1, 1963. Some 20 miles (30 km) west of Tokyo city proper, Sayama today is a bedroom suburb. In 1963 it was still a rural village. Sixteen-year-old woman attended the local high school. It was her birthday.

The fourth of five children, she came from a prosperous farming family. That afternoon on the 1st, she did not return from school. Her oldest brother drove to the high school to look for her, but found it empty.

As her family ate their dinner, her brother noticed an envelope in the front door. It contained a note. Bring 200,000 yen ($555 at the prevailing exchange rate) tomorrow at midnight, the writer declared, and he would return their daughter. Talk to anyone, and he would kill her. The family went to the police anyway, and they

---

[1] Kuni v. Ishikawa, 369 Hanrei jiho 6 (Urawa D. Ct. Mar. 11, 1964), modified, 756 Hanrei jiho 3 (Tokyo High Ct. Oct. 31, 1974), aff'd, 864 Hanrei jiho 22 (Sup. Ct. Aug. 9, 1977). Details on the case are taken primarily from Ryoji Kanno, Saibanin jidai ni miru Sayama jiken [The Sayama Case, Examined in the Age of Jury Trials] (Tokyo: Gendai jimbun sha, 2009). These details are well-known, and are are widely available from a variety of books and internet sites.

in turn staked out the designated area with 50 officers. Her sister arrived at midnight, but the kidnapper sensed something awry and escaped. Two days later, the police found her body in a shallow grave, raped and strangled.

After three weeks (May 23), the police arrested Kazuo Ishikawa, an unemployed 24 year-old from the adjacent outcaste ("*dowa*" or "*buraku-min*") community. In the arrest warrant, they listed attempted extortion (demanding the ransom) and an unrelated theft and battery. They then interrogated him for three weeks (as apparently allowed by the Criminal Procedure Code), nearly every day, all day.[2] He had nothing to do with the kidnapping, he insisted. But he gave an alibi that was an obvious lie.[3] He failed a polygraph test.[4] He wrote with a handwriting that resembled that of the ransom note. And over the course the interrogations, he confessed to a variety of other crimes.

At the end of the three weeks (June 13), the police charged Ishikawa on the original theft and battery counts, along with another seven crimes (mostly thefts and acts of battery) to which he had confessed during the detention. They then (June 17) nominally released him on 50,000 yen bail. Before he could leave the police station, however, they re-arrested him for rape and murder. They re-started interrogations, and continued them until July 6. They let him talk to an attorney only 12 times, and never for more than

---

[2] The Criminal Procedure Code gives police a total of 23 days to interrogate suspects. See Keiji sosho ho [Code of Criminal Procedure], Law No. 131 of 1948, Secs. 203, 205, 208. For discussions in English, see generally Daniel H. Foote, The Benevolent Paternalism of Japanese Criminal Justice, 80 Cal. L. Rev. 317, 335 (1992); Daniel H. Foote, Confessions and the Right to Silence in Japan, 21 Ga. J. Int'l & Comp. L. 415, 429-30 (1991).

[3] See Kanno, supra note 1, at 199-200.

[4] See Kanno, supra note 1, at 202-04.

40 minutes.[5] On June 20, Ishikawa finally confessed. The police continued the interrogation until they learned the necessary details, and then formally charged him with rape and murder.

On September 4, Ishikawa appeared at the Urawa District Court to stand trial. As evidence, prosecutors introduced his uncontested confession. They added several pieces of evidence (*e.g.*, Yoshie's fountain pen) that they claimed to have found only through his confession. After 11 sessions, the judge found Ishikawa guilty on all counts, and on March 11, 1964, sentenced him to hang.

Ishikawa's attorneys appealed the death sentence, and the Tokyo High Court proceedings began on September 10, 1964. As soon as his attorneys finished reading their appeal at the first session, Ishikawa jumped up. "I didn't kill her!," he shouted. "I haven't told my attorneys," but "I didn't kill her."

Effectively, the appellate proceedings now became a retrial on the merits. In the District Court, Ishikawa had not contested his confession. He now asserted his innocence. He had earlier confessed, he insisted, only because the senior detective told him that he could send him away for a decade anyway on the basis of his thefts and batteries —— and would keep the sentence to those 10 years if only he confessed.[6]

As the Tokyo High Court proceedings progressed, activists in the outcaste civil rights movement transformed the case into a cause célèble. The policing had been "discriminatory" (*i.e.*, they had employed ethnic profiling), they claimed. The prosecution had been discriminatory. The trial had been discriminatory. Groups in the

---

[5] See Kanno, supra note 1, at 213. Arrested suspects have a right to consult a lawyer in Japan, but not a right to demand that he attend the interrogations. See Foote, Benevolent, supra note 2, at 338; Foote, Confessions, supra note 2, at 432.

[6] See Kanno, supra note 1, at 222-33.

New Left (this being the 1960s and 1970s) adopted Ishikawa's cause, and the defense team ballooned to 85 lawyers. After ten years and 83 sessions, on October 31, 1974, the Tokyo High Court slashed his penalty to life in prison and affirmed the conviction. Ishikawa appealed his conviction and prosecutors appealed the sentence, but the Supreme Court affirmed both (August 9, 1977).

No sooner did the Supreme Court issue its opinion than Ishikawa petitioned for a retrial. The courts denied the petition, and on 1986 he filed a second. They denied this retrial petition too, but released him on parole in 1994. In 2006, Ishikawa filed his third retrial petition, and as of 2019 the case is pending still. In 1996, he married a woman he learned to know in the course of his highly politicized protests. He continues to try to clear his name, and outcaste activists celebrate him as a martyr in the quest for equality. They organize rallies. They publish a monthly magazine about his case.[7] At least one of them wrote a song about his plight.[8] And in 2013 a resident-Korean director filmed a sympathetic documentary.[9]

When Ishikawa first confessed at the police station (June 20, 1963), he claimed to have kidnapped, raped, and killed woman with two friends. He never named the pair, and within three days recanted and said he had killed her alone.[10] But one might reasonably wonder. Two days after the police located her body (May 6, 1963), one of the workers on her family farm was found dead in an empty well. The police called it suicide, and explained that he had drunk pesticide and dived into the well. Five days later, a farmer who had reported a group of three suspicious men to the police on the evening of her

---

[7] Available at: http://burakusabe.exblog.jp/16068853/.

[8] See https://www.youtube.com/watch?v=pKAsbpIZTkU.

[9] See http://sayama-movie.com.

[10] Kanno, supra note 1, at 233-238.

kidnapping ended up dead too. The police called this one a suicide as well: he had stabbed himself in the heart with a knife. Four months after the district court sentenced Ishikawa to hang, her older sister was found dead.

She had drunk poison (maybe agricultural pesticide), concluded the police. In 1966, a laborer on the Sayama pig farm where Ishikawa had once worked lay dead on the train tracks. In 1977, one of her brothers was found hanged. And again in 1977, unidentified assailants beat to death a journalist covering Ishikawa's case.[11]

Meanwhile, Ishikawa's New Left supporters turned the macabre more extreme still.[12] In 1969, they threw molotov cocktails at the Urawa District Court and occupied the building. In 1974, they organized a 110,000-strong march in support of Ishikawa; broke into the Tokyo High Court and attacked the staff with steel pipes; and tried to firebomb the home of the judge presiding over the high court appeal. In 1976, they attacked that high-court judge in his car with bats, and in 1977 tried to firebomb the home of the judge handling the Supreme Court appeal. In 1979 they tried to firebomb a Ministry of Justice housing complex, in 1990 they did firebomb the home of the district court judge who initially sentenced Ishikawa to death, and in 1995 the home of the high-court presiding judge finally burned to the ground.

▼11　See, e.g., Kanno, supra note 1, at 301-03; Jiken kankeisha ga 6nin jisatsu, henshi shita Sayama jiken [The Sayama Case in which 6 People Connected with the Case Commited Suicide or Died Under Mysterious Circumstances], available at: http://ww5.tiki.ne.jp/~qyoshida/jikenbo/057sayama.htm.

▼12　See page 15-20. See also, e.g., Kanno, supra note 1, at 298-299, and a variety of other sources on the internet.

2 Guilt and innocence

In the voluminous range of articles, books, and internet sites on the case, Ishikawa's supporters dissect every piece of evidence. Relentlessly, they identify apparent ambiguities. They emphasize inconsistencies in the prosecutorial logic, the unexplained events, the unexplored alternatives.

These ambiguities and inconsistencies reflect the fact that Ishikawa initially told the police he would not contest his guilt. He confessed to the crime, and throughout the district court trial showed no sign of retracting that confession. Given a defendant who acknowledged his guilt, the police had little reason to pursue every detail. When that defendant now retracted his confession and denied responsibility, prosecutors faced a daunting task. Having prepared for uncontested proceedings, they found themselves prosecuting a defendant who denied his guilt —— and prosecuting him with evidence that police had collected for a trial in which no one expected him to deny his guilt.

What makes the *Sayama* case so unusual —— and pedagogically invaluable —— is the wealth of information available to evaluate the court's verdict. In most cases, readers cannot see the evidence introduced at trial. Rather, they know only what a judge chooses to tell them in his opinion. Given that he writes the opinion to justify his decision, that recitation of the evidence is inherently biased. In the *Sayama* case, however, the leaders of the Burakumin Liberation League (*Buraku kaiho domei*) turned Ishikawa into a community martyr. As a result of the ensuing publicity, readers have direct access to the material actually introduced at trial.

Because of this material, readers can judge Ishikawa's guilt or innocence for themselves. Perhaps Ishikawa confessed because he actually committed the crime. Given that he confessed only after

127

the police interrogated him long and hard, however, perhaps he confessed to a crime he did not commit. Innocent people sometimes do this, after all. Exactly because they do, judges, scholars, and the public worry when police can point to little evidence other than the confession itself.

In the *Sayama* case, readers can evaluate that evidence directly. Crucially, they can compare the handwriting in the murderer's ransom note against the Ishikawa's own handwriting. They will find this material in a wide variety of books and other public sources. They will find a small sample of it even in the Wikipedia article on the *Sayama* case.

Readers should examine these handwriting samples and judge for themselves. If they conclude that someone other than Ishikawa wrote the ransom note, then the case may epitomize the risks to aggressive police investigations: Ishikawa confessed to a crime he never committed. If they conclude that he probably wrote the ransom note himself, then the case no longer exemplifies that wrongful conviction. They might still conclude that police should take less draconian tactics. But the case itself would no longer illustrate a wrongful conviction at all.

3 Police misbehavior

Scholars and activists vociferously complain that the police interrogated Ishikawa at outrageous length. In particular, they complain that the police improperly extended the amount of time they questioned him. All along, the police suspected that Ishikawa had raped and killed woman. Rather than arrest him on those grounds, though, they first arrested him for the failed extortion and two unrelated crimes. They questioned him for three weeks (primarily about kidnapping), released him, and then re-arrested him for rape and murder. By taking this two-stage approach (*bekken taiho, bekken koryu*), they could question him for six rather than three weeks. Japanese judges traditionally allowed the practice (and they allowed it here), but scholars have long complained. Recently, several lower court judges have begun to criticize it as well.[13]

Circumstantial evidence suggests the police may have planted some evidence. To validate the confession, they needed Ishikawa to tell them about evidence they could not otherwise find. They needed him to provide information, in other words, that only the killer would now. At trial, they introduced a fountain pen that (they claimed; the defense objected) the murderer had stolen from the victim. They found it in Ishikawa's house (on June 26, 1963), they said, after he told them where he had hidden it. In fact, they had searched his house exhaustively twice before (May 23, June 18). Perhaps they did not find it then because they did not know where to look. Perhaps, though, they did not find it then because they had not yet planted it there to validate the confession.

Crucially, however, neither the length of the interrogation nor any planted evidence proves Ishikawa innocent. People will sometimes confess if interrogated alone for weeks on end, including people who did nothing at all. They are especially likely to confess if they have no attorneys with them. Yet even interrogation that well-meaning scholars would like to ban can still produce truthful information. The Nazis tortured French resistance fighters during their occupation. Despite the length and brutality of their sessions, they still learned where to find other resistance fighters. Torture can

---

[13] See, e.g., [No names given], 1329 Hanrei taimuzu 276 (Osaka High Ct. Mar. 3, 2009); [No names given], 610 Hanrei taimuzu 27 (Fukuoka High Ct. apr. 28, 1986); [No names given], 2012WLJPCA01056001 (Fukuoka D. Ct. Kokura Branch Off. Jan. 5, 2012).

sometimes yield the truth, and so can long interrogation sessions.

What is more, even if Ishikawa did write the ransom note as the courts found, he may not have kidnapped her alone. For whatever reason, the police apparently wanted a sole-kidnapper confession. Yet Ishikawa ran with a bad crowd, and he committed nearly all of his other thefts and batteries with other delinquents. He initially claimed to have raped and killed her with two friends, and several of the macabre deaths that followed the initial kidnapping suggest that someone may have been eliminating unwanted witnesses.[14] Unfortunately, the police seem to have left this possibility largely unexplored.

4 Ethnic profiling

The police focused on Ishikawa soon after they discovered the body. The murderer had buried her with a shovel from the nearby pig farm, so they turned to men who would have known about the shovel. That group included the former pig-farm employee Ishikawa. The owner of this pig farm came from the outcaste community, and so did his employees. But the police insisted that they did not focus on the pig farm workers because they were outcastes. They focused on the pig farm workers —— they explained —— because the murderer had stolen a shovel from the farm.

Nonetheless, outcaste leaders and their allies on the left accused the police of "ethnic profiling." The police targeted Ishikawa, they asserted, out of sheer bias. Given that bias, they continued, the police assumed from the start that the kidnapper must have been an outcaste. The prosecutors and judges sent Ishikawa to prison because

---

[14] See Kanno, supra note 1, at 27-30.

they shared the same bias.

Over the past two decades, this question of "ethnic profiling" has become an extraordinarily sensitive topic in the U.S. American police do disproportionately arrest African American young men, and such men constitute a large fraction of the prison population. The question is whether police do target them because of their race, and (if they do) whether that targeting is proper.

African-American men in the U.S. violate the law at extremely high rates. Consider murder victimization rates. In 2013, 5,024 whites died of murder —— a rate of 2.25 deaths per 100,000 population. In the same year, 7,950 African Americans died of murder —— 20.42 per 100,000 population.[15] Blacks, in other words, were 9 times more likely to be murdered than whites.

Most American murder victims die at the hands of someone of their own race. According to 2013 FBI data, whites killed 91.1 percent of the white murder victims, and blacks killed 83.2 percent of the black victims.[16] Given the 9-times higher black victimization rate, these numbers necessarily imply substantially higher rates of violent crime in the African-American community. When they investigate a murder, rational police would obviously focus on suspects of the victim's race —— and given the numbers involved, police who do so will disproportionately investigate African-Americans.

When violent crime correlates with ethnic status, police who adopt a cost-effective approach will use racial profiling. Police have finite resources. Necessarily, the more they spend on one investigation, the less they have for another. If young Islamic men

---

[15] Centers for Disease Control and Prevention, Deaths: Final Data for 2013, tab. 18, available at: http://www.cdc.gov/nchs/fastats/homicide.htm.

[16] Federal Bureau of Investigation, Uniform Crime Reports, available at www.fbi. gov.

hijack planes and Islamic men disproportionately come from the Middle East, then cost-effective airport security staff will focus on young men from the Middle East. If young African-American men disproportionately commmit violent crime in U.S., then cost-effective police will disproportionately investigate African-American young men.

Rational police will not end their search with these target groups. If airport investigators searched only Middle Eastern young men, then Islamic terrorists would recruit others to carry their bombs. If U.S. police investigated only African-Americans, then more white Americans would turn to crime. But in a world of limited resources, cost-effective police will focus first on sub-populations most likely to yield a positive return. Sometimes, that focus may entail racial profiling.

Police who take these cost-effective measures deter crime ——and save lives. Nowhere will taxpayers fund crime control at unlimited levels. If (as evidence and logic indicate) policing deters crime, then the more *in*efficiently police use their funds, the higher the crime levels will rise. The higher the crime rate, the more innocent citizens will suffer. In the U.S., African-American criminals prey on the African-American community —— so the more *in*efficiently U.S. police perform their job, the more African-Americans will suffer criminal attacks. To put this conversely: when police focus disproportionately on young men from high-crime groups, they save the property and lives of other —— innocent —— members of those groups themselves.

5 Police discretion

a. Introduction Police must make split-second decisions. They must react to criminals, to possible criminals, and to dangerous situations more generally, and do this with little chance to plan. In

132

turn, criminals choose their own strategies by what they think police will do. Given that criminals try to game the system by anticipating police responses, the police will need to act unpredictably. They will need the discretion to choose from among a wide range of tactics, and to exercise that discretion in an apparently random way.

This discretion, though, poses risks: because of the authority modern governments give them, police can threaten not just criminals, but innocent citizens as well. Police need the ability to choose from among a broad range of tactics. Yet the broader their discretion, the greater the risk that they will threaten people who did nothing wrong.

b. U.S. approach The U.S. and Japanese governments take fundamentally different tacks toward limiting the risks posed by police discretion. Through the courts, the U.S. government cabins police within a detailed set of rules. By "constitutionalizing" these rules (nominally, they "interpret" the Constitution), the judges impose these rules on all police officers across the country. They tell police which suspects they can approach. They tell them whom they can arrest. They limit whom they can search, whom they can question, how long they can question him, what interrogation tactics they can use, what warnings they must issue, and when they must give suspects access to attorneys.

Necessarily, this U.S. approach has its costs. By limiting the range of tactics that police can adopt, judges may lower the odds that courts will convict innocent citizens. Yet they also the lower the odds that they will convict the actual criminals. Because punishment deters, they thereby also raise the level of violent crime that other citizens will experience.

c. Japanese approach By contrast, the Japanese government largely restricts police discretion through internal bureaucratic incentives. It does impose some rules on the police. It bans torture, for instance, and gives suspects the right to consult an attorney. Still, it imposes far fewer rules than do American courts —— as the interrogations in this case illustrate. After all, the police interrogated Ishikawa (without an attorney present) nearly every day, all day, for over a month.

Rather than impose restrictive rules, the Japanese government limits the risk of police misconduct by embedding the police force within a tightly organized national bureaucracy. Officers answer to supervisors who monitor their work closely. They promote them if they make sensible decisions, and punish them if they seem to abuse their authority. Prosecutors and judges work within analogous worlds. They too find their work monitored. They too place their careers at stake when they work. Do the work that their supervisors want done, and they enjoy the perquisites of promotion. Do anything else, and they find their careers stymied. For the most part, the system works: Police, prosecutors, and judges mostly behave as voters want them to behave; they solve most serious crimes; they seldom convict the innocent; and they keep crime rates at astonishingly low levels.

d. Policing and government structure Part of the reason for the cross-national difference lies in the federal structure of the American government. In the U.S., police departments are local. The states have their police forces too, and the FBI investigates some national crimes —— but most police are municipal. They answer to local politicians and local voters.

Unfortunately, this U.S. approach magnifies the variance in police performance. Some towns elect bright, ambitious mayors with good judgment. These mayors supervise (and sometimes appoint) police chiefs who show the same good judgment. Together, they outperform any police force that a national government might send, no matter how tight that national bureaucracy might be. Other places, however elect badly dysfunctional local governments. City voters can elect flagrantly corrupt governments —— think Tammany Hall in New York, or the controversies that have plagued New Orleans. Some small town voters elect incompetent and dishonest mayors, year after year.

The U.S. federal courts keep police within constitutionalized rules to limit the risks that the worst local governments can pose. Given the wide variance in police performance, the best American police perform at high levels. Those voters who elect a good mayor (or police chief) enjoy excellent police protection. Those who select the incompetent or corrupt, however, can find themselves with police who let crime rates soar and harass innocent citizens routinely. American judges impose the rules they do to limit the harm that these bad departments can cause.

By contrast, the Japanese government limits the threats police pose to public welfare through internal organizational structure. The government monitors and contrains the police by embedding them within a tightly run bureaucracy that ruthlessly ties career incentives to performance. To be sure, national governments need not run good bureaucracies. Many (if not most) national governments do not. And when a national police force operates dysfunctionally, the entire country suffers. At least since World War II, though, the Japanese government has run the national police force well. It keeps most officers off the mob payroll, it solves most serious crime, and it seldom convicts innocent victims.

e. The exclusionary rule To enforce their "constitutional" rules, American judges exclude evidence that police obtain through tactics that break the rules they (the judges) invent. Japanese courts avoid this U.S. "exclusionary rule" for a reason: absent jury trials, the rule does not make sense. In America, jurors decide guilt. If a judge prevents them from hearing a confession, they will not know that the defendant ever admitted to the crime. In Japan, however, the judge himself (at least until the recent introduction of quasi-juries) decides guilt. He decides both what evidence to admit, and what verdict to announce. If the police obtain an otherwise-believable confession through illegal means, a judge may formally exclude it. But in later deciding whether to convict the defendant, he will make the decision knowing that the defendant confessed. In the absence of jury trials, the exclusionary rule degenerates into a largely senseless "mind game" within the judge himself.

6 Erroneous convictions

Disputes like the *Sayama* case can imply that Japanese courts may be convicting the innocent. As often noted, anyone prosecuted will almost always find himself convicted. The fraction of criminal defendants convicted runs about 99.9 percent: in 2010, the Japanese district courts acquitted 80 of their 61,816 criminal defendants.[17] By contrast, in the U.S. federal courts, the conviction rate runs about 93 percent: in 2010, the district courts acquitted 8,893 of the 96,311 criminal defendants.[18] Most American defendants plead guilty, and most Japanese defendants confess. Yet among the remaining contested cases, the basic contrast between the U.S. and Japan remains.[19]

---

[17] Homu sho, ed., Hanzai hakusho [Crime Whitepaper] tab. 2-3-2-1 (Tokyo: Homu sho, 2011).

[18] Adm. Office of the U.S. Courts, ed., Judicial Facts and Figures, tab. 5.4 (Washington, D.C.: Adm. Off. U.S. Courts, 2014), available at http://www.uscourts.gov/statistics-reports/judicial-facts-and-figures-2014.

Activists regularly assert that Japanese judges routinely convict a large number of innocent defendants. For this proposition, they typically point to prisoners acquitted on retrial. In fact, however, whether a judge convicts a prisoner upon retrial says nothing about his actual guilt. Courts typically retry a prisoner only many years (sometimes several decades) after the original crime. Over those years, memories will fade. Witnesses will die. Evidence will disappear. Whether prosecutors can prove a defendant guilty beyond a reasonable doubt so long after a crime says nothing about whether he actually committed the original crime.

Popular accounts routinely suggest that judges who acquit defendants suffer in their careers. Judges convict defendants, in other words, because court administrators will assign them to less prestigious posts, transfer them to less attractive cities, or move them up the pay scale more slowly if they do anything else. In the popular 2007 movie about a young man unfairly accused of groping in a commuter train, "I Just Didn't Do It," a central character makes the claim explicitly: judges who acquit a defendant jeopardize their career.[20]

In 2001, Professor Eric Rasmusen and I studied exactly this claim.[21] We took all 455 opinions in criminal cases published in either 1976 or 1979. We identified the judges involved, and collected multiple variables to proxy for their diligence and intelligence. Holding constant these indices of judicial ability, we then use multiple regression analysis to ask whether those judges who acquitted

CASE
11

狭山事件
Kuni v. Ishikawa

---

[19] J. Mark Ramseyer & Eric B. Rasmusen, Measuring Judicial Independence: The Political Economy of Judging in Japan 101 (Chicago: University of Chicago Press, 2003).

[20] Masayuki Suo, dir., Soredemo bokuha yattenai [I Just Didn't Do It] (2007).

[21] J. Mark Ramseyer & Eric B. Rasmusen, Why Is the Japanese Conviction Rate So High?, 30 J. Legal Stud. 53 (2001); Ramseyer & Rasmusen, supra note 19, at ch. 6.

defendants received worse postings during the ten years after a case than those who convicted them. In ordinary criminal cases, we found no evidence that they did.

Relevant to the discussion in the *Sunagawa* case,[22] we do find that judges who acquit defendants in politically sensitive cases suffer in their careers. If a prosecutor brought criminal charges against a Japan Communist Party candidate for violating election campaigning laws, a judge who acquitted him could jeopardize his career. In an ordinary criminal case where a judge merely believed the police had arrested the wrong suspect, however, judges who acquitted the defendant incurred no such career penalty. In short, in routine criminal cases we find no evidence of any administratively driven conviction bias.

解 説　COMMENT　捜査・訴追の規制

　本件は，被告人が，女子高校生を誘拐し，強姦して殺害したうえ，被害者宅に現金を要求する脅迫状を送ったという事実により，有罪判決を受けた事案である。被告人は，控訴審の段階から無実を主張し，有罪判決が確定した後も，3度にわたる再審請求を行った。第3次再審請求は，現在も東京高裁に係属中である。その意味で，本件の最大の争点は，被告人が犯人であるかどうかであったが，裁判では，それ以外にも，いくつかの法律上の争点が提起された。

　第1は，別件逮捕・勾留の問題である。本件では，被告人は，まず，脅迫状を送りつけた恐喝未遂と，暴行および窃盗で逮捕・勾留され，その期間中に，それらの事実と並行して，強盗強姦殺人および死体遺棄についても取調べを受け，その後，それらの事実で逮捕・勾留されて自白をしたという経緯があった。

---

[22]　See pages 1-26.

そのため，弁護人は，それが違法な別件逮捕・勾留であるとの主張を行ったが，最高裁は，それを退けた。別件逮捕・勾留という捜査手法は，取調べによる自白獲得を重視してきたわが国に特有のものであり，アメリカでは，そのような手法がとられることがないこともあって，直接にそれを扱った裁判例も存在していない。そのため，ラムザイヤー教授の「解説」においても，別件逮捕・勾留自体の適法性よりも，長期間にわたって身柄を拘束した状態で，弁護人の立会いもなく行われた取調べによって獲得された自白の信用性に着目した検討がなされている。

　アメリカでは，ミランダ判決に代表されるように，憲法の人権条項を根拠とした連邦最高裁による一連の判例により，捜査権限に対して厳しい制約が課されている。日本においても，憲法や刑事訴訟法，さらには判例により，捜査権限に対する規制がなされており，分野によっては，アメリカよりも厳しい部分もあるが，本件で問題となった取調べに関しては，規制は緩やかであるといえよう。「解説」では，それを前提に，日本では，むしろ，警察内部の組織的な監督体制が権限の濫用を抑制する機能を果たしているとの評価がなされている。そして，両国の違いは，警察機構が中央集権的か地方分権的かという点に由来し，警察内部で統一的な規制ができないアメリカでは，裁判所が憲法を根拠にその権限を統制するという方法によらざるを得ないのだとされている。

　第2の争点として，弁護人は，本件の捜査および裁判は，部落出身者である被告人に対する予断と偏見に基づくものであって憲法14条に反するという主張を行った。しかし，最高裁は，捜査から裁判に至る本件の手続が予断と偏見に基づく差別的なものではなかったとして，その前提自体を否定している。本件以外にも，捜査や訴追において差別的な取扱いがあったとして憲法14条違反が主張された事例はあるが，それらは，共犯関係にある者の間での取扱いの差異や，同種事案における取扱いの差異が問題となったものである。そして，最高裁は，いずれの事案においても，その主張を退けている（最判昭和26・9・14刑集5巻10号1993頁，最判昭和33・10・24刑集12巻14号3385頁，最判昭和56・6・26刑集35巻4号426頁）。

　他方，アメリカでは，以前から，警察により，人種を理由とした不均衡な法執行が行われているのではないかが問題とされてきた。「解説」では，特定の人種に属する者をターゲットにして捜査を行うことも，捜査資源の効率的な配分

CASE
11

狭山事件
Kuni v. Ishikawa

の観点から許容されるという結論が示されている。もっとも，これは，特定の犯罪について，特定の人種等の集団に属する者による犯罪率が，そうでない場合に比べて明らかに高いことを基礎とするものであり，そもそもそのような状況が存在しないわが国には妥当しないであろう。

PART 5 民事法

CASE	
12	サブリース事件
13	学納金返還請求事件
14	更新料返還請求事件
15	懲罰賠償
16	松下電器カラーテレビ事件

Sumitomo fudosan, K.K. v. Senchurii tawaa, K.K.

57 Saihan minshu 1213 (Sup. Ct. Oct. 21, 2003)

サブリース事件
(最判平成15年10月21日民集57巻9号1213頁)

1 The facts

Along the banks of the Kanda River near the Suidobashi railroad station stands the swank, post-modernist Century Tower. As a simple internet search will show, the building currently houses a hospital affiliated with the Juntendo medical school, but a decade ago it had gone completely vacant. When the Nomura Research Institute left in 2003, it had been the last tenant to go.

Architecturally striking in the extreme, Century Tower was an odd building to stand empty. Designed by Norman Foster's firm, the tower wears its frame on the outside. Unlike the stark elegance of Mies van der Rohe's Seagram Building or the hundreds of Seagram-imitations around the globe, Century Tower encircles its obligatory glass walls with a criss-crossed steel grid, and houses a soaring atrium in the middle.

The Oobunsha publishing house had owned the land. The firm had invented the test-prep industry in the 1930s, but by 1970s faced brutal competition from rivals like Kawai juku. When the founder died in 1985, he left the firm to his 30-something son, Kazuo Akao.

Upon inheriting the company, the young Akao promptly bet the firm on real estate. The test-prep publishing market may have

Figure Urban Commercial Land Indexed Prices

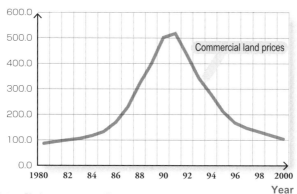

Notes: Six largest metropolitan areas.
Sources: Urban land price index, March 2000 = 100. From Japan Statistical Yearbook, as found at: http://www.stat.go.jp/english/data/nenkan/1431-17.htm

seemed glutted, but the commercial real estate rental market boomed ( Figure). To exploit the firm's land along the Kanda River, Akao negotiated a deal with the massive (86.7 billion yen capitalization) Sumitomo Real Estate, K.K. Akao would form a new firm, Century Tower, K.K., and capitalize it at a trivial 260 million yen. He would place his firm's river-side land in Century, and then borrow additional funds from a bank. Century would build the tower and lease it to Sumitomo, and Sumitomo would sublease it to commercial tenants. If the rental market continued its meteoric rise, Sumitomo would pocket the difference between its receipts and the rent it paid Century. If the market collapsed, Sumitomo would bear the corresponding loss.

Under the terms of Akao's final (1991) agreement with Sumitomo, the real estate giant promised to pay Century 4.9 billion yen upfront (*shikikin*), and at least 2 billion yen per year for 15 years. High rent or low rent, a glut of tenants or a dearth, it promised to pay Century at least 2 billion. At the end of the 15 years, the firms would discuss possible renewals.

Akao and Sumitomo explicitly addressed rental adjustments. More specifically, they explicitly agreed that the rent would rise. They negotiated the necessary mechanism: every 3 years the rent would rise 10 percent (subject to modification if economic circumstances changed radically). To lower the rent, they provided no mechanism: 2 billion per year was the absolute minimum.

To build the tower that Foster designed, Century hired the Oobayashi gumi construction firm. It paid Foster's architectural firm 1.8 billion yen, and Oobayashi 21.2 billion. To pay these amounts, it used Sumitomo's 4.9 billion upfront fee, and borrowed another 18.1 billion from a bank.

Once the tower opened in 1991, the commercial rental market promptly collapsed (➡ Figure). Sumitomo had promised Century 2 billion yen per year (plus triennial increases) for 15 years. By 1994, its receipts from its sublessees had dwindled to 120 million per month, and by 1999 to 46 million per month. Desperate to stem its losses, in early 1994 it asked Century to cut the rent to 1.4 billion yen. A few months later, it begged Century to cut it to 870 million, in 1997 to 790 million, and in 1999 to 530 million.

Century refused all of Sumitomo's requests. It had negotiated these questions with Sumitomo at elaborate length, and Sumitomo had promised to bear the risks. Notwithstanding those promises, it now refused to pay. When Century sued, Sumitomo argued that Section 31(a) of the Land and House Lease Act let it slash the rent —— notwithstanding the contract it had negotiated and signed: [1]

> *If,*
>
> (a) because of a change in the taxes or oth-

---

[1] Shakuchi shakuya ho [Land and House Lease Act], Law No. 90 of Oct. 4, 1991.

er costs associated with the land or building,

(b) because of a change in the price of the land or building,

(c) because of changes in other economic circumstances, or

(d) in comparison to rents charged at nearby or similar buildings, the rent for the building becomes unreasonable, *then*, regardless of the terms of the contract, the parties may demand a change in the future rent of the building. If the contract specifically provides that the building's rent shall not be increased for a stated period, that provision shall be followed.

Century sued for the unpaid rent.

2 The decision

Two large firms had explicitly allocated the risks associated with the market demand for rental real estate. On the strength of Sumitomo's promise to bear that risk, Century had agreed to borrow a massive amount from a bank. It further agreed to assume the risks entailed in designing and building the tower.

To the Tokyo District Court, the dispute between the two firms was simple matter of contract.[2] Having agreed to bear the rental market risk, Sumitomo was now liable. As the District Court put it:

The defendant [Sumitomo] proposed to guarantee the rental stream. It promised the plaintiff [Century] a stable

---

[2] Senchurii tawaa, K. K. v. Sumitomo fudosan, K. K., 1654 Hanrei jiho 23 (Tokyo D. Ct. Aug. 28, 1998).

long-term stream of revenue. ... The defendant's rental guarantee lay at the core of this contract. The plaintiff realized it was borrowing a large amount of money, and realized the risks that the loan entailed. For exactly that reason, it wanted the defendant's rental guarantee. In response, the defendant repeatedly explained to the plaintiff that, because of the rental guarantee, it (the defendant) would bear the risk.

In exchange, Century let Sumitomo keep the gains that would accrue if the demand for commercial rental real estate continued to rise.

Should the revenue increase beyond the amount of the original rent, the defendant stood to earn a potentially unlimited amount of profit. By contrast, the plaintiff would receive only the contractually specificied rental revenue.

The District Court enforced the contract, and held Sumitomo to its agreement. The High Court modified the judgment, and the parties appealed.

The Supreme Court reversed. Section 31 (a) of the Land and House Lease Act applied, and Sumitomo could pay a lower rent. Section 31 (a) is not a default term, explained the Court. It is a mandatory term. It applies to all building leases, and this is a lease. True, the parties were sophisticated firms. They explicitly negotiated a rental guarantee. The guarantee was crucial to their deal, and Century borrowed funds from the bank on the strength of the guarantee.

Rational and sophisticated firms had decided to allocate the risk to Sumitomo, but the Supreme Court did not care. Section 31 (a) was mandatory. The parties could not negotiate around it. The term applied, and Sumitomo could throw part of the loss on Century.

3 Discussion

a. Statutory application There is a bit of the Oliver Wendell

Holmes to this. "If my fellow citizens want to go to Hell," he once declared, "I will help them. It's my job."[3] A statute may make no sense. It may hurt both parties. It may slash social welfare. But statutes are law and a judge's job is to enforce the law. Good or bad, announced Holmes, he would enforce whatever statutes his fellow citizens might enact.

Something of that mechanical, damn-the-consequences quality appears in the Supreme Court decision. It is a mechanical quality that appears often in Japanese jurisprudence —— probably for two reasons. First, generally the Japanese government can amend, repeal, or replace statutes that voters do not want. The U.S. government cannot do this. The U.S. government takes presidential form, and power alternates regularly between two rival parties. In many years, neither party has the requisite power —— i.e., the control over the House, the Senate, and the Presidency —— to pass statutes.

By contrast, Japan has a parliamentary government with a strong lower house that has been under the control of the Liberal Democratic Party (LDP) for most of the post-war years. For the most part, that party has won elections by giving voters in its coalition the legislation and programs they wanted. If a statute reduced social welfare in a way that its coalition did not want, the LDP did not need the Supreme Court to void it. It could simply repeal it. As a result, the courts routinely —— and rationally —— leave it to the legislature to fix bad statutes.

Second, as discussed in pages 2–14, Japanese lower-court judges effectively work as bureaucrats. Fast-track judges in the Secretariat's (*Jimusokyoku*) personnel office monitor the performance of other judges. They evaluate their work. And they move them from

---

[3] Justice Oliver Wendell Holmes, letter to Harold J. Laski, March 4, 1920, in 1 *Holmes-Laski Letters*, ed. Mark DeWolfe Howe (1953), at 249.

post to post at (generally) three-year intervals. On the basis (in part) of that evaluation, the judges in the personnel office reward other judges with posts in attractive cities or penalize them with years in a provincial branch office. They give the other judges prestigious administrative responsibilities or send them to family court. They promote the other judges up the pay scale quickly or at a more leisurely pace.

Given this monitoring and evaluation, Japanese lower-court judges have an incentive to conform. For the most part, the Secretariat does not reward them for creativity. It rewards them for disposing of cases quickly, predictably, and by precedent. As a result, precedent probably binds more tightly in the civil-law Japan than in the common-law U.S. Once a precedent is established, judges follow it even when the precedent is highly dysfunctional (note the labor law cases in PART **7**).

In this case, the Supreme Court applied the statute straightforwardly. It was a bad statute. It limited the ability of firms to allocate risk to the parties best able to bear it. In the process, it imposed a significant —— and entirely unnecessary —— cost on economic transactions. The District Court judge seems to have understood this, and avoided the statute (a courageous move, given the bureaucratic organization of the courts).

The Supreme Court had no such qualms. It did not criticise the statute, and it certainly did not quote Holmes. Perhaps it missed the basic economic logic involved. After all, because most Japanese judges have majored in law as undergraduates, many will never have taken a course in economics. Or perhaps the Court understood the dysfunctional nature of the statute and simply did not care. It applied it anyway, consequences-be-damned.

b. Landlord-tenant law The case fits smoothly within the general disaster that is Japanese landlord-tenant law. The case in-

148

volved price adjustments, but the better known terms of Japanese landlord-tenant law involve evictions. Under these terms, Japanese landlords usually may not evict their tenants at the expiration of the lease. The law dramatically reduces social welfare, but in a way that spreads the loss broadly over the population at large. It simultaneously enhances the wealth of incumbent renters, and incumbent renters are a discrete group with intensely held interests. Democracies often reward groups with intensely held interests —— and that is exactly what the government does in Japan.

Suppose a landlord and tenant negotiate a year-to-year lease. Despite the terms of the lease, at the end of the year the landlord cannot freely evict his tenant. Suppose the landlord needs the house for his own family. If the tenant declares that he would prefer to stay in the house (and the law gives him every incentive to pretend that he wants to stay), the landlord cannot enforce the contractual terms. Instead, he can evict the tenant only if he needs the space more than the tenant does (typically, only if the landlord intends to live there himself), and —— in addition —— pays the tenant several years' rent.

This law produces several obvious consequences. First, it keeps rental units small. In most comparable modern democracies, tenants can rent units almost as large as those they can buy. In Japan, they will look hard to find anything but the most miniscule units to rent. Because judges will not let a landlord evict a tenant at the end of a lease, they effectively give tenants an interest close to a life estate. Yet landlords need periodic turnover. They need the turnover both to keep rents near market levels, and to renovate units or replace buildings as necessary. Given the law, they can maintain this turnover only by limiting rentals to units so small that no couple would want to stay in them beyond a few years.

Second, landlords keep many units —— particularly units in the best locations —— off the market. Suppose a landlord owns a house in suburban Tokyo. It stands 5 minutes from a commuter line station in an increasingly desireable neighborhood. Built in the late 1960s, the building is starting to look old, and lacks many of the amenities modern Japanese would prefer. Within a few years, the landlord would like to replace it with a modern, attractive apartment building. He lacks the funds to do so now, but hopes to obtain that money within five years.

The obviously efficient arrangement is for the landlord to rent the house for five years, and then replace it with the modern apartment building. If he did so, he would collect rent for five years. The public would obtain access to the ideally located house. Given Japanese landlord-tenant law, however, he will not lease the house. No matter how explicitly a tenant agreed to let the landlord evict him, the court would not enforce the agreement. Instead, when the landlord asked the tenant to leave, the tenant (if well-advised) would refuse. The landlord would sue to evict, and the judge would declare that he can do so (if in fact it gives him that right at all) only if he pays the tenant an enormous sum of money. Rather than take this risk, the landlord will simply keep the unit off the market.

It is worth noting where this law began. During the war in China, the Japanese military took increasingly brutal control over the economy. It imposed wage and price controls in 1938.[4] It imposed rent controls in 1939.[5] And landlords reacted to the controls in predictable fashion. If the law limited the rent they could charge incumbent tenants, then they would evict those tenants and rent to new tenants at prices closer to market.[6] In response, the government imposed the limits on evictions.[7] In the years since the war, it dropped

---

[4] Kokka sodo in ho [National Mobilization Act], Law No. 55 of 1938.

[5] Chidai yachin tosei rei [Ground and House Rent Control Order], Chokurei No. 704 of 1939.

the controls on rent, but kept the effective ban on evictions. The result is the situation in place today.

c. Bubbles The case also illustrates something about the real estate price prices of 1985-1995. As the Figure shows, these prices climbed rapidly in the late 1980s, and fell just as precipitously in the early 1990s. The question is what to make of this. As suggested by the popular description (and the description in the District Court opinion) of the period as a "bubble," readers may assume that market incorporated a classic "speculative bubble."

In a speculative bubble, investors know that asset prices are too high (higher than market fundamentals warrant), but buy the asset anyway. They do so because they hope prices will rise further and plan to sell the asset before prices collapse. They know prices will inevitably fall, in other words, but buy at the inflated price because they hope to sell before that collapse.

Observers typically discuss bubbles by citing tulips and the South Sea Company. In 17th century Netherlands, investors bid up the price of selected tulip bulbs to stratospheric levels —— and prices promptly plunged. In 18th century England, investors bid up the price of shares in the South Sea Company —— and again, prices plunged. The observers who first called the 1980s Japanese economy a "bubble" used the term because they saw a similarity to the South Sea Company.

Yet the fact that prices rise and then fall need not imply a bubble. In bidding for assets, investors estimate the future prices of

---

▼6 It tried to control rents on new leases too, of course. Chokurei No. 678 of 1940.

▼7 See generally Jun'ichi Honda, Shakuya ho to seito jiyu no hanrei sogo kaisetsu [Comprehensive Commentary on the Case Law Concerning the House Lease Act and Appropriate Reasons](2010)

those assets. And to reach those estimates, they use all information available to them. If that information suggests that the demand for the asset will rise, they will bid up its price. If it indicates that the demand will fall, they will bid it down. If they believe the Japanese economy will grow, they will anticipate higher demand for commercial real estate and bid up rents. If the news suggests slower growth, they will bid them down. When they do all this, they do not create a bubble. They simply price by market fundamentals.

Investors bid in a speculative bubble when they buy and sell the asset at prices that they realize do not reflect market fundamentals. They buy it for prices above those fundamentals because they plan to sell the asset before the price crashes. They understand, explains economist Peter Garber,[8] that a "venture has no chance of paying large dividends, but [believe] that a sequence of share buyers at ever increasing prices is available." They then "buy in on a gamble that they will not be in the last wave of buyers."[9]

The Japanese real estate market in the 1980s was *not* a bubble —— and this case shows why. Investors may buy tulip bulbs in a bubble. They are not placing their wealth in long-term investments. They are merely buying tulip bulbs, and plan to sell them before the price collapse. Japanese firms in the 1980s did not buy tulips. Instead, Oobunsha built a 21 billion yen skyscraper, and Sumitomo guaranteed the rents on the building for 15 years. Investors do not construct 21 billion yen buildings at prices they think will collapse any day. Neither do they guarantee rental payments for 15 years at levels that they know exceed market fundamentals. Century and Sumitomo were wealthy and sophisticated investors. Century built the massive

---

[8] Peter M. Garber, Famous First Bubbles, J. Econ. Perspectives, vol. 4, no. 2, 35 (1990).

[9] Garber, supra note 8, at 41.

152

office tower that it did precisely because it did *not* expect prices to fall. Sumitomo guaranteed rents payments for 15 years precisely because it did *not* expect prices to fall either.

Given those expectations, the market was not a speculative bubble at all.

解 説 COMMENT サブリースと借地借家法 32 条の適用

サブリース事件（「住友不動産 vs センチュリータワー」事件）は，いわゆるサブリースにつき，契約当事者に賃料増減請求権を認める借地借家法 32 条が適用されるか否かが争われた事件である。

借地借家法 32 条は，当事者の合意がない場合にも裁判所に賃料を変更する権限を付与する規定である。事情変更の原則が具体化された規定であると言われることもあるが，契約交渉において劣位に立つ当事者（借地借家の場合には賃借人）を保護する趣旨を含む規定であることに留意する必要がある。同様の規定としては，身元保証人の責任範囲の決定を裁判所に委ねる身元保証法 5 条がよく知られている。このような立法は，戦時期に限らず，短い世紀としての 20 世紀（1920 年代～1980 年代）を通じて，日本において支持されてきたものである。そこにあるのは，賃借人にせよ身元保証人にせよ，当初の契約時に既に不利な契約内容を承認させられていることが多いという状況認識である。

ここで注意すべきは，「住友不動産 vs センチュリータワー」事件において賃借人として現れている住友不動産は，情報・交渉力の両面においてセンチュリータワーに劣後するわけではないという事実である。一般的に言ってサブリースにおいては，このビジネスモデルを主導するのは賃借人たる事業者なのである。これは，少なくともサブリースにおいては，借地借家法がもともと想定する賃借人の保護の必要は存在しないということを意味する。本件においても，センチュリータワーが賃料増額条項を強要したというわけではない。

そこで，センチュリータワー側は，本件契約には借地借家法 32 条は適用されないと主張した。その理由づけはいくつかありうるが，主として問題となった

のは，本件契約は借地借家法の適用される「建物の賃貸借」にあたらない，む
しろここで約されているのは一種の共同事業であるという主張の当否であった。

　この点について，最高裁は原審の判断を否定して，本件契約にも借地借家法
が適用されることを明らかにした。その結果，当事者が事前に協議をして賃料
の増額につき合意をしたにもかかわらず，当該合意は裁判所が変更しうること
となる。①これは不当な結果をもたらすのではないか，②日本の最高裁の法令
解釈は硬直的に過ぎるのではないか。こうした疑問が生ずることになる。

　②に関しては，法令解釈が硬直的か否かというよりは，最高裁はどのように
契約の性質決定を行っているのか，という観点が重要であるように思われる。
もし本件契約を賃貸借ではない契約として性質決定することができれば，その
時点で借地借家法の適用の余地はなくなるので，借地借家法の解釈以前のレベ
ルで問題は解決されることになるからである。確かに，本件契約は共同事業的
な性質を帯びている。しかしながら，そこで用いられた契約類型が賃貸借でな
いとは言いがたい。最高裁はそう考えたのであろう。このような態度を硬直的
と評することは可能かもしれない。しかしながら，最高裁は常にこのような契
約解釈をしているのかと言えば，必ずしもそうではない。また，契約類型を尊
重した解釈方法は常に硬直的な帰結を導くと断ずることもできない。

　①に関しては，借地借家法32条が適用されれば，必ず賃料減額請求は認めら
れるのかという点に注意する必要がある。最高裁によれば，同条の適用にあたっ
ては，当事者間の特約の存在を考慮に入れることが求められているからである。
これは，強行規定と特約との関係につき，一つの見方を提示したものとして注
目される。すなわち，ある規定が強行規定であると評価されるならば，特約は
当該規定を排除することはできない。しかしながら，当該規定の適用にあたっ
ては特約の存在を考慮に入れる余地がある。こうした見方が提示されていると
言える。

[No name given] v. Gakko hojin Nihon daigaku

60 Saihann minshu 3732 (Sup. Ct. Nov. 27, 2006)

学納金返還請求事件
(最判平成18年11月27日民集60巻9号3732頁)

1 Fees at the Arts and Science Departments

In 2001, several high school students sued the arts and sciences departments of the "safety" (*suberidome*) schools to which they had applied.[1] To hold their place at these private universities, they had paid the required admission fee (*nyugaku kin*), usually a modest 300,000 yen. They had paid the first years' tuition (*jugyo ryo*), generally in the 350,000 to 900,000 yen range. A few days later, however, they had found themselves admitted to a school they preferred. Rather than attend their safety, they retracted their acceptance and asked for a refund. When the schools refused, they sued.

On appeal, the Supreme Court let the schools keep the admission fee, but told them to refund the tuition charges to those students who had retracted their acceptance promptly. By paying the admission fee, reasoned the Court, a student acquired the contractual right to attend. He might or might not choose eventually to enroll, but

---

[1] [No name given] v. Gakko hojin Nihon daigaku, 2004 WLJP 03300021 (Tokyo D. Ct. Mar. 30, 2004), rev'd, 60 Saihan minshu 3514 (Tokyo High Ct. Mar. 10, 2005), rev'd in part and aff'd in part, 1958 Hanrei jiho 12 (Sup. Ct. Nov. 27, 2006).

155

by paying the fee he could hold the spot. In turn, through the fee the school obtained compensation for the administrative costs it incurred in holding that spot for him. Unless it charged an unreasonably high amount (which none did here), it did not need to refund the fee.

Tuition was different, said the Court. Schools charge tuition for the educational services they supply. A school need not refund the tuition for education it already supplied, of course. But if a student voided his contract with it prospectively, then it could not necessarily keep the money.

A school could keep tuition, reasoned the Court, only if the student did not notify it promptly. Schools admit students every year. They realize that not everyone admitted will accept their offer, and that not everyone who accepts will eventually matriculate. Because of this experience, they know how to mitigate damages. They can admit extra applicants from the outset. They can admit students off their wait-list. Given that the school year starts April 1, if a student withdraws before that date they can take a variety of steps to minimize their losses.

After April 1, continued the Court, universities will find it harder to avoid losses. They will incur fixed costs they cannot eliminate. They will face greater resistance when they try to recruit students off their waitlists. To the extent that they cannot mitigate their losses, they will not violate the "public order and good morals" requirement in the Civil Code if they refuse to refund the first year's tuition. Neither will they violate the Consumer Contracts Act (which, in a parallel case decided the same day, the Court held constitutional).[2] Section 9(a) of the Act voids "penalties" that exceed "the average

---

[2] [No name given] v. Gakko hojin Aoyama gakuin, 1849 Hanrei jiho 29 (Tokyo D. Ct. Oct. 23, 2003), aff'd, unpub'd (Tokyo High Ct. Feb. 24, 2005), aff'd, 424 Hanrei jiho 10 (Sup. Ct. Nov. 27. 2006).

damages incurred by firms in the industry from the cancellation of consumer contracts of the same category as the contract at hand." When a student withdraws after April 1, reasoned the Court, the forfeited tuition will seldom exceed the school's average damages.

And if a school tells applicants they can retract their acceptance after April 1, then students who follow its instructions necessarily retract in a timely fashion as well. Two parallel cases (again, decided the same day) concerned students who had skipped orientation.[3] The schools involved had announced that they would treat anyone absent from their April 2 orientation ceremonies (*nyugaku shiki*) as having retracted acceptance. Several students skipped orientation and asked for a refund. The Court ordered the schools to pay. A school should anticipate, it noted, that students will take it at its word. If it tells them non-attendance constitutes retraction, some students will retract by not attending. When they do, they necessarily have retracted their acceptance in a timely fashion, and deserve a refund.

2 Fees at the Medical Schools

a. Introduction   Many years ago, I visited a medical professor in his office. He taught at a low-ranking private medical school. Walking through the school parking lot, I noticed a large fraction of Mercedes Benzes, BMWs, and Jaguars. I suggested that the school must pay its professors well. He laughed, and explained that we were in the student parking lot.

---

[3]   [No names given], 1424 Hanrei jiho 62 (Sup. Ct. Nov. 27, 2006); [No names given], 60 Saihan minshu 3651 (Osaka D. Ct. Mar. 5, 2004), modified, 60 Saihan minshu 3698 (Osaka High Ct. Apr. 22, 2005), modified, 1958 Hanrei jiho 24 (Sup. Ct. Nov. 27, 2006).

Medical students are different, it seems. The students above who sued their safety schools attracted enormous attention. Most of them had applied to departments in the "arts & sciences" (*i.e.*, humanities or social sciences). These departments enroll most Japanese students, and by suing them the plaintiffs touched the lives of most students.

But if the suit affected many students, it involved only modest amounts of money. The case (this one decided the same day as well) that raised much higher stakes concerned a medical student. Very few students go to medical school —— perhaps 9000 of the more than 600,000 college freshmen in Japan.[4] But the students who attend the private medical universities have parents who earn high incomes. The schools charge them high fees —— and, when admitted students retract their acceptance, refuse to refund those high fees.

b. The medical services industry Since the early 1960s, the Japanese government has provided universal medical care through a patchwork of several insurance programs. For the services they render, it pays doctors fixed prices. It sets these prices low, but low in ways that skew delivery toward rudimentary care.[5]

Like everyone else, physicians respond to prices. If the government skews prices toward rudimentary care, then physicians will focus on rudimentary care. The most successful doctors do this by running small clinics. Typically, they purport to specialize in both internal medicine and surgery (the two fields have nothing in common), and often claim to handle several other specialities as well. They

---

[4] http://www.mext.go.jp/b_menu/houdou/26/10/1352932.htm.

[5] J. Mark Ramseyer, The Effect of Cost Suppression under Universal Health Insurance on the Allocation of Talent and the Development of Expertise: Cosmetic Surgery in Japan, 52 J.L. & Econ. 497, 498-500 (2009).

treat nearly anyone who walks in the door, and bill the government for services rendered; they keep a few beds, and warehouse patients for long periods at government expense.[6]

Do it right, and a physician can turn a rudimentary clinic into a money making machine. Physicians earn high incomes in Japan, but the physicians running the small clinics earn the most. Through their clinics, they earn very high incomes. As they age, they will try to pass their wealth to their children. Given the high gift and estate tax rates in Japan, many will not want to pass it as cash. Instead, many try to pass it in the form of the clinic itself —— as an income-generating capital asset.[7]

c. Private medical schools When they do try to convey their profitable clinic to their children, many physicians come face-to-face with an uncomfortable fact: their children cannot pass the medical school entrance exam. Half of the children in this world may be smarter than their parents, but the other half are dumber. Fathers or mothers may have passed the medical school entrance exam, but their children need not pass it. Many such children will indeed pass, but others will find it hard. To address this "problem," educational entrepreneurs have created a cohort of private medical schools that effectively cater to the not-quite-as-bright children of doctors owning profitable clinics.

Lower-tier private medical schools charge their students extremely high fees. Arts and sciences departments at the private universities charge about 300,000 yen in entrance fees. Many

---

[6] Ramseyer, supra note 5, at 500-03.

[7] J. Mark Ramseyer, Universal Health Insurance and the Effect of Cost Containment on Mortality Rates: Strokes and Heart Attacks in Japan, 6 J. Empirical Legal Stud. 309, 316-22 (2009).

medical schools charge 1 or 1.5 million yen. The Juntendo, Kawasaki, Kanazawa, Saitama, and Hyogo medical schools charge 2 million.[8] Indeed, Kawasaki Medical (with a *hensachi* score of 60, one of the least selective medical schools)[9] charged an entrance fee of 2 million yen, annual tuition of 2 million yen, and an "educational enhancement fee" (*kyoiku jujitsu hi*) of 6.5 million yen in the first year and 5 million every year thereafter. It charged 12 million yen in fees in March upon acceptance,[10] and a total of 45.5 million over the course of the next six years.[11]

In the case summarized at the outset, three of the plaintiffs had applied to the Nihon University medical school as their safety university.[12] Admitted elsewhere, they opted not to attend Nihon and sued for a refund of what they had paid. One of them won at trial, and the court ordered the school to repay all fees (about 7 million yen) except the entrance fee. The two losing plaintiffs did not appeal to the Supreme Court, and Nihon University did not appeal the one it lost.

Instead, the case that brought the medical school question to the Supreme Court involved an applicant to the Osaka Medical University.[13] The school notified the student that he passed the exam on Friday, March 2, 2011. It told him to pay —— by 3:00 p.m.,

---

[8] As found in http://www.igakubujuken.jp/ranking/payment.html.

[9] http://daigakujuken-plus.com/nyuushi-hensati-ranking/igakubu/.

[10] http://www.igakubu.com/archives/53_gakuhi/index.html; http://www.daigaku-gakuhi.com/igakubu.html.

[11] As found on the university's website: https://www.kawasaki-m.ac.jp/med/examination/07.html.

[12] [No name given] v. Gakko hojin Nihon daigaku, 2004 WLJP 03300021 (Tokyo D. Ct. Mar. 30, 2004), rev'd, 60 Saihan minshu 3514 (Tokyo High Ct. Mar. 10, 2005), rev'd in part and aff'd in part, 1958 Hanrei jiho 12 (Sup. Ct. Nov. 27, 2006).

[13] [No names given], 60 Saihan minshu 3792 (Osaka D. Ct. Nov. 11, 2003) (pf loses), modified, 1882 Hanrei jiho 44 (Osaka High Ct. Sept. 10, 2004) (pf wins), rev'd, 1958 Hanrei jiho 12 (Sup. Ct. Nov. 17, 2006).

March 8 —— an entrance fee of 1 million yen, first-year's tuition of 610,000 yen, and an educational enhancement fee of 5 million. The plaintiff duly paid all amounts on the following Monday, March 5.

On Thursday, March 22, the student learned that he had passed the entrance exam to the medical school at Kobe University. Kobe was one of the national universities, and the national schools published their acceptances on March 22. The student accepted Kobe's offer the next Monday, March 26, and retracted his acceptance at Osaka Medical on March 27. Unfortunately for the plaintiff, Osaka Medical had announced that it would refund fees (other than the entrance fee, which it vowed never to refund) only if a student retracted his acceptance by March 21. Obviously, it refused to volunteer as a safety school for the national universities.

The plaintiff would not have traded Osaka Medical for Kobe for the prestige. The two schools enrolled roughly equivalent students. According to one website, the mean selectivity score among the exam preparation services for Osaka Medical (in 2015) was a *hensachi* score of 67.5. For Kobe, it was 68.5.[14] Instead, the plaintiff would have traded the schools for the money. Over the course of his six years, he would have paid (2015 rates) Osaka Medical about 31.4 million yen. As a national university, Kobe charged only 817,000 per year. Over the course of six years, he would have paid it about 5 million yen. Even if he forfeited the entire 7 million he paid Osaka Medical upon acceptance, he saved money by switching schools.[15]

Many students made exactly that decision. Whether voluntarily or not, Osaka Medical was a safety. In 2001, it initially admitted 83 students. Only 59 of those 83 even accepted the offer,

---

[14] http://daigakujuken-plus.com/nyuushi-hensati-ranking/igakubu/.

[15] http://www.igakubu.com/archives/53_gakuhi/index.html; http://www.daigaku-gakuhi.com/igakubu.html.

and 40 of the 59 then retracted their acceptance. Osaka Medical admitted another 125 off its waitlist, but only 101 accepted. Of those 101, 20 retracted their acceptance as well. Of the 83 students it initially admitted, 19 enrolled. Of the 125 it admitted off its waitless, only 81 enrolled.

If students hoped to use Osaka Medical as their safety, the school would make them pay for the service. More precisely, it would make them pay 7 million yen. The students who did enroll at Osaka Medical may have taken the phenomenon as a blow to their pride, but the high retraction rate saved them nontrivial funds. In 2001, 60 students who accepted the Osaka Medical offer retracted their acceptance. If they each forfeited 7 million yen, the school earned 420 million yen from their strategy. To raise that amount from the 600 students enrolled in its six-year program, it would have had to raise tuition by 700,000 yen per year.

The Supreme Court held for the school: Osaka Medical did not need to refund any of the money that the plaintiff had paid. It charged astronomical fees, and the plaintiff retracted his acceptance promptly. In due course, the school would properly fill its 100-student class. To the Court, however, none of that mattered. It would not require the school to refund the money.

The Court did little to explain why Osaka Medical won when the other universities lost. It noted that the government heavily regulated medical schools. It noted that the government strictly enforced the 100-student cap at Osaka Medical, and brutal economics required the school fill the 100 spots it had. Otherwise, though, it left the diametrically opposed case outcomes largely unexplained.

３ U.S. Universities

a. Early decision American schools do not like students

treating them as "safeties" either, but they bind admitted students even more tightly than Osaka Medical. Osaka at least let students switch to another school if they paid 7 million yen. Most premier American schools will not let some of the students they admit switch at any price.

Many U.S. universities bind their applicants through what they call an "early decision" (ED) option. These schools let students apply either "regular decision" (RD) or ED. When they admit a student who applied RD, the student will pay a modest deposit (usually about $500) to hold his place. If he decides to go elsewhere, he will forfeit that money. But the schools do not charge "education enhancement fees," and refund tuition well into the semester. At the University of Chicago, for example: [16]

> Students allowed to drop all or part of their registrations will be granted a reduction of a portion of the original charges according to the schedule below. ... [The] [l]ast day for full refund of charges is the end of first week of a quarter or equivalent ....

MIT similarly provides: [17]

> A student withdrawing before the start of a term is not charged any tuition for that term, and any tuition payments previously made for that term will be refunded. Students withdrawing during the fall or spring term are charged one-twelfth of the stated tuition for the term for each week from the starting date of the term ....

If a student applies ED, however, he loses all flexibility. If the school offers him admission, he must accept the offer —— he has

---

[16] https://bursar.uchicago.edu/tuition-refund-schedule. Note that Chicago does not use an ED system.

[17] http: // web.mit.edu/catalog/overv.chap3-cost.html.

no choice whatsoever. He must retract all other applications, and may not accept any admissions offer anywhere else. As Columbia University explains on its website:[18]

> If you are admitted under the Early Decision program, you are obligated to accept Columbia's offer of admission. Once you accept Columbia's offer of admission, you may file no further college applications and must withdraw any other applications that have already been submitted.

In exchange for sacrificing flexibility, the student who applies ED will enjoy a higher acceptance rate. Top students choose the ED option because they find the admissions process at the premier schools so unpredictable. Rather than a Japanese-style school-specific entrance exam, the best U.S. universities choose their undergraduate students through a mix of standardized exams (called the SAT), high school performance, and other (hard to quantify) characteristics. This gives the admissions officers such an enormous amount of discretion that even an applicant with an apparently perfect record will have only a modest chance of admission.

The result is a process that to outside observers will seem heavily random. At the Massachusetts Institute of Technology (MIT —— generally considered the best engineering school in the world), a student who scores in the 750-800 range on the SAT math test (800 is a perfect score; this range is equivalent to 75-80 on the Japanese *hensachi* scoring) has only a 12 percent of admission. A student who scores in the 750-800 range on the reading test has only a 13 percent chance. At the slightly lower-ranked Cornell University, a student scoring

---

[18] https://undergrad.admissions.columbia.edu/apply/first-year/early-decision. Original in part in bold.

[19] http://mitadmissions.org/apply/process/stats; http://irp.dpb.cornell.edu/wordpress/wp-content/uploads/2015/04/Profile2014-Freshmen-update.pdf

at least 750 on the math test has an 18 percent chance of admission. One scoring over 750 on the reading test has a 27 percent chance.[19]

Suppose a high school student wants to become an engineer. He is extremely talented. He has near perfect SAT scores, and ranks near the top of his high-school class. He is captain of the school math club, an enthusiastic member of the debate team, and helps at the local shelter for the homeless. Given this background, he has a plausible chance of admission at his first-choice MIT—— but much less than 50 percent. Even at Cornell, he has less than a 50 percent chance. He does, however, face very good odds of admission at the State University of New York.

This student will be strongly tempted to apply "early decision" at Cornell. Given his record, he has as good a chance as anyone at MIT. Nonetheless, he may sacrifice the chance to attend MIT in order to increase his odds at his second-choice Cornell by applying ED. In general, schools do claim that their ED applicants are slightly more talented than their RD applicants, but the contrast in admission rates is stark. Of the students applying RD, Cornell takes 12.3 percent. Of those applying ED, it takes 27.7 percent. Of its entering class, it chose 41.5 percent from among those applying ED:[20]

Admission rates		
RD	ED	% class filled by ED
Columbia: 5.5%	19.7%	46.8%
Cornell: 12.3	27.7	41.5
Dartmouth: 9.9	27.9	42.3

[20] http://ivycoach.com/2018-ivy-league-admissions-statistics/. Note that MIT does not use an ED system.

Recall that this student has a near-perfect record. Although he would prefer to attend MIT, and although he has as high odds of success at MIT as anyone, he may voluntarily decide to sacrifice his hopes of MIT. He will promise to attend Cornell in order to increase his chance of acceptance there. He will do so because, under the highly unpredictable admissions process at elite American universities, he faces non-trivial odds of being rejected by both MIT and Cornell. In order to reduce the risk of ending at the state university, he may choose to apply ED to his second choice.

b. Tuition   The lower-tier Japanese medical schools charge very high fees. U.S. universities charge high fees too, but not quite in the way that journalists report. In Japan, the higher-ranking medical schools tend to be cheaper than the lower-ranking ones. So too in the U.S.: subject to a variety of qualifications, some of the top-ranking universities charge less than many of the lower-ranking schools.

The confusion follows from the fact that the top U.S. universities do not charge anything close to the tuition journalists report. Typically, journalists quote the nominal tuition rates. Consider the rates at several of the better-known schools (as of about 2015):

Harvard	$44,000
MIT	$45,000
University of Chicago	$48,000
Columbia	$51,000
Cornell	$47,000
Dartmouth	$48,000

Crucially, these are the nominal rates. These are not the anounts that most U.S. high school students would pay if admitted.

The premier schools levy charges that depend crucially

on family income, and only the richest families pay the full amount. At Harvard, for example, students whose parents earn less than $65,000 attend for free (as of about 2015). Even those with parents earning $150,000 pay only $15,000. Note that the median national household income is $52,000 in the U.S., and $150,000 is the 88th income percentile. At Stanford, students from families earning less than $65,000 similarly attend for free, and the school offers financial aid to those from families earning up to an astonishing $225,000 (the 96th percentile). Columbia offers grants (*i.e.*, a discount) to half of its students, and those grants average $47,000 —— 92 percent of the nominal tuition.

For students from most American homes, the premier universities are cheap; it is the lower-ranked schools that are so expensive. These lower-ranked schools charge lower nominal tuition rates, but offer less financial aid. Consequently, their students incur higher levels of debt, (being less talented) are less likely to graduate, and face fewer job opportunities if they do.

For example, take the public universities. Although they charge a lower nominal tuition than Harvard or Stanford, they pay less financial aid. As a result, for students from most households they charge a higher effective tuition. The mean cost of a four-year state university for full-time state residents is only $23,200, but the average student pays $18,000. The mean cost of a public two-year college is only $15,000, but the average student pays $11,700.[21] A student at Stanford from a family earning the national median income would pay $0, and enjoy a wide variety of job offers upon graduation. The same student at the average state university would pay $18,000 per year and find it harder to locate a job.

---

[21] http://www.aacc.nche.edu/Publications/Reports/Documents/CCStudents_A_Primer.pdf.

Students graduate from the less selective schools with substantial debt. Among all students who graduated from four-year colleges in 2012, 72 percent had student loan debt, and among those who borrowed the mean debt was $29,000.[22] At some schools, however, the numbers were much worse. At St. Francis University (in Pennsylvania), 87.7 percent of the students borrowed to pay for their education, and those who borrowed (and graduated) graduated with an average debt of $50,275. At Anna Maria College (Massachusetts), 92 pecent borrowed, and graduated with an average debt of $48,750. At Mt. Ida College (Massachusetts), 84.9 percent borrowed, and graduated with a debt of $43,860.[23]

Aggravating matters, most of the students at these lower-tier schools are not good students. Arguably, they should not be attending college at all. Many will never graduate. Even if they do, they will find it hard to obtain a good enough job to repay the money they borrowed to pay the tuition. SAT scores range from 200 to 800 with a median of 500, so the sum of the math and reading tests would have a median of 1000. At St. Francis University, 75 percent of the students scored below 1160 on the two tests combined—— analogous to a *hensachi* score of 58 at a Japanese university. At Mount Ida College, 75 percent of the students scored 980 or below, and at Anna Maria College, 75 percent scored 975 or below. At St. Francis 71 percent of the students graduate within six years. At Anna Maria only 46.9 percent graduate in six years, and at Mt. Ida only 39.2 percent.[24]

---

[22] http://ticas.org/sites/default/files/legacy/files/pub/Debt_Facts_and_Sources.pdf.

[23] http://www.usnews.com/education/best-colleges/the-short-list-college/articles/2015/02/17/10-colleges-that-leave-graduates-with-the-most-student-loan-debt.

[24] http://graphics.wsj.com/accredit-2015/.

| 解 説 | COMMENT | 学納金の法的性質と機能 |

学納金返還等請求事件（日本大学事件）は，2006 年 11 月 27 日に下された一
連の学納金事件判決のうちの一つである。

日本においては，様々な形で利用可能な統一試験（センター試験）があるも
のの，各大学は，最終的に合否を判定するための入学試験をそれぞれに行い，
合格者もそれぞれに発表している。受験者は複数の大学を受験することが可能
であるため，試験日・発表日の設定は，より良質の受験者をより多く獲得した
いという私大各校の思惑によってなされる。結果として，入学試験は，私立大
学から国立大学へという順序で，私立大学の間では，事実上いわゆる下位校か
ら上位校へという順序で行われるという「秩序」が形成されている。これに対
して，受験者の側は合格した下位校に対してまず入学手続を取った上で，上位
校の発表を待つという行動をとり，首尾よく上位校に合格した場合には，下位
校の入学手続の際に納入した学納金（入学金・授業料等の納入金の総称）を放棄
して，上位校に入学する。

このような「慣行」は，疑問が呈されることもなく存続してきた。しかしな
がら，消費者契約法の施行を契機に，学納金不返還条項は同法 9 条の定める不
当条項にあたるとして，この「慣行」の当否が争われる事例が相次ぐようになっ
た。

一連の判決で最高裁は，入学金と授業料を区別した上で，前者については大
学に入学する地位の対価であるとして不返還を認めるが，後者については損害
賠償の予定であるとして新年度が始まる前に（すなわち 3 月中に）辞退がなされ
たか否かで返還の要否が分かれるという考え方を示した。

このような判断枠組はおおむね肯定的に受け止められているが，いくつかの
疑問がないわけではない。たとえば，半年分の授業料を「平均的な損害」とす
るのは本当に合理的なのだろうか，また，この判断枠組は大学以外（高等学校
や専門学校）にも及ぶのか，といった疑問が直ちに思い浮かぶ。前者はなかな
か難しい問題であるが，後者についてはいくつかの後続判例が現れて一定の回
答を与えている。

ところで，本件を含む一連の訴訟は，いわゆる政策形成型の訴訟であったと

169

言える。実際のところ，多くの大学は判例の判断枠組に従って，新年度開始前の入学辞退者に対しては学納金の全額を返還するという態度をとるようになっている。

しかしながら，判例に対する反応として考えられる方策はこれに尽きるかと言えば，そうではなかろう。判例は入学金の不返還を認めているのだから，大学側としては入学金・授業料の割合を変更して入学金に重点を置くならば，学納金のうち不返還部分の割合を上昇させることが可能になる。もっとも，これは「入学金」とは何か，そもそも「入学金」ならば不返還でよいと一律に断ずることができるのかという問いを惹起しそうである。

他方，判例は推薦入学などについては別途の取扱いを認めている。そうであるならば，推薦入学のほか通常の入試とは別の形式での合格者の割合を増やすことによって，全体として不返還部分を増やすことができることになる。入試形態の多様化が進みつつある今日の状況を考えるならば，判例法理が直ちには妥当しない入学者は今後増えていくことが予想される。そうなると，推薦入学者は別扱いにするという例外の当否は再検討を求められるかもしれない。

（費用の徴収を含めて）大学入学者選抜制度は，国によって時代によって一様ではない。アメリカのように学納金が高額に達する国がある一方で，フランスのように公教育における無償原則が貫かれている国もある。また，韓国では，ある意味では日本と似た制度が採られてきたが，しばらく前から大学には，入学辞退者の学納金の全額返還が義務づけられているようである。

K.K. Choei v. Kuroki

65 Saihan minshu 2269 (Sup. Ct. July 15, 2011). [1]

更新料返還請求事件
(最判平成 23 年 7 月 15 日民集 65 巻 5 号 2269 頁)

1 The facts

When spring came to Hokkaido in 2003, one high school senior found himself bound for the Kyoto City University of the Arts. Before he left, his mother scoured the internet and found him a one-room apartment. He promised the landlord he would pay 38,000 yen/month for a year, and agreed to pay two months' rent each time he opted to renew.

Within a year, the landlord started to complain to the art student about his bringing girlfriends home for the night. The landlord also called his mother in Hokkaido and complained to her besides. Nonetheless, the student stayed. Three times he duly paid the renewal fee. On the fourth time, he refused to pay and sued.

The art student argued that the renewal fee violated Section 10 of the Consumer Contract Act:[2]

Any consumer contract clause is void if it (a) limits a consumer's rights or increases his obligations ... and (b) one-

---

[1] Reversing 1372 Kinsho 14 (Osaka High Ct. Feb. 24, 2010), affirming 2066 Hanrei jiho 95 (Kyoto D. Ct. Sept. 25, 2009).
[2] Shohisha keiyaku ho [Consumer Contract Act], Law. 61 of 2000, Sec. 10.

171

sidedly harms his interests in violation of the principles of Sec. 1 (b) of the Civil Code.

Section 1 (b) requires that legal rights and obligations follow principles of "truthfulness and integrity."

2 The decision

The District and High Courts held the renewal fee void, but the Supreme Court reversed. The contract did indeed increase the art student's obligations beyond that of a standard rental contract, observed the Supreme Court. Given the fee's modest size, however, the contract did not one-sidedly harm his interests in violation of norms of truthfulnes and integrity. Hence, the court concluded, it could not have violated Section 10.

3 Discussion

a. The role of the price term in one-sided contracts Landowners supply housing, and tenants pay rent. Landowners compete for tenants, and prospective tenants compete for housing. Under these circumstances, tenants cannot pay landowners less than a market return on their investments —— because if they tried, landlords would provide the space to other tenants instead. Landowners cannot demand "exploitative" terms —— because if they tried, their prospective tenants would find housing elsewhere.

In gauging the price of a housing unit, renters and landlords will consider the total amounts charged. Renters will sum the rent, renewal fees, "key money" (*reikin*), and anything else they will need to pay. Landlords will aggregate everything they expect to receive. If a tenant expects to stay in a unit, he will worry about the total he will pay —— but will not care whether a landlord denominates an amount

172

a monthly rental or an annual renewal fee.

For example, suppose a tenant plans to rent an apartment for 4 years. He thinks living in the unit for 4 years is probably worth 2 million yen. As a result, he would willingly pay 42,750 per month (42,750 × 48 = 2,052,000). He would, however, just as willingly pay 38,000 per month with a 2-month annual renewal fee (38,000 × 48 + 38,000 × 6 = 2,052,000 yen). Indeed, he would willingly pay 26,308 yen per month with a 10-month annual renewal fee (26,308 × 48 + 26,308 × 30 = 2,052,000 yen). Under any of these contracts, he would pay 2,052,000 yen to use the apartment for four years —— and ultimately, that is all that matters.

Obviously, a tenant would prefer to rent an apartment for 38,000 yen per month with no renewal fee rather than pay the same monthly rent and 2 months' rent to renew. But he does not prefer the former because he dislikes renewal fees. He prefers the former because he will pay a lower total. If a tenant expects to stay in the apartment for four years, how his landlord allocates the total charge among monthly rents and annual renewal fees is beside the point. Ultimately, if the market annual rental on an apartment is 456,000 yen (=38,000 × 12), a landlord who wants a renewal fee will have to charge a lower monthly rent. Do anything else, and his tenants will simply go elsewhere.[3]

Unfortunately, the lower courts and the legislature that passed the Consumer Contract Act seem to have missed this lesson in basic economics. The best protection a tenant can have is not a statute like the Consumer Contract Act. Rather, it is a competitive housing market. In a competitive market, a tenant will choose among

---

[3] Somewhat bizarrely, the High Court considered the claim that the landlord charged a lower rent to offset the renewal fee, but declared it unproven. In fact, of course, it is simply a function of the market.

alternative housing options. Should a landlord try to charge more than the market price, he can simply rent an apartment somewhere else.

In competitive markets, there are no "one-sided" contracts, for a simple reason: all terms (whether "fair" or "unfair") are "priced." [4] If a landlord insists on a term (like a renewal fee) that a tenant does not want, the tenant will demand an off-setting cut in the monthly rent. And so it is with any apparently one-sided term. If one of the parties insists on it, the other party will demand a lower price. If the insisting party refuses to lower the price, the other party will go elsewhere. Necessarily, any price to which both parties agree will capture the value of the contract as a whole. Even if any term seems "unfair," the offending party will have paid for the "unfair" term by adjusting the price to the point at which the "victim" was willing to agree to it. [5]

---

[4] In fact, the point is not limited to competitive markets. Even in monopolies, all terms (included "unfair" terms) will be priced. The monopolist cannot profitably charge more than the monopoly price. As a result, should he try to add a term to which the buyer objects, he will have to lower the price terms or else lose a sale.

[5] This logic applies even when consumers are imperfectly informed. Consumers vary in the extent to which they search and acquire information. Some search carefully and are informed; some do not. But as Alan Schwartz and Louis Wilde put it, "The presence of at least some consumer search in a market creates the possibiity of a 'pecuniary externality': persons who search sometimes protect nonsearchers from overreaching firms. This result can obtain because in mass transactions it is usually too expensive for firms to distinguish among extensive, moderate, and nonsearchers. ... Thus, if enough searchers exist, firms have incentives both to compete for their business and to offer the same terms to nonsearchers." See Alan Schwartz & Louis L. Wilde, Intervening in Markets on the Basis of Imperfect Information: A Legal and Economic Analysis, 127 Univ. Penn. L. Rev. 630, 638 (1979). Indeed, not only will the unfair terms be priced in the contract, but the landlord generally will be dissuaded by reputational concerns from taking advantage of the consumer anyway. See Lucian A. Bebchuk & Richard A. Posner, One-Sided Contracts in Competitive Consumer Markets, 104 Mich. L. Rev. 827 (2006).

174

Table 1 Hypothetical Rental Unit

Posit a housing unit with a market rental value of 1,000,000 yen per year.

Contract A: No renewal fee

Monthly rent:	83,333 yen
Annual rent for renewing tenant:	1,000,000 yen
Annual rent for vacating tenant:	1,000,000 yen

Contract B: Renewal fee of 2 months' rent

Monthly rent:	71,429 yen
Annual rent to renewing tenant:	1,000,000 yen
Annual rent to vacating tenant:	857,143 yen

In a competitive market, statutes like the Consumer Contract Act provide consumers no benefit. They do not provide "little" benefit. They provide no benefit at all. To the extent that they limit the shape of the contractual options from which landlords and tenants can choose, they actually lower the welfare of both.

b. Why some landlords demand renewal fees Consider the contractual choice landlords face. Take a landlord who owns an apartment with a market rental value of 1 million yen per year. Suppose that most but not all tenants want to stay in an apartment for more than a year. The landlord can either charge a monthly rental with no renewal fee (Contract A in **Table 1**) or couple a renewal fee with the monthly rental (Contract B). If he chooses not to charge a renewal fee, he will charge a monthly rental of 1,000,000/12 = 83,333 yen. If he decides instead to charge a renewal fee, he cannot keep the rent at 83,333 yen. If he did, he would be charging more than 1 million yen per year for an apartment worth only 1 million. Given that tenants will only pay 1 million a year to stay in his apartment, if he opts to charge a 2-month renewal fee he will need to lower the rent to 1,000,000/14 = 71,429 yen.[6]

To ask why a landlord might opt for Contract B over Contract A is to ask why a tenant would care. More precisely, it is to ask what kind of tenant would prefer Contract B over Contract A. Contrast the tenant who wants to stay indefinitely, with the tenant who wants to stay only for a limited time. If a tenant plans to stay in an apartment indefinitely, he will be indifferent between Contract A and Contract B. In either case, he will pay the landlord 1 million yen per year.

If a tenant plans to stay only for a limited time, however, he will prefer Contract B. Suppose he plans to live in the apartment exactly one year. Under Contract A, he would pay 1 million yen in rent. Under Contract B, he would pay only 857,143 yen for the year. In effect, a landlord who demands a renewal fee offers short-term tenants a discount —— in this case, a price cut on an annual basis of 14 percent. As a result, tenants who plan to stay in an apartment indefinitely will not care whether a landlord offers Contract A or Contract B; those who plan to stay only a short time will prefer Contract B.

As this example illustrates, landlords demand renewal fees when they hope to attract short-term tenants. A contract that couples a monthly rental charge with a renewal fee (Contract B) will cause

---

[6] In fact, if tenants sort themselves successfully (as described above) , the short-term renters will compete the rent on these renewal-fee apartments up beyond 71,429 yen.

tenants to sort themselves by their expected term at the apartment. Disproportionately, it will cause those who expect to stay only a short time to self-select into apartments demanding renewal terms.

This logic tracks the way landlords most often demand renewal fees in the metropolitan Tokyo area. They will most commonly hope to attract short-term tenants if they want either to adjust the rent regularly, or to renovate or replace their buildings soon. They will most likely want to take these steps in booming real estate markets. Such is exactly the case in the greater Tokyo area. Indeed, in neighboring Kanagawa prefecture (containing Yokohama city), over 90 percent of the landlords charge renewal fees.[7]

c. The restrictions on contract   Tokyo landlords work to attract limited-term tenants because of the peculiarly dysfunctional nature of Japanese landlord tenant law. Landlords everywhere will want mostly long-term tenants. They will want to avoid vacancies, and want to avoid the cost of recruiting and replacing tenants.

Even when landlords want mostly longer-term tenants, however, they need some turnover. For one thing, primarily only with turnover can they experiment toward finding the market rental charge. For another, if they plan to rennovate or replace an aging building, they obviously will need to convince all of their tenants to leave.

Unfortunately for landlords, Japanese landlord-tenant law does not let landlords evict tenants. People who rent their own home can evict a rent-paying tenant only at ruinous cost; those who rent commercial apartments cannot evict rent-paying tenants at any price.

---

[7]   Minkan chintai jutaku ni kakaru jittai chosa [Empirical Survey Regarding Private Rental Housing], June 2007, posted at http://www.mlit.go.jp/kisha/kisha07/07/070629_3/02.pdf.

These draconian restrictions date from 1941. The Japanese army had over-run Manchuria in 1931, and invaded the rest of China in 1937. Soon, the government found the war bitterly intractable and ruinously expensive. Trying desperately to fund the effort, it ordered wage and price controls in 1938.[8] It imposed rent controls in 1939.[9]

These economic controls generated predictable avoidance tactics: facing rent control, landlords tried to evict their tenants in order to reset the rent at a higher level.[10] To stop landlords from doing this, the government added the statutory section that lies at the root of the modern disaster.[11]

Unless the owner of a building needs it for his personal use or for other justifiable reasons, he may not either refuse to renew the lease or petition to vacate the lease.

After the war ended, the new democratically elected governments steadily dismantled the economic controls. They dropped rent controls in one sector after another, and repealed what remained in 1986.[12] The ban on all evictions except where a landlord could point to "justifiable reasons," however, they retained.[13] Only in 1999 did they finally allow landlords and tenants to negotiate enforceable eviction terms in their leases, and only if they agreed at

---

[8]   Kokka sodo in ho [National Mobilization Act], Law No. 55 of 1938.

[9]   Chidai yachin tosei rei [Ground and House Rent Control Order], Chokurei No. 704 of 1939.

[10]   It tried to control rents on new leases too, of course. Chokurei No. 678 of 1940.

[11]   Sec. 1-2 of the Shakuya ho [House Lease Act], Law No. 50 of 1921, as amended 1941.

[12]   Kyoka ninka to minkan katsudo ni kakaru kisei no seiri oyobi gorika ni kansuru horitsu [Act Concerning the Rationalization and Ordering of Regulatory Measures concerning Permits and Recognition in Civil Activities], Law No. 102 of 1985.

[13]   Shakuchi shakuya ho [Land and House Lease Act], Law No. 90 of 1991, at Sec. 28.

the outset that the lease would last for one-year only.[14]

The law leaves landlords in an impossible situation. One Hiroshima University professor, for example, owned a house in Tokyo that he rented for 60,000 yen per month. When he obtained an appointment to a Tokyo university, he and his wife came to Tokyo. They planned to move into their house as soon as their current tenant's lease expired. Until then, they lived with their son and his wife in Chiba, 2-1/2 hours from the university. When the lease expired, the professor asked his tenant to leave, but the tenant refused. When the professor sued to evict, the judge ordered him to pay the tenant 7 million yen. The amount came to 117 months' rent. In effect, the professor could retrieve his house only if he paid his tenant a decade's rent.[15]

Or take the firm that owned a crumbling building it hoped to replace. Its tenant had run a modest (he earned 20,000-30,000 yen per month) electrical repair business. The foundation was crumbling, the roof threatened to collapse, the walls had rotted, and government inspectors had declared the place a safety hazard. The firm wanted to demolish the hazard, and erect a new building. The court let it evict the tenant only if it paid him 1.5 million yen. In effect, the firm could retrieve its building only by doubling its tenant's income for the past half decade.[16]

The Oshio family had four children. Having out-grown their house, they wanted a new, larger space. Toward that end, they bought an old house with crumbling walls, a leaking roof, and fire-hazard wiring. They did not care. They planned to tear down the

---

[14] Shakuchi shakuya ho, supra note 13, at Sec. 38.

[15] Tsuji v. Ejiri, 785 Hanrei taimuzu 177 (Tokyo D. Ct. Sept. 6, 1991).

[16] Kimura v. Goshi gaisha Yamaguchi shoten, 527 Hanrei taimuzu 119 (Tokyo D. Ct. Feb. 28, 1984).

building and build a new one. The house, however, came with a tenant named Yokoyama. He paid 15,000 yen a month to live there, and when the Oshios bought the house and asked him to leave, he refused. They even offered him 5 million yen, but the court declared the amount too low. They could evict him only if they paid him 7 million. In effect, the Oshios could retrieve their house only by refunding four years' rent.[17]

Sometimes courts will not let landlords have their homes back, no matter what they might pay their tenant. And indeed, in the case at hand, the plaintiff argued exactly that —— that he had no obligation to pay the renewal fee because his landlord had no right to refuse to renew his lease anyway. One couple operated an office supply busines on their first floor, and lived on the second. They rented part of the first floor to a clothing boutique. When they ran out of room, they asked the boutique owners to leave. The boutique owners refused. The summary court ordered them to leave if the owners paid them 5 million yen. The tenants appealed, and the district court reversed. No matter what the landlords might offer, the clothing boutique could stay.[18]

d. The implications of the legal regime   Courts almost always slash social welfare when they refuse to enforce voluntary contracts, and they do so here. Landlords and tenants contract over a competitive market. Many landlords compete to offer space, and many tenants compete to rent it. The leases they negotiate maximize their joint welfare —— otherwise, obviously, they would not agree to them. If a landlord wants the right to evict a tenant upon the end of the term and the tenant does not want to give him that right, the

---

[17]   Oshio v. Yokoyama, 714 Hanrei taimuzu 193 (Fukuoka D. Ct. June 7, 1989).
[18]   Mori v. Sano, 1136 Hanrei jiho 116 (Yokohama D. Ct. Mar. 2, 1984).

180

Table 2 Owned and Rented Housing, International Comparison

	Owned	Rented	Owned/Rented
Japan	124 ㎡	46 ㎡	2.70
U.S.	157	113	1.40
England	95	75	1.27
France	114	76	1.50
Germany	124	76	1.63

Sources: J. Mark Ramseyer, The Virtues of Japanese Private Law ch. 6 (Chicago: University of Chicago Press, 2015); Somusho, ed., Jutaku, tochi tokei chosa [Survey of Housing and Land] (2003), available at: Kokudo kotsu sho, ed., Ju seikatsu kihon keikaku (zenkoku keikaku) (an) kankei shiryo [Basic Plan (National, Proposed) for Housing: Materials] Fig. 9 (2011).

landlord will have to pay for the term (through lower rent). Otherwise, the tenant will rent space elsewhere. A landlord and tenant will agree to a right to evict only where the right is worth more to the landlord than to the tenant —— and the landlord pays the tenant for it. The resulting contract maximizes the joint welfare of the landlord and tenant, and a court that refuses to enforce it simply lowers the welfare of both.

Japanese courts refuse to enforce rights to evict, and several straightforwardly inefficient consequences follow. First, landlords rent only very small units. Large living units are available in Japan, but not for rent. Instead, someone who wants to live in one of the larger units will need to buy it. Rental units in Japan average 44 square meters; owned units average 124 square meters. The average owned unit, in other words, is 2.7 times as big as the average rented unit. In the U.S., the ratio is only 1.4 (Table 2).

The absence of a rental market for larger units reflects a landlord's inability to retrieve a unit from his tenant. Landlords need regular turnover to keep rents at market levels, and in due course need the right to evict tenants to renovate or replace buildings. If a tenant refuses to leave when asked (and given the huge payments courts will order landlords to pay unwilling tenants, even tenants who might otherwise happily leave will feign refusal), the courts will let a landlord evict a tenant only upon paying him several years' rent. Landlords respond by renting only units so small that no family would want to stay in them beyond a few years.

Second, landlords will keep off the market any unit that they hopes to replace or renovate within a few years. Obviously, they will most likely want to replace or renovate units in a prime locations. Suppose a family owns a old house near a suburban Tokyo train station. It would like to tear the house down and build a nice 3-storey apartment house. It does not have the funds to do so now, but hopes to inherit the money in 5 to 10 years from an elderly relative.

The family will not rent the house. They could use the income that renting the unit would provide. Many people would appreciate the chance to live in the old but conveniently located house for a few years. Yet notwithstanding the mutual benefit that renting the house would provide, the owners will not rent. If they did rent the house, they would be able to evict their renters when they inherited the funds only by refunding all (or possibly more than all) of the rent they received during the interim. Rather than take that risk, they will keep the house empty.

Table 3 shows some of the consequences. The table gives the location of empty housing in the Tokyo area. Note the large number of empty units conveniently located to central Tokyo. Obviously, social welfare in Tokyo would increase if landlords would rent these units. They do not rent them, for the obvious reason that once they did the law would prevent them from reacquiring the units unless they paid huge amounts (if it even let them reacquire the units at all).

Table 3   Tokyo Area Vacant Housing

Tokyo area housing left vacant (2009) --

1. Distance to railroad station:

Under 500 m:	26.7 %
500 m - 1 km:	40.6 %
Over 1 km:	32.8 %

2. Time (Walking) to railroad station:

Under 5 minutes:	22.2 %
5 -10 minutes:	40.6 %
10 -15 min:	21.7 %
Over 15 min:	8.3 %

Sources: J. Mark Ramseyer, The Virtues of Japanese Private Law ch. 6 (Chicago: University of Chicago Press, 2015); Tokyo to, ed., Tokyo no akiya no jittai [The Circumstances of Empty Houses in Tokyo] (2010), available at: http://www.toshiseibi.metro.tokyo.jp/juutaku_kcs/shiryou_h22_02_03.pdf.

Last, landlords demand lease renewal fees. They do so for a simple reason: to cause prospective tenants to sort themselves by their plans to stay in the unit. As **Table 1** illustrates, landlords who charge lease renewal terms effectively offer a discount to tenants who plan not to stay. They do so because they hope those prospective tenants who plan not to stay indefinitely will self-select into their units. And they do this because Japanese courts refuse to let them enforce the eviction clauses that both they and their tenants would like to include.

解説　COMMENT　更新料条項の不当性判断

　更新料返還請求事件（長栄 vs 黒木事件）は，学生が借りたアパートの更新料をめぐる紛争であり，借主側の（既払）更新料返還請求に対して，家主側は反訴において（未払）更新料を請求した。最高裁は，更新料条項は，賃貸借契約の要素を構成しない債務を特約によって賃借人に負わせるものであり，その意味で，任意規定の定めるところに比べて消費者たる賃借人の義務を加重するものであるとしつつ，契約書に一義的かつ具体的に記載された更新料条項は，特段の事情がない限り，信義則に反して一方的に消費者の利益を害するものであるとは言えないとして，消費者契約法 10 条によって無効とはならないとした。ほぼ同時期に現れ，いわゆる敷引特約（敷金の一部の不返還特約）を原則有効とした最判平成 23・3・24 民集 65 巻 2 号 903 頁，最判平成 23・7・12 判時 2128号 43 頁とともに注目を集めたものである。

　本判決による消費者契約法 10 条の適用には，いくつかの特色が認められる。第一に，基準となる任意規定は明文のものに限られず，一般法理も含まれるとしたこと。第二に，本件賃貸借契約に消費者契約法が適用されることは前提としつつも（すなわち，定型的には本件の当事者間には情報・交渉力の格差があるという前提に立ちつつも），10 条による無効判断に際して，当事者間の情報・交渉力の格差を改めて考慮に入れていること（具体的には更新料の額を勘案していること）。第三に，契約条項が一義的・具体的に契約書に記載されていることを重視していること。

　ここには次のような見方が現れている。①契約類型ごとに当事者が負うべき義務の内容は定まり，そこから逸脱する合意に対しては違法の嫌疑が向けられる。しかしながら，②支払うべき総額が明らかになっていれば，賃借人は合理的な選択を行ったと評価できる。もっとも，③更新料の額が高額に過ぎる場合には，情報・交渉力の格差の影響があると考える余地がある。最高裁は，②を支える要素として契約条項の一義性・具体性を取り出しており，最終的な判断にはこの点が大きな影響を及ぼしている。とはいえ，①によって違法判断の間口が広げられていることや，③によって例外的な無効化の余地が残されていることにも留意しなければならない。

また、②そのものに関しても、選択可能性が契約条項の一義性・具体性のみによって確保されるのか、そもそも、ここでいう一義性・具体性とは何を意味するのか、という点については議論の余地がある。契約条項に基づいて計算をすれば賃借人の負担総額は明らかになるとしても、見かけ上の賃料額に幻惑されて適切な判断ができないことがあるのではないか。平成23・7・12判決の岡部反対意見が、敷引金の額だけでなく性質についても認識できることが必要であるとしたのは、同様の趣旨であろう。

数年前にニューヨークの大学でこれら一連の判決について講義をしたところ、学生たちからは、日本の賃貸借市場における情報提示は不透明・不公正ではないか、という批判が聞かれたが、同様の方式による情報提示は日本の賃貸借市場においてのみ観察されるものではない。ニューヨークでは、価格＋チップを合算しないと本当の価格が明らかにならないことに私は困惑したが、彼らはこれは不透明・不公正だとは感じないらしい。日本に限らず行われている航空料金に上乗せされた燃料サーチャージャーなどというのも同様である。

最後に、本判決が持つかもしれない波及効果について一言しておこう。本判決は更新料の性格は複合的なものであるとしつつも、結局は、賃料とあわせて賃貸借の対価となっていると考えている。そう考えるのであれば、契約期間（賃料据置期間）の途中で賃貸借が終了した場合には、更新料につき割合的な清算がなされるべきではないかという疑問も出てきそうである。この疑問は（必要な修正を加えれば）権利金にも及びうるかもしれない。

Northcon I v. Katayama

51 Saihan minshu 2573 (Sup. Ct. July 11, 1997).

懲 罰 賠 償
(最判平成9年7月11日民集51巻6号2573頁)

1 The facts

In 1982, the Oregon partnership Northcom I won a suit over a real estate lease against the Japanese industrial firm Mansei. The jury awarded Northcom $425,000 in compensatory damages, and $40,000 in attorneys' fees. On the ground that Mansei had engaged in "intentional misrepresentation and intentional concealment of material facts,"[1] it added another $1.125 million in punitive damages. Norcom 1 then sued in Japan to enforce the judgment.

2 The decision [2]

The Japanese courts awarded Northcom 1 the compensatory damages, but denied the punitive damages at every level. The

---

[1] Kerry A. Jung, How Punitive Damage Awards Affect U.S. Businesses in the International Arena: The Northcon I v. Mansei Kogyo Co. Decision, 17 Wis. Int'l L.J. 489, 492 (1999).

[2] Northcon I v. Katayama, 1376 Hanrei jiho 79 (Tokyo D.C. Feb. 18, 1991, aff'd, 1471 Hanrei jiho 89 (Tokyo High Ct. June 28, 1993), aff'd, 1624 Hanrei jiho 90 (Sup. Ct. July 11, 1997); see also Katayama v. Northcon I, __ Hanrei jiho __ (Sup. Ct. July 11, 1997) (plaintiff may collect interest on compensatory portion of California judgment).

law authorizes civil suits, the Supreme court eventually explained, to make injured parties whole. It does not authorize civil suits to punish. Punishment lies within the ambit of criminal suits, yet punitive damages resemble nothing so much as criminal fines. To impose these fine-equivalents in a civil suit violates the public order. And to enforce a punitive damage award issued by a California court would violate the public order just as much as if the Japanese court had issued the award itself.

３ Discussion

These Japanese opinions contain an unstated "subtext": that from time to time, U.S. state courts have turned entirely unprincipled and highly dysfunctional, and that punitive damage judgments can embody that unprincipled dysfunction.

The subtext is entirely warranted. The source of the problem lies in two places: the use of jurors to decide facts, and the selection of judges in some states through contested elections. Together, these factors can transform courts into institutions that strategic attorneys can manipulate to redistribute wealth from out-of-state defendants to local claimants.

Japan is not the only modern country to avoid the civil jury. Courts in civil-law jurisdictions have always avoided them, and today even courts in most common-law countries do. New Zealand "has relegated [them] to only one or two cases per year."[3] Canada retains them "in some jurisdictions in name only," and in other places abolished them entirely.[4] And in the United Kingdom, "less than one percent of civil trials" use juries, and in personal injury cases plaintiffs

---

[3] Neil Cameron, et al., The New Zealand Jury: Towards Reform, in Neil Vidmar, ed., World Jury Systems (2000).

cannot use a jury at all.[5]

Even without punitive damages, juries are unpredictable. Juries in those jurisdictions favored by the plaintiffs' bar do not just award large amounts. Instead, they award the largest amounts to local plaintiffs against defendants from out-of-town.[6] Take a stark comparison from Erik Helland and Alexander Tabarrok.[7] In suits over traffic accidents, the plaintiffs mostly sue local defendants, but in products liability suits sue corporations from other states. In wealthier counties (those with a poverty rate below 5%), plaintiffs recover a mean $244,000 in automobile accident cases and $1.18 million in products liability. Shrewd attorneys generally file product liability claims in poor counties —— for a reason: in poor counties (poverty rates above 25%), plaintiffs recover $760,000 (3.1 times as much as in the rich counties) in automobile accidents and $6.74 million (5.7 times as much) in products liability.

When judges face contested elections to keep their jobs, they effectively decide cases before lawyers who are their actual or potential campaign contributors. Plaintiff's lawyer Richard "Dickie" Scruggs described the dynamics:[8]

The trial lawyers have established relationships with the judges that are elected; they're State Court judges; they're populists. They've got large populations of voters [who serve on the juries] who are in on the deal, they're getting

---

[4] W.A. Bogart, Guardian of Civil Rights ... Medieval Relic: The Civil Jury in Canada, in Vidmar, ed., 2000, supra note 3.

[5] Sally Lloyd-Bostock & Cheryl Thomas, The Continuing Decline of the English Jury, in Vidmar, ed., 2000, supra note 3.

[6] Eric Helland & Alexander Tabarrok, Race, Poverty, and American Tort Awards: Evidence from Three Data Sets, 32 J. Legal Stud. 27, 38 (2003); Eric Helland & Alexander Tabarrok, Judge and Jury: American Tort Law on Trial chs. 2, 3 (2006).

[7] Helland & Tabarrok, 2003, supra note 6; Helland & Tabarrok, 2006, supra note 6.

[8] Peter J. Boyer, The Bribe, New Yorker, May 19, 2008.

their piece in many cases. And so, it's a political force in their jurisdiction, and it's almost impossible to get a fair trial if you're a defendant in some of these places... . The cases are not won in the courtroom. They're won on the back roads long before the case goes to trial. Any lawyer fresh out of law school can walk in there and win the case, so it doesn't matter what the evidence or law is.

If jurors want to transfer wealth from an out-of-state corporation to their neighbors, some state judges declare themselves happy to help. As one retired justice of the West Virginia Supreme Court wrote:[9]

The anarchy that currently prevails among American state jurisdictions absolutely guarantees politically that no line of any sort will be drawn. After all, I'm not the only appellate judge who wants to sleep at night. As long as I am allowed to redistribute wealth from out-of-state companies to injured in-state plaintiffs, I shall continue to do so. Not only is my sleep enhanced when I give someone else's money away, but so is my job security, because the in-state plaintiffs, their families, and their friends will reelect me.

The same judge continued (in discussing a particular case):[10]

From what I know about myself and my colleagues, I have the distinct impression that in a product liability case the vote would have been 3 to 2 the other way, and the whole $10 million judgment would have been sustained. Had a defective Ford automobile killed the little boy, even I would have had none of the enthusiasm for reducing the judgment that I had when the judgment against the defendants would

---

[9] Richard Neely, The Product Liability Mess 4 (Free Press: 1988).
[10] Neely, supra note 9, at 70-72.

affect business and consumer costs in West Virginia. What do I care about the Ford Motor Company? To my knowledge Ford employs no one in West Virginia in its manufacturing processes ... . The best that I can do, and I do it all the time, is make sure that my own state's residents get more money out of Michigan than Michigan residents get out of us.

Kip Viscusi quoted another state judge who made much the same point:[11]

I may not always congratulate myself at the end of the day on the brilliance of my legal reasoning, but when I do such things as allow a paraplegic to collect a few hundred thousand dollars from the Michelin Tire company - thanks to a one-car crash of unexplainable cause - I at least sleep well at night. Michelin will somehow survive (and if they don't, only the French will care), but my disabled constituent won't make it the rest of her life without Michelin's money.

Elections affect outcomes. Suppose, Eric Helland and Alexander Tabarrok ask, one could shift a case from a state court where the government picked judges through a non-partisan process to a court where the judges faced partisan elections. The likely award will climb 23%.[12] They add:[13]

In cases involving out-of-state defendants and in-state plaintiffs, the average award (conditional upon winning) is $362,988 higher in partisan states than in nonpartisan states; $230,092 of the larger award is due to a bias against out-of-state defendants, and the remainder is due to generally high-

---

[11] W. Kip Viscusi, Reforming Products Liability 56 (Cambridge: Harvard University Press, 1991).

[12] Helland & Tabarrok, 2006, supra note 6, at 88-90.

[13] Helland & Tabarrok, 2006, supra note 6, at 92.

er awards against businesses in partisan states.

Punitive damages exacerbate these effects. In awarding them, juries face very few constraints. They can instead award amounts with virtually no relation to the damages that a victim actually suffered. By 2004, Kip Viscusi counted 64 punitive damage awards of at least $100 million.[14] According to Joni Hersch and Viscusi, juries (rather than judges) had awarded nearly all of the extremely large punitive awards. Juries were more likely to award punitive damages, to award larger amounts, and to award amounts less correlated with the actual damages suffered.[15] Overall, punitive damages averaged 22 times the compensatory awards.[16]

The U.S. Supreme Court has tried to limit the disaster. In 2008, for example, it declared that punitive damages in maritime cases could not exceed actual damages. The case concerned the Exxon Valdez oil spill in which the jury had awarded compensatory damages of $287 million and punitive damages of $5.0 billion.[17] In other cases, it has tried to impose both substantive and procedural limits on the awards.[18] The problem, however, remains largely unresolved.

---

[14] W. Kip Viscusi, The Blockbuster Punitive Damages Awards, 53 Emory L.J. 1405 (2004).

[15] Joni Hersch & W. Kip Viscusi, Punitive Damages: How Judges and Juries Perform, 33 J. Legal Stud. 1 (2004).

[16] Joni Hersch & W. Kip Viscusi, Punitive Damages by Numbers: Exxon Shipping Co. v. Baker, 18 Sup. Ct. Econ. Rev. 259, 273 tab. 1 (2010).

[17] Joni Hersch & W. Kip Viscusi, Punitive Damages by Numbers: Exxon Shipping Co. v. Baker, 18 Sup. Ct. Econ. Rev. 259 (2010).

[18] BMW of North Am., Inc. v. Gore, 517 U.S. 559 (1996); Pacific Mutual Life Ins. Co. v. Haslip, 499 U.S. 1 (1991); see generally Victor E. Schwartz, Mark A. Behrens & Joseph P. Mastrosimone, Reining in Punitive Damages "Run Wild": Proposals for Reform by Courts and Legislatures, 65 Brooklyn L. Rev. 1003 (1999).

| 解 説　COMMENT | 懲罰賠償の意義 —— 陪審制及び裁判官の公選制との関係で |

　本判決（最判平成9・7・11民集51巻6号2573頁）は，日本の国際民事訴訟法の文脈においては，外国判決の承認の要件の一つである，判決内容が日本の公序良俗に反しないこと（現民訴118条3号）の解釈を示したものと位置付けるのが一般的であるように思われる。即ち，懲罰賠償を命じたカリフォルニア州裁判所の判決は，実損害を超える賠償を命ずる点で刑罰とほぼ同様の意義を有することから，実損害の補塡という日本の損害賠償制度の基本原則と相いれず，判決内容が「公序良俗」に反するので，日本において承認できない，と判示したのである。

　しかし，ラムザイヤー教授の「解説」は，本判決をアメリカ法から見たときに別の2つの問題——陪審制と裁判官の公選制——が存することを指摘する。

　民事事件において，陪審（小陪審〔petty jury〕）とは，一般市民から無作為抽出で選ばれた陪審員の合議体であり，トライアルにおいて事実認定（損害賠償請求訴訟においては賠償額を含めて）を担当する機関である。また，アメリカ合衆国は，連邦制の国家であるため，裁判所も連邦裁判所と各州の裁判所とがあるところ，州裁判所の裁判官の選任方法は州によって異なり，州知事の任命による州もあれば，裁判官を党派的選挙（partisan election）により選任する州もある（浅香吉幹『現代アメリカの司法』〔東京大学出版会，1999〕140頁以下）。党派的選挙とは，政党（例えば共和党あるいは民主党）が裁判官候補者を選抜し，候補者が政党名を付して公示され，投票が行われる仕組みである。政党名付きの方が，候補者の思想信条が有権者に伝わりやすい，という指摘がされている。陪審制と裁判官の公選制とに通底するのは，民主主義国家における司法のあり方という問題である。民主主義国家においては，司法権も民主的でなければならず，国民に対して責任を負わなければならない。一般論としては，裁判は，民意を反映したものであるべきである（少なくとも民意から乖離したものであってはならない），と言えよう。

　しかし他方，民主主義の過程において少数派の権利が多数派によって侵害された場合に，その救済をするのが司法権の重要な役割であることから，立法や行政と同じような意味で司法が民主化するのが望ましいとは言い難い。他州の

被告から自州の原告に富を過剰に移転するのが自州州民の多数意思であるとしても，それをそのまま裁判において認めるのは不当である。裁判官が，選挙の際に支持してくれた自州の住民に有利な裁判をすることも不適切である。「民主司法のジレンマ」（兼子一＝竹下守夫『裁判法〔第4版〕』〔有斐閣，1999〕24頁）と言われる所以である。

　他州の被告から自州の原告への富の過剰な移転という問題を，一層深刻にするのが懲罰賠償制度である。実損害を超える賠償を命ずることは，本判決が指摘するように，制裁の側面を有することになるところ，従来我が国においては，法違反の抑止機能という視点から，私人による法の実現を促進する制度であるという肯定的な紹介がされたこともあった（田中英夫＝竹内昭夫『法の実現における私人の役割』〔東京大学出版会，1987〕133-172頁）。他方で，懲罰賠償制度は，陪審制と結びつくことによって，命じられる賠償額の予見可能性が乏しくなり，また賠償額が時として莫大になることもある点も，しばしば指摘されてきた。懲罰賠償制度には，このような側面もあることに留意すべきであろう。

Taishi kensetsu kogyo, K.K. v. Matsushita denki sangyo, K.K.

842 Hanrei taimuzu 69, 1493 Hanrei jiho 29
(Osaka D. Ct. Mar 29, 1994).

松下電器カラーテレビ事件
(大阪地判平成6年3月29日判例時報1493号29頁)

1 The facts

Noboru Hatamoto ran a construction firm in the Osaka suburb of Yao. Upon opening an office in 1987, he received a gift of a Panasonic television set. A few months later, an employee noticed smoke rising from around the set. She called the fire department, but the set caught fire. By the time the firemen arrived, the flames had destroyed the office. Hatamoto collected from his insurer, and sued Matsushita Electric (owner of the Panasonic brand) for the 7.3 million yen damages not covered.

2 The decision

a. **The reasoning** Matsushita Electric was liable, held the Osaka District Court. To reach that decision, it cited the tort damage provisions of Civil Code Section 709.[1] The section declares defendants liable if they injure others intentionally or negligently:

> He who infringes a right of another, either

---

[1] Minpo [Civil Code], Law No. 89 of Apr. 27, 1896.

194

intentionally or negligently, must compensate that person for any damages he causes.

To decide whether a defendant acted negligently, Japanese courts have often (not always) adopted a balancing test much like Learned Hand's famous *Carroll Towing* formula:[2]

> Possibly it serves to bring [the rule] into relief to state it in algebraic terms: if the probability [of the accident] be called P, the injury, L; and the burden [of preventing the accident] B; liability depends upon whether B is less than L multiplied by P; i.e., whether $B < PL$.

Due care is that which "a person of ordinary care would show under the circumstances," the Japanese Supreme Court explained in 1911.[3] And those circumstances, in turn, may require people to weigh risks (Hand's P), harms (L), and precautionary costs (B).

In the case at hand, the Osaka District Court began by announcing a stringent and wide-ranging duty of care:[4]

> In the course of designing, manufacturing, and distributing a product, a manufacturer bears a high duty of care. He owes a duty to insure that the product is safe, and that users will not suffer damage from any dangers that might inhere in it. Should he breach that duty and distribute an unsafe product, he must compensate users for any damages that result.
>
> This duty to distribute only safe products is one the manufacturer owes to anyone who uses his product. If he violates the duty, he is liable in tort to all users, regardless of

---

[2] United States v. Carroll Towing Co., 159 F. 2d 169, 173 (2d Cir. 1947).

[3] Fukuyama v. Nakamura, 17 Daihan minroku 617, 622 (Sup. Ct. Nov. 1, 1911).

[4] Taishi kensetsu kogyo, K.K. v. Matsushita denki sangyo, K.K., 842 Hanrei taimuzu 69, 85 (Osaka D. Ct. Mar 29, 1994).

whether he stands in contract with them.

The court then applied the principle to Matsushita. Television sets, it reasoned, should not catch fire. This one did. It was defective, and if Matsushita acted negligently it was liable for any resulting damages. The court had no evidence either of negligence or of non-negligence —— so it presumed that Matsushita had been negligent, and left it to the firm to rebut the presumption. Given that Matsushita could not prove its non-negligence, it lost.

Matsushita chose not to appeal.

b. Strict liability Of course, it would never apply strict liability, insisted the Osaka District Court. After all, Section 709 governed, and the Section did not hold manufacturers to strict liability. It held them only to negligence:[5]

> The case raises the questions of (a) who should bear the losses caused by the use of a product, and (b) under what circumstances that person should bear those losses. The question involves the allocation of risks inherent in living within a social enviroment. Citizens must decide that allocation through a community-wide consensus —— through the legislative process. If they have not yet followed that process, a court cannot impose strict (or non-negligent) liability unilaterally.

Democratic sentiments to be sure. Section 709 required plaintiffs to show negligence or intent, and Sec. 709 was the law. The court was not about to hold Matsushita strictly liable. Instead, it would hold it only to duties premised on "rationality" and governed by "social convention" (p. 86).

---

[5] Taishi kensetsu kogyo, K.K., 842 Hanrei taimuzu at 86.

And so it was that the court protested its fealty to democratic values. After declaring that it would not hold Matsushita strictly liable, however, it reasoned:

(i) That all television sets "must meet the standard of absolute safety under reasonable use" (p. 87);

(ii) That a set which did not meet that "standard of absolute safety" was "defective;"

(iii) That a television set which caught fire was necessarily unsafe and therefore defective (p. 87): "Given that this television set started smoking and caught fire under reasonable use ..., it must have been unreasonably dangerous. Necessarily, it was defective."

(iv) And that once a plaintiff "proved that a product was defective," the court would "presume the manufacturer's negligence." (p. 86).

The court protested that it avoided strict liability in the interest of democratic government. But perhaps it protested a bit too much —— a bit like Hamlet's mother Gertrude.

What the court faced was the question of how to allocate the loss when it had no evidence about fault. The fire itself obviously destroyed much of the evidence, and by the time of trial, the remains of the television set were nowhere to be found (p. 70). Only one person —— Yoko Yamanaka —— claimed to see the smoke, but as Hatamoto's employee her testimony was obviously self-serving.

c. The choice On the one hand, television sets seldom burn. Newspapers do report cases of television fires, but only rarely. Matsushita claimed to have sold 84,000 of the sets in question, and to have had no fires. And on the other hand, owners can cause fires by misusing the sets. They can fray the wires inside power cords by pulling on them improperly. They can use extension cords with inadequate electrical capacity. They can block the unit's vents. Indeed, they can even cause fires through other means (cigarettes, candles, space heaters) which they then blame on the television sets.

Were the court to have required Hatamoto to prove Matsushita's negligence, it would have imposed a burden he could not meet. People whose television sets caught fire would bear the loss themselves. If television sets rarely caught fire, the approach would arguably make sense.

Instead, however, the court required Matsushita to prove that it had not acted negligently, or —— what is probably the same thing —— that Hatamoto's employees had somehow caused the fire. This Matsushita could not do. If employees rarely fray wires, use wrong extension cords, block vents, smoke, light candles, or run space heaters, this makes sense. If they do periodically make these mistakes, the approach becomes much more problematic.

3 The 1994 statute

In 1994, the Japanese Diet passed a statute (effective 1995) holding manufacturers strictly liable for any injury that their products might cause.[6] The Diet modeled the law on the European Community directive of 1985.[7] At its core lay Section 3:

A manufacturer must pay compensation for any damages to the life, health, or property of another person, if those damages were caused by a defect in a product that it manufactured, processed, or imported ... .

Query what the statute might have changed. After all,

---

[6] Seizobutsu sekinin ho [Products Liability Act], Law No. 85 of July 1, 1994, effective July 1, 1995.
[7] Council Directive of July 25, 1985 (OJ L 210, 7.8.1985, p. 29).

198

Hatamoto collected damages from Matsushita under the Civil Code without introducing any evidence of negligence. The court simply declared that Matsushita had an obligation to sell safe television sets. This one caught fire, so it must not have been safe. It was defective. Given the defect, the manufacturer could avoid liability only if it could prove that it had not been negligent.

What is more, if Matsushita had sold Hatamoto the television set directly, it would have been strictly liable by contract. Japanese courts often declared product safety an "implied" contractual term. A seller implicitly promised to deliver a safe product, they explained. If it sold an unsafe product, it was liable for breaching that implied term. For example, consider the family that bought a toy archery set. When the suction cup at the end of one of the arrows fell off, the daughter blinded her brother. Held the judge: the manufacturer had a duty to sell a safe set; this set was not safe; hence, the manufactuer was liable.[8]

If the Matsushita court transformed the negligence in Section 709 into strict liability, other courts transform strict liability into negligence. "When it comes to the liability of manufacturers for design defects and insufficient warnings, strict liability is often tempered with elements normally associated with negligence," writes comparativist Mathias Reimann.[9] Suppose a buyer claims that a design was defective, for example. Even under a strict liability regime, a judge may find the design defective only if the buyer can show that the manufacturer it devoted insufficient resources to designing or testing the product. If the judge uses a cost-benefit analysis to determine whether it invested "insufficient resources," he essentially introduces

---

[8] K.K. Tokiwa shoji v. Yamamoto, 1196 Hanrei jiho 132 (Osaka D. Ct. Feb. 14, 1986).

[9] Mathias Reimann,. 2003. Liability for Defective Products at the Beginning of the Twenty-First Century: Emergence of a Worldwide Standard, 51 Am. J. Comp. L. 751, 775-76 (2003).

negligence back into strict liability.

Given the porous boundaries between the two legal regimes, Japanese courts often ignored the new statute anyway. Apparently, they knew the Civil Code. If they could obtain the result they wanted through the Code without bothering to learn the new statute, they did not bother with the new statute. One young woman sued a cosmetics firm under tort and products liability. In 2001, the judge held the firm liable under tort without worrying about the products liability statute.[10] One buyer sued a manufacturer over an engine compartment fire. In 2007, the judge held it liable without distinguishing the various legal theories.[11]

4 Product safety

Proponents of the 1994 statute often claimed it would improve product safety. Hold manufacturers liable for dangerous things they sold, and they would keep their products safe. "[M]anufacturers [in Japan] have become much more conscious of PL issues," claimed Japanese law scholar Luke Nottage, "and accordingly have adopted counter-measures to improve product safety."[12] Indeed, he continued, there is "clear evidence of widespread attempts by manufacturers to improve their product safety and complaint handling procedures, initiated mainly over 1994-6."

In fact, there is no evidence of improved safety at all. Back in 1970, the government opened a network of "consumer centers"

---

[10] [No name given] v. Ion keaa, K.K., 1765 Hanrei jiho 67 (Tokyo D. Ct. May 22, 2001).

[11] Y.G. Hikari kyuso saabisu v. Fuji jukogyo, K.K., 1994 Hanrei jiho 65 (Tokyo D. Ct. Apr. 24, 2007).

[12] Luke Nottage, Product Safety and Liability Law in Japan 196, 198 (2004).

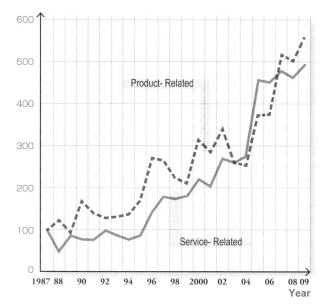

Figure 1 Health & Safety Inquiries Relating to Products and Services, Indexed at 1987= 100

Sources: Kokumin seikatsu sentaa, ed., Shohisha seikatsu nempo [Consumer Living Annual] (Tokyo: Kokumin seikatsu sentaa, various years); J. Mark Ramseyer, The Virtues of Japanese Private Law (Chicago: University of Chicago Press, 2015).

recently renamed "Citizens' Life Centers." Ostensibly, the government uses the centers to coordinate its efforts to improve product safety. By 1997, it had established 330 offices.

In **Figure 1**, I give the number of product-related and service-related accidents reported to these Citizens' Life Centers. For ease of comparison, I index the numbers at their 1987 values. Crucially for this purpose, the 1994 statute covered products but not services. If it did improve safety levels, it should have raised the safety of products relative to services; after 1995, the number of product-related claims should have fallen relative to the number service-related claims.

Nothing of the sort occurred. The number of product and service claims stayed stable until the mid-1990s, and then began to climb, but at the same rate.

Nor did the statute cause the number of serious accidents to fall. In **Figure 2**, I give the number of non-traffic accidental deaths from 1950 to 2010 (numbers on left axis), and rates per 100,000 population (right axis). For four decades from 1950 to about 1990, the rates fell. From 30.4 deaths per 100,000 in 1950, they fell to 11.9 in 1987. From the mid-1990s, the death rate then began to rise: roughly coincident with the passage of the strict products liability statute, the number and rate of accidental deaths began to climb.

Figure 2 raises two questions: why did the rate of accidental deaths fall from 1950 to 1990, and why did it increase thereafter. The reason for the initial fall reflects the essential irrelevance of products liability law. From 1950 to 1990, per capita Japanese income rose steadily and rapidly. As Japanese grew rich, they demanded safer goods. The demand for product safety rises with income. After all, poorer people do not necessarily want safer goods. Product safety is costly, and many poorer families would prefer to buy cheaper goods and use the money saved to feed and house their children.

As incomes rose, Japanese increasingly demanded safer products. For a simple reason, manufactuers offered them those safe products in response: manufacturers who respond to consumer demand make money. If consumers want safer (but more expensive) products rather than dangerous (but cheaper) products, then manufacturers who offer safer products increase profitability. From 1950 to 1990, Japanese incomes rose, manufacturers offered safer products, and the rates of accidental deaths fell.

The rise in accidental deaths after 1990 captures an underlying demographic shift. As Japanese grew richer, they began to survive the diseases that had killed so many before. In 1943,

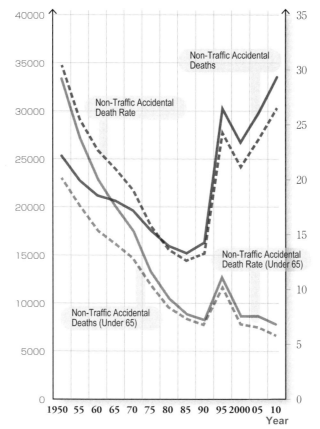

Figure 2 Non-Traffic Accidental Deaths --Numbers and Rates (per 100,000)

Notes: Number of deaths on left axis, rates per 100,000 on the right.
Sources: Kosei rodo sho, ed., Jinko dotai tokei [Vital Statistics] (Tokyo: Kosei tokei kyokai, various years); J. Mark Ramseyer, The Virtues of Japanese Private Law (Chicago: University of Chicago Press, 2015).

tuberculosis killed 170,000 Japanese; it now kills fewer than 3000 a year. Much the same tale accounts for the other diseases that killed so many Japanese during the first half of the 20th century.

Notwithstanding modern medicine, however, everyone

eventually dies. In societies that have learned to weather tuberculosis, cholera, and dysentary, accidents are like cancer, strokes and heart disease: they kill people who survive everything else that nature throws their way. A Japanese man may have survived the war, the occupation-era food shortages, and the dozens of mid-century epidemics. Now in his late 80s, he will slip on the stairs and fall. He will break his hip. After a few weeks in the hospital, he will die. Crucially, however, he will not die because the stairs were defective. He will die because he was old and unsteady.

Overwhelmingly, the accidental deaths in **Figure 2** involve the elderly. Of the 28,000 deaths in 2004, 42.1 percent involved people age 80 or older; 79.7 percent involved those 60 or older. To capture this dynamic, in **Figure 2** I add two additional curves: the non-traffic accidental deaths among those 65 or younger, and the accidental death rate (per 100,000 population) among this group. Among the non-elderly the accidental rate does not rise after 1990. Instead, it continues its steady decline.

解 説　COMMENT　　**製造物責任の法的意義と社会的影響**

松下カラーテレビ事件（太子建設工業 vs 松下電器産業事件）は，製造物責任法の制定以前に（しかし，これと近接した時期に），民法709条の過失責任主義の下で，「欠陥」を理由とする責任が認められた事例として知られている。原告が購入した松下電器製のテレビから発火があったことは認められたものの，欠陥部位や発火に至るメカニズムは明らかではなかった。しかしながら，大阪地裁は発火の事実から「欠陥」の存在を認定し，「欠陥」があれば過失が推定されるとした。

製造物責任法の制定をめぐっては，欠陥や因果関係につき推定規定を設けるか否かが論じられたが，最終的には推定規定は置かれないこととされた。しか

しながら，本判決のように，発火の事実を安全性の欠如ととらえて「欠陥」があると解するならば，具体的な欠陥部位（本判決はこれを「欠陥原因」と呼ぶ）を特定する必要がないことになる。その意味では欠陥の存在は推定されると言ってもよい。またこれは，特定の部位の欠陥から発火に至るまでのメカニズムを証明する必要はないということであり，この部分についての因果関係を推定するということに他ならない。以上のような意味で，本判決は，立法論として主張されていた二つの推定を行った判決として位置づけることができる。

　このように製造物責任法の制定以前に，その内容を先取りするような，場合によってはその内容を超えるような判決が登場していたことは興味深い。しかしながら，考えてみると，それ以前の不法行為判例に照らしてみれば，本判決の内容はそれほど奇異なものではない。たとえば，新潟水俣病判決（新潟地判昭和46・9・29下民22巻9=10号別冊1頁）は次のように考えていた。すなわち，①被害疾患の原因物質，②原因物質が被害者に到達する経路（汚染経路），③生成・排出に至るメカニズムのうち，①②が証明されれば，③については企業側が反証の責任を負うとしていた。本判決には，これと同様の発想が認められる。

　以上に見たように，製造物責任法の制定を待つまでもなく，民法709条の下でも相当程度までの救済が可能であること，それゆえ，製造物責任立法にはそれほど大きな意味があるわけではないことは，立法当時からすでに指摘されていた。しかし，このような推論が可能であることと現にそれを行うこととの間には，越えるべき谷間があったこともまた確かである。大阪地裁が本判決を下した背後には，製造物責任法制定の機運が盛り上がっていたという事情が作用していたのではなかろうか。そうだとすると，製造物責任立法には少なくとも象徴的な効果はあったと言えるかもしれない。

　実際のところ，製造物責任法の立法を通じて，世論だけでなく企業の安全性に対する意識も高まりを見せたということは，様々な形で指摘されてきた。こうした見方に対して，ラムザイヤー教授はデータを掲げて疑念を示している。確かに，同教授が説くように，国民生活センターに報告されている事故事例は，製造物責任法制定後も減っていない。しかし，このデータは，製造物責任法制定によって事故に対する意識が高まり，結果として報告数が増えたと解釈することもできる。児童虐待防止法の制定後も虐待認知件数は右肩上がりで増え続けているが，法律を制定しても虐待は減らないというのではなく，虐待に対す

る社会的な関心の高まりによるところが大きいという見方もある。同様の事情が製造物責任法の場合にもあるのではなかろうか。

　こう考えた方が，ラムザイヤー教授が提示するもう一つのデータも理解しやすい。同教授は，高齢者に限って言えば，（交通事故以外の）事故率は戦後一貫して減少していると説いている。確かに，全体的な傾向としてはその通りであるが，1995年前後にいったんは事故数が増加していることにも注意する必要があろう。この時期には製品の安全性に対する関心が高まったために，事故報告数が増えたと見ることはできないだろうか。もっとも，そうだとすると，虐待の場合とは異なり，安全性に対する関心の高まりは一過性のものであったことになる。

PART 6

会社法

CASE

17	ブルドックソース事件
18	UFJ銀行事件
19	アパマンショップ事件

	CASE
Steel Partners Japan Strategic Fund (Offshore), L.P. v. Bull-Dog Sauce Co., Ltd.	**17**

61 Minshu 2215 (Sup. Ct. Aug. 7, 2007).[1]

ブルドックソース事件

(最判平成19年8月7日民集61巻5号2215頁)

1 The case

The Bull-Dog Sauce firm makes the thick, heavy flavored sauce so popular on the nominally *yoshoku* (western-style) dishes that Japanese consumers learned to enjoy in the wake of World War II. Japanese tourists may wonder what U.S. sushi chefs could be thinking when they lace their rolls with cream cheese. Americans find themselves just as puzzled that anyone would consider *tonkatsu* (breaded pork cutlets) "western." But no matter —— post-war Japanese thought the Bull-Dog sauces a perfect fit for the new recipes.

Warren Lichtenstein runs a collection of hedge funds under the Steel Partners brand. On the firm website,[2] his spokesman ex-

---

[1] Affirming 1806 Shojihomu 40 (Tokyo High Ct. July 9, 2007), affirming 1805 Shoji homu 43 (Tokyo D. Ct. June 28, 2007). Translations of the Supreme Court opinion are available at Curtis J. Milhaupt, J. Mark Ramseyer & Mark D. West, eds., The Japanese Legal System 819 (New York: Foundation Press, 2d ed., 2012); J. Mark Ramseyer & Masakazu Iwakura, eds., Keesu bukku M&A [Casebook Mergers & Acquisitions] 134 (Tokyo: Shoji homu, 2015); Nels Hansen, Japan's First Poison Pill Case, Bulldog Sauce v. Steel Partners: A Comparative and Institutional Analysis, 13 J. Japanese L. 139, 146 (2008); translation of the High Court opinion is available at Ramseyer & Iwakura, supra, at 123.

[2] www.steelpartners.com.

plains that the funds help transform companies and "increase long term corporate value." Critics claim he looks only to obtain fast returns. He has, as one observer put it, "a reputation for being aggressive and pursuing short term positions for a quick gain -- a tendency that has caused some people to call him a vandal." [3]

Early in the 2000s, Lichtenstein took Steel Partners to Japan. Quickly, the funds began to acquire interests in Japanese firms, several of them in the food industry. By 2007, they had invested $4 billion in 30 Japanese companies. [4]

The Steel Partners funds turned to Bull-Dog in 2002. By the end of the year, they held 5.05 percent of the firm's stock, and by 2007, They held 10.25 percent. On May 16, 2007, they announced an any-and-all tender offer for the firm. Where Bull-Dog stock had traded for 1,336 yen per share, the Steel Partners funds offered an 18.56 percent premium —— 1,584 yen per share. On June 7, Bull-Dog management announced that it would oppose the takeover, and on the 15th, the funds responded by raising their offer to 1,700 yen.

Simultaneously, Bull-Dog management announced what some observers called a "poison pill" defense. Under its plan, the firm would distribute one "warrant" for every outstanding share. Each warrant would entitle the stockholder to three additional shares during the month of September. The firm effected, in other words, a 4-to-1 stock split. Prior to September, Bull-Dog retained the right to repurchase Steel Partner's warrants (but not the warrants of anyone else) for 396 yen each. Effectively, the firm repurchased 3/4 of Steel Partners' shares, at a price exactly equal (given the 4-to-1 stock split) to what Steel Partners originally offered for Bull-Dog shares (1584 yen/4 shares

---

[3] Warren Lichtenstein Bio, Returns, Net Worth, Insider Monkey, available at: http://www.insidermonkey.com/hedge-fund/steel+partners/68/.

[4] See Ramseyer & Iwakura, supra note 1, at 128 (High Ct. opinion).

= 396 yen/share).

Bull-Dog shareholders overwhelmingly approved the strategy. At a late-June meeting, they voted 83.4 percent of the outstanding shares in favor of the plan.

Steel Partners sued to enjoin the defense. The Tokyo District Court refused the injunction, and the Tokyo High Court affirmed. The High Court justified its decision by characterizing —— at elaborate length —— Lichtenstein as an "abusive" shareholder.[5] The Supreme Court then affirmed the High Court, albeit without the almost-pamphleteering prose.

Although Bull-Dog treated Steel Partners differently from the other shareholders, explained the Supreme Court, it did not act in an "inequitable or unreasonable" manner.[6] After all, the Court reasoned[7]

The shareholders passed the allotment proposal at their shareholders meeting by about 83.4% of the total voting shares. Virtually all shareholders other than Steel Partners and its related entities decided that the acquisition of control by that group would impair the firm's value.

The Supreme Court added that Bull-Dog redeemed Steel Partner's warrants at a price that reflected the "tender offer price that [Steel Partners] themselves determined," and that it had not accomplished the defense "through an extremely unfair method."[8]

As the tender offer closed in August, shareholders had tendered 1.89 percent of the stock.[9]

---

[5] See Ramseyer & Iwakura, supra note 1, at 131-33 (High Ct. opinion).

[6] See Ramseyer & Iwakura, supra note 1, at 137 (Sup. Ct. opinion).

[7] See Ramseyer & Iwakura, supra note 1, at 137-38 (Sup. Ct. opinion).

[8] See Ramseyer & Iwakura, supra note 1, at 138 (Sup. Ct. opinion).

[9] Tomoko Yamazaki, Steel Partners Bid for Japan's Bull-Dog Sauce Fails (Update 1), Bloomberg, Aug. 23, 2007, available at: http://www.bloomberg.com/apps/news?pid=newsarchive&sid=alSO7RblFcVg.

⊇ The substance

a. Introduction Predictably, some foreign observers lambasted the court opinions as being based on jingoistic bias. One Internet writer described them as "a disturbing effort by the Japanese courts to prevent foreign money and ownership permeating into an important aspect of the Japanese cultural dinner table."[10] The British Telegraph described Lichtenstein' s bid as going "to the heart of intensifying Japanese fears about an influx of foreign corporate predators with designs on some of the country' s prized assets."[11] Forbes wrote that the Supreme Court opinion "reflects the prevailing distaste in corporate Japan for foreign invaders like Steel Partners that threaten the long-cherished coziness of its management ranks."[12]

In fact, however, these writers fundamentally misunderstood the transaction. Given the High Court' s diatribe against "abusive" acquirers, the reaction is easy enough to understand. The plan itself did not, however, hurt Steel Partners. As Nels Hansen correctly observed, it instead took money from the other stockholders and paid it to Lichtenstein as "greenmail."[13] If the High Court misunderstood

---

[10] Japan's High Court Rules Against Saucy Gaijins, Japan: Stippy, July 20, 2007, available at: http://www.stippy.com/japan-work/bull-dog-sauce-feeds-steel-partners-poison-pill/.

[11] Mark Kleinman, The Battle For Bulldog Sauce, The Telegraph, June 14, 2007, available at: http://blogs.telegraph.co.uk/finance/markkleinman/3845701/The_battle_for_Bulldog_Sauce/.

[12] Shu-Ching Jean Chen, Japan High Court Keeps Bull-Dog Sauce from Steel Partners' Jaws, Forbes, Aug. 8 2007, available at: http://www.forbes.com/2007/08/08/bulldog-steel-partners-markets-equity-cx_jc_0808markets03.html

[13] Nels Hansen, Japan's First Poison Pill Case, Bulldog Sauce v. Steel Partners: A Comparative and Institutional Analysis, 13 J. Japanese L. 139, 160 (2008). Stephen Givens, Looking Through the Wrong End of the Telescope: The Japanese Judicial Response to Steel Partners, Murakami, and Horie, 88 Wash. U.L. Rev. 1571, 1582 (2011), makes the point as well.

the nature of the corporate control market, the Supreme Court did not:[14]

> Indeed, if Bull-Dog acquires the options held by Steel Partners and its related entities through the call clause, it will pay them a large amount of cash. That itself may impair its corporate value and harm the collective interests of shareholders.

To see the economics of the Bull-Dog plan, consider two hypothetical transactions.

b. Two examples Suppose a company has 100,000 shares outstanding. It owns a bank account with 100 million yen, and nothing more. Obviously, each share is worth 1,000 yen.

Suppose investor Steel buys 10,000 shares in this company. Steel will own a 10 percent interest in a firm worth 100 million yen. And suppose that the other 90,000 shares are owned in equal part by 90 stockholders.

Transaction A Under Transaction A, the company will adopt a two-part plan. First, it will redeem all of Steel's shares at 1,000 yen per share. Second, to the other stockholders it will distribute 3 additional shares for each share that the stockholder currently holds.

Consider the result of this Transaction A —— both on Steel, and on the other stockholders. Through the transaction, Steel will receive (1,000 yen/share * 10,000 shares =) 10 million yen. Prior to Transaction A, Steel owned 10 percent of a company worth 100 million yen —— i.e., stock worth 10 million yen; after Transaction A, it will hold 10 million yen in cash. Steel has neither gained nor lost.

After Transaction A, the other stockholders will hold shares

---

[14] See Ramseyer & Iwakura, supra note 1, at 138.

212

worth exactly the value of the shares they held before. Prior to the transaction, they each held 1,000 shares worth 1,000 yen each. After the transaction, they will hold four times as many shares. The company will now be worth (100 million yen - 10 million yen =) 90 million yen. It will have 360,000 shares outstanding (the original 100,000 shares − 10,000 shares = 90,000 shares, plus the new 90,000 shares×3 = 270,000 shares). As a result, each share will be worth 90 million yen/360,000 shares = 250 yen/share. Prior to Transaction A, each shareholder held 1,000 shares worth 1,000 yen each (1 million yen total); after Transaction A, each stockholder will hold 4,000 shares worth 250 yen each (1 million yen total). These shareholders, too, have neither gained nor lost.

Transaction B Now suppose that the company decides to redeem Steel's shares at a 20 percent premium over market price. Where the shares had been worth 1,000 yen/share, the company will redeem Steel's shares at 1,200 yen/share. Steel will receive (1,200 yen/share * 10,000 shares =) 12 million yen. Prior to this Transaction B, Steel owned shares worth 10 million yen; after Transaction B, it will hold 12 million yen in cash. Steel has gained 2 million yen.

Because the firm paid Steel 12 million, Transaction B will cause the value of the firm to fall to (100 million yen - 12 million yen =) 88 million yen. The remaining shares (a total of 360,000 shares; see calculation above) will still be owned in equal part by 90 shareholders, so the value of each stockholder's interest will equal (88 million yen/90 =) 978,000 yen. Prior to Transaction B, each stockholder held shares worth 1 million yen; after Transaction B, each stockholder will hold shares worth 978,000 yen. What Steel has gained, the other shareholders have lost.

c. The Bull-Dog pill Bull-Dog adopted a variation on Transaction B. For expositional simplicity, the hypothetical simplifies the timing of the transactions, and posits that the firm redeems all of Steel Partners' shares. In fact, of course, Bull-Dog first issued warrants to all shareholders, redeemed the warrants it gave Steel, and then let the other shareholders exercise their warrants. In effect, it split the stock 4-to-1 and redeemed 3/4 of Steel Partners' shares. Otherwise, however, the Bull-Dog transaction is similar to Transaction B.

Crucially, Bull-Dog redeemed Steel Partners' stock at a premium. It pegged its redemption price to Steel Partners' tender offer price, but the Steel Partners funds did not offer to buy shares at the market price. Instead, they offered to buy the shares at a price 19 percent above market. Had Bull-Dog redeemed Steel Partners' stock at market, it would have tracked Transaction A. Given that it redeemed the shares at 19 percent above market, it tracked Transaction B.

To pay the Steel Partners funds that premium, Bull-Dog took value from the other shareholders. Given that a firm cannot create value out of thin air, Bull-Dog had to obtain the premium it used to pay the funds from the other shares. When it redeemed the shares of the Steel Partners funds at a premium, it transferred wealth from its other shareholders to the Steel Partners funds. In effect, it paid the funds "greenmail."

3 The American parallel

Delaware courts let firms adopt a wide variety of poison pills, and the Japanese Supreme Court let Bull-Dog adopt the poison pill here. Curtis Milhaupt notes a broad similarity between Delaware and modern Japanese corporate jurisprudence.[15] And that similarity ap-

---

[15] Curtis J. Milhaupt, In the Shadow of Delaware? The Rise of Hostile Takeovers in Japan, 105 Colum. L. Rev. 2171 (2005).

pears in the disposition of the Bull-Dog pill.

Through tender offers and other corporate control transactions, assets and personnel move to their highest valued uses (this logic appears in more detail in the **Case18**). Because acquirers buy firms at a premium, these takeovers increase target shareholder value. Because the threat of a takeover induces all other managers to work harder, the possibility of a takeover increases the welfare of shareholders everywhere. And because assets and workers shift to managers best able to use them productively, society as a whole gains. The rule that best promotes aggregate social welfare is (as Frank Easterbrook and Daniel Fischel explain —— see **Case18**) a rule that bans all defensive tactics.

A ban on takeover defenses may be the rule that best promotes social welfare, but it is not the law. Subject to a variety of restrictions, incumbent managers may fight unsolicited bidders. They may adopt poison pills. At that level of generality, such is the rule in Delaware, and such is the rule in Japan.

Understand, however, that the Bull-Dog warrants do not resemble the typical American poison pill. As Stephen Givens rightly observed, U.S. firms usually adopt a pill before an unsolicited bidder arrives.[16] Through the pill, they threaten to impose large losses on anyone who tries unilaterally to take over the firm. Concomitantly, however, they also offer a way for that bidder to avoid those losses: negotiate with the incumbents first. In other words, through a poison pill, incumbent U.S. managers push hostile bidders to sue for peace before proceeding with an acquisition.

By contrast, the Bull-Dog pill simply redeems 3/4 of the hostile bidder's shares at a premium. Through warrants, it splits

---

[16] Givens, supra note 13, at 1582.

the stock into quarters. By repurchasing Steel Partners' warrants, it effectively redeems 3/4 of its equity interest. And all this it does at a 19 percent premium.

To illustrate the typical American pill, consider *Moran v. Household International*.[17] The Delaware court explained how the poison pill (called the "Plan" or the "Rights") worked:

> [The] Plan provides that [target] common stockholders are entitled to the issuance of one Right per common share under certain triggering conditions. There are two triggering events that can activate the Rights. The first is the announcement of a tender offer for 30 percent of [target] shares ("30% trigger") and the second is the acquisition of 20 percent [target] shares by any single entity or group ("20% trigger").

> If an announcement of a tender offer for 30 percent of [target] shares is made, the Rights are issued ... and are redeemable by the Board for $.50 per Right. If 20 percent of [target] shares are acquired by anyone, the Rights are issued and become non-redeemable .... If ... thereafter, a merger or consolidation occurs, the Rights holder can exercise each Right to purchase $200 of the common stock of the tender offeror for $100.

In other words, the *Moran* pill did four things:[18]

> (a) The [pill] is triggered by the announcement by a hostile bidder of plans to buy at least 30 percent of [the target].

> (b) Initially, the [target] board can redeem these "pills"

---

[17] Moran v. Household Int'l, Inc. 500 A.2d 1346, 1348-49 (Del. 1985).

[18] J. Mark Ramseyer, Business Organizations 362 (New York: Wolters Kluwer, 2012).

216

at 50 cents each.

(c) If the bidder actually buys a 20 percent stake in the firm, the board can no longer redeem the pills.

(d) If the acquirer merges the firm into another firm ..., then [target] shareholders obtain a right to buy acquirer stock at a high price.

Should anyone try to acquire a significant stake in the target firm, in short, the pill limited what he could do. If he tried to merge the target into another company, target shareholders obtained the right to buy the acquirer's stock at a deep discount. He could make this problem disappear, but only if he pacified the target board first. If he wanted the pill cancelled before he took control, in other words, he needed to talk to the target board. Only after he made peace and the target board canceled the pill could he safely proceed.

The puzzle in *Bull-Dog* is why the shareholders did what they did. Unlike *Moran*-style pills, the Bull-Dog pill did not impose a cost on the Steel Partners funds. It did not threaten to punish them if they proceeded with the acquisition without negotiating first with Bull-Dog management. Instead, by redeeming Steel Partners' stock at a premium, it imposed a cost on everyone else.

Why pay Steel Partners funds a premium? Indeed, why redeem them at any price at all? The funds only held 10 percent of Bull-Dog stock. If stockholders controlling 80 percent of the shares voted in favor of this defense tactic, then they were not about to tender their shares to Steel Partners funds in a tender offer.[19] The offer was bound to fail for a simple reason: no one would sell. If the funds held only 10 percent and had no chance of acquiring control, why buy their shares?

---

[19] Again, as Stephen Givens, supra note 13, observed.

解説 COMMENT	敵対的買収への対抗策

　日本では，2005年の夏以降，平時において事前警告型と呼ばれる買収防衛策を導入する上場会社が登場した（これを導入している上場会社は，2018年夏現在，約400社）。ブルドックソース社は，このような防衛策を導入しておらず，スティールパートナーズによる敵対的な株式公開買付けがされたことに対し，株主総会決議によって防衛目的の対抗策を打ったのが本件である。会社法上の原則ルールでは，新株予約権無償割当ての決定は，取締役会設置会社においては取締役会の権限であって株主総会の権限ではない（会社法278条3項参照）。そこで，ブルドックソース社は，株主総会決議で定款を変更して新株予約権無償割当ての決定権限を株主総会に付与したうえで，株主総会決議でこれを決定して実行した。差別的な行使条件が付された新株予約権は株主が行使することが可能と設計されているものの，税制上の理由で会社が一定時期に強制取得するという条項が付され，これが実施された。

　本件での対抗策実施の特徴は，株主総会決議に基づいて実行されたことと，対抗策の実行によって敵対的買収者が受ける経済的な損失に相当する額（公開買付価格×保有株式数）を会社がその買収者に支払うこととしたことの2点にある。いずれも，アメリカにおけるライツプランでは見られない実務である。イギリスでは取締役会決議による防衛策や対抗策は認められていないが，株主総会決議によるときは認められる（アメリカ・イギリス・日本の比較について，John Armour, Jack Jacobs and Curtis J. Milhaupt, The Evolution of Hostile Takeover Regimes in Developed and Emerging Markets: An Analytical Framework, 52 Harvard International Law Journal 221 (2011) 参照）。後者の金銭補償については，ラムザイヤー教授ご指摘のような理由で，日本でも批判が強いが，平時に防衛策を導入していなかったため，有事すなわち敵対的買収者が現れて公開買付けが開始した後の対抗策の実行は，それにより公開買付けが実質的に功を奏しないようにする効果があるため違法と解されるおそれがあり，公開買付者に生じる経済的損失は補償されるべきとの意見が一部にあったこと等を考慮しての対応であったと見受けられる。なお，本件の後に公表された経済産業省の企業価値研究会の報告書では，事前警告型の買収防衛策において，

防衛策に沿って有事に発動される対抗策の実行に際してそのような損失の補償をしないと明記しておいた場合には，金銭補償は不要である旨の見解が述べられている（企業価値研究会「近時の諸環境の変化を踏まえた買収防衛策の在り方」〔2008 年 6 月 30 日〕）。

本件における最高裁の考え方は，平時に買収防衛策を導入していない会社が有事となって行う新株予約権無償割当て型の対抗策は，それが適法であるためには必要性と相当性を必要とするが，前者は株主総会決議があったときは推定され，後者は株主総会決議があったときであっても裁判所が審査するというものということができる（田中亘『企業買収と防衛策』〔商事法務，2012〕第 6 章参照）。そして最高裁は，本件ではいずれの点も満たされていると判断した（株主総会決議によらないで取締役会決議かぎりで本件と同種の対抗策を打ったところ，対抗策である新株発行が差し止められた事例として，東京高決平成 20・5・12 判タ1282 号 273 頁がある）。これは，原審（高裁）がスティールパートナーズは濫用的買収者であるとの理由で対抗策の適法性を認めたこととは対照的な法理である。

ラムザイヤー教授ご指摘のように，本件では，対抗策を打たなくても一般株主の多くは公開買付けに応じて持株を売却しなかったであろうから公開買付けは成功しなかったとの見方もある。実際，本件と近い時期にスティールパートナーズが敵対的な公開買付けをした天龍製鋸社では，ほとんどの株主が公開買付けに応じず，公開買付けは失敗に終わっている。ブルドックソース社は，公開買付けが開始された時点においては，そのように楽観的には考えなかったということになる。

なお，日本の会社法のもとでは，本件におけるようなタイプの対抗策とは別に種類株式を用いた防衛策（黄金株などと呼ばれる）が可能であるが，東京証券取引所はこの防衛策を原則として認めていない。また，平時において事前警告型の買収防衛策を導入している会社が有事となって新株予約権無償割当て型の対抗策を発動した事例は，未だ見られない。

CASE

Sumitomo Trust Bank, K.K. v. K.K. UFJ Holdings

58 Minshu 1763 (Sup. Ct. Aug. 30, 2004).

UFJ銀行事件
(最判平成16年8月30日民集58巻6号1763頁)

1 The facts

Many banks competed in the Japanese financial market of 1990: 22 major institutions, 132 regional banks, and 451 cooperative (*shinkin*) banks.[1] By then, however, the stock and real estate markets had already begun their precipitous collapse (see real estate price trends in the Figure accompanying **Case 12**). For banks, these falling prices brought disaster. Investors had bought their shares and land with money they had borrowed from banks. With those assets nearly worthless, they could not (or at least would not) repay their loans. The banks found themselves holding debt they could not collect.

Facing financial peril, banks began to merge. One should pause and ask "why?" "Adding two weak banks [does] not produce a strong bank,"[2] observed economists Kimie Harada and Takatoshi

---

[1] Kaoru Hosono, Koji Sakai & Kotaro Tsuru, Consolidation of Banks in Japan: Causes and Consequences, in Takatoshi Ito & Andrew K. Rose, eds., Financial Sector Development in the Pacific Rim, East Asia 265, 271 tab. 8.1 (Chicago: Univ. Chicago Press, 2009).

[2] Kimie Harada & Takatoshi Ito, Did Mergers Help Japanese Mega-Banks Avoid Failure? Analysis of the Distance to Default of Banks, NBER Working Paper 14518 (Dec. 2008), at 6 (published as 25 J. Japanese & Int'l Eco. 1 (2011)).

Ito. It just produces one big weak bank. And indeed, they conclude, "mergers of Japanese banks did not make them financially healthier."[3] The merging banks typically claimed that the transaction would let them close redundant outlets or fire duplicative employees. According to economist Tae Okada, though, after the merger the banks were simply less efficient.[4]

In the 1990s, banks merged to game government guarantees, conclude Harada, Ito, and Okada. Implicitly, the Japanese government had promised to rescue banks it deemed "too big to fail." As its revenues declined, the government began to reduce the number of banks it implicitly promised to save. It increased its definition of "too big" in the "too big to fail" formula, in other words. As it did, failing banks merged to stay big enough to qualify.[5]

Banks again started to merge in the early 2000s. This time, they merged because regulators had tightened the accounting rules about non-performing loans and deferred taxes. These changes threatened to disqualify many of the largest banks.[6] In particular, the new rules pushed the capital ratio at some of the biggest banks below the 8 percent necessary to operate internationally.[7] Banks now merged to game the accounting rules.

The UFJ Bank was in distress. In 2002, the Osaka-based Sanwa Bank had merged with the Nagoya-based Tokai bank. They had named the resulting entity "UFJ," for United Financial of Japan. This new UFJ group actually included several institutions: UFJ Hold-

---

[3] Harada & Ito, supra note 2, at 5-6.

[4] Tae Okada, Ginko gappei no doki to sono koka [The Motives and Effects of Bank Mergers], Osaka University Graduate School of Economics, DP 07-18, at 14.

[5] Hosono, Sakai & Tsuru, supra note 1, at 269; Harada & Ito, supra note 2, at 25-26; Okada, supra note 4.

[6] Harada & Ito, supra note 2, at 2-3.

[7] Harada & Ito, supra note 2, at 2-3.

ings, which in turn owned UFJ Bank, UFJ Trust Bank, and several other firms. When regulators imposed their more stringent accounting rules, the UFJ Bank unit needed more capital badly.

To obtain that capital, in May 2004 UFJ Holdings contracted to sell its trust unit to the Sumitomo Trust Bank. For UFJ Trust, Sumitomo Trust would pay 300 billion yen.[8] And to protect their planned transaction, Sumitomo and UFJ executed a "memorandum of understanding" (MOU). In it, they promised to negotiate in good faith toward a final contract, and not to negotiate with anyone else in a way that might compromise their planned transaction (a "no-talk" agreement). They did not promise to reach a final agreement, though, and did not agree to pay liquidated damages should either breach the contract.[9]

But the Sumitomo arrangement did not last. To meet the 8 percent capital ratio, UFJ needed 700 billion yen. It thought it could raise 400 billion through a stock issue, and obtain the other 300 by selling its trust bank to Sumitomo. The regulators, however, declared its balance sheet unacceptable and threatened criminal prosecution. That was not an environment in which UFJ could issue 400 billion yen's worth of new stock. It needed the full 700 billion through other means.[10]

Faced with this regulatory presure, in July 2004 UFJ cancelled its agreement with Sumitomo Trust. In its place, it announced a merger with Mitsubishi Tokyo Financial Group. The product of a

---

[8] Veronica L. Taylor, Japanese Commercial Transactions and Sanctions Revisited: Sumitomo v. UFJ, 8 Wash. U. Global Stud. L. Rev. 399, 404 (2009).

[9] Veronica Taylor, supra note 8, at 404.

[10] Takayasu Kamiya, Kigyo baishu no kihon goisho chu no kyogi kinshi joko no koryoku [The Effect of Non-Negotiation Clause in a Memorandum of Basic Understanding Regarding a Firm Acquisition], 205 Bekkan Jurisuto: Kaisha ho hanrei hyakusen 194.

merger between Mitsubishi Bank and Bank of Tokyo, Mitsubishi-Tokyo was relatively healthy. Quite what it saw in UFJ is unclear. After all, UFJ was perilously close to bankruptcy. In their press releases, the two groups claimed they wanted to slash their combined work force. Mitsubishi claimed it wanted UFJ's branch network and corporate clients.[11]

Whatever the reason, Mitsubishi-Tokyo agreed to invest 700 billion yen in UFJ. Sumitomo quickly counter-offered with 500 billion, and may have considered a hostile takeover. In response, however, Mitsubishi-Tokyo restructured its 700 billion investment as a preferred stock purchase. Although the shares initially did not vote, Mitsubishi-Tokyo negotiated the right to convert them into voting stock (a 35 percent interest) if anyone acquired a 20 percent stake in UFJ.[12] In effect, it structured its investment as a poison pill: should Sumitomo acquire a 20 percent interest through a hostile takeover, Mitsubishi-Tokyo would hold 35 percent of the bank's voting stock.[13]

2 The decision

When UFJ repudiated the MOU and turned to Mitsubishi-Tokyo, Sumitomo Trust sued. UFJ had promised not to negotiate with other parties, and Sumitomo Trust wanted that no-talk clause enforced. The Tokyo District Court agreed, and ordered UFJ to comply. The no-talk clause was legal, and a violation would leave Sumitomo substantially harmed financially.[14]

Within a week, the Tokyo High Court vacated the injunc-

---

[11] Tokyo Mitsubishi, UFJ Set Merger Terms, World Business on NBC News.com, Feb. 18, 2005.

[12] Veronica Taylor, supra note 8, at 407.

[13] Scramble for UFJ, Sumitomo Mitsui Seen at Dead End, Nikkei Business, Sept. 20, 2004.

tion.[15]   The trust between Sumitomo and UFJ had already disappeared, it noted. The odds that they would successfully negotiate a final contract was close to zero. The point of the no-talk clause was to help them reach that final agreement. If they could no longer realistically hope to agree, they had no reason to enforce the no-talk clause.

The Supreme Court affirmed. Again, it observed that the parties had negotiated the no-talk in order to reach a final contract. Yet now they no longer trusted each other. In the absence of that trust, reasoned the Court, they would never negotiate a final agreement:[16]

> In this case ..., UFJ reneged on the MOU, and on July 14, 2004 informed Sumitomo Trust .... UFJ [then] concluded a preliminary agreement with Mitsubishi-Tokyo Financial Group concerning the business integration between UFJ group and Mitsubishi-Tokyo group .... [This] preliminary agreement is successfully progressing towards a final and definitive agreement on the business integration. Under these circumstances, ... it is very unlikely that Sumitomo Trust and UFJ will reach a final and definitive agreement ...., [and] the MOU does not guarantee that a final and definitive agreement will exist ....

Without a realistic chance of agreement, the no-talk clause served no purpose.

---

[14] Sumitomo Trust Bank, K.K. v. K.K. UFJ Holdings, 1708 Shoji homu 22 (Tokyo D. Ct. July 27, 2004), confirmed, 1708 Shoji homu 22 (Tokyo D. Ct. Aug. 4, 2004).

[15] Sumitomo Trust Bank, K.K. v. K.K. UFJ Holdings, 1708 Shoji homu 23 (Tokyo High Ct. Aug. 11, 2004).

[16] Sumitomo Trust Bank, K.K. v. K.K. UFJ Holdings, 1872 Hanrei jiho 28 (Sup. Ct. Aug. 30, 2004), as translated by Miyuki Ishiguro at Curtis J. Milhaupt, J. Mark Ramseyer & Mark D. West, eds., The Japanese Legal System (New York: Foundation Press, 2d ed., 2012).

If the two firms were not likely to reach a final agreement, the Court continued, Sumitomo suffered no damages due to UFJ's no-talk clause violation. UFJ had indeed violated the clause. But given that the firms would never agree anyway, Sumitomo could not point to any damages. According to the statute at issue:[17]

> A provisional injunction may be issued to preserve a provisional status with respect to disputed rights when the injunction is necessary to protect the rights-holder from significant damage or imminent danger.

If Sumitomo would suffer no damage, then the statute authorized no provisional injunction. Even if Sumitomo did suffer damage, it did not need an injunction to protect itself. It could simply sue for compensation:

> [I]t is not possible to assert that [Sumitomo Trust's] damages cannot be compensated by subsequent monetary compensation ....

The Supreme Court refused to enforce the no-talk clause on the grounds that Sumitomo Trust had an adequate remedy in damages, so Sumitomo Trust did sue for damages.[18] It claimed a loss of 233.3 billion yen, and (for reasons unclear) sued UFJ for 100 billion. The Tokyo District Court noted that UFJ had agreed not to talk to a third party. When it repudiated the MOU and turned to Mitsubishi-Tokyo, it breached that agreement.

Yet to the Tokyo District Court it was a breach on which Sumitomo Trust could not collect. Having lost at the Supreme Court on the grounds that it had an adequate remedy in damages, it now found at the District Court —— bizarrely —— that it could collect no dam-

---

[17] Minji hozen ho [Civil Preservation Act], Law No. 91 of 2000, Sec 23(b).

[18] Sumitomo Trust Bank, K.K. v. K.K. UFJ Holdings, 1928 Hanrei jiho 3 (Tokyo D. Ct. Feb. 13, 2006).

ages. It might have made a profit from a final contract with UFJ, but UFJ had no obligation to agree to any final contract. UFJ may have breached its promise not to talk with Mitsubishi-Tokyo, but it need not have agreed to sell its trust bank to Sumitomo anyway. Sumitomo could not claim lost foregone profits from the UFJ Trust Bank purchase, because it had no right to that purchase. UFJ breached its no-talk clause; Sumitomo lost the profits it would have made from buying UFJ Trust; but given that Sumitomo had no right to those profits, it lost nothing from UFJ's breach.

Having lost at the Tokyo District Court, Sumitomo Trust appealed. Before the High Court issued a decision, the two firms settled. On November 21, 2006, UFJ agreed to pay Sumitomo Trust 2.5 billion yen.[19]

3 Discussion

a. The market for corporate control   Hostile takeovers comprise part of a "market for corporate control"[20]: a metaphorical forum where rival groups of managers can buy and sell the right to control firms. Suppose one group of managers runs a firm. That firm's shares will sell for a price that reflects the value other investors ascribe to the firm under the control of those managers.[21]

Suppose another group of managers thinks it can run the firm better. These outsiders will try to buy enough stock to acquire control over the firm. To buy that stock, they will pay a premium

---

[19] Shin'ichi Nemoto, Sumitomo shintaku ginko vs kyu UFJ horudinguzu jiken dai isshin hanketsu ni tsuite [Regarding the Trial Court Decision in the Sumitomo Trust v. Old UFJ Holdings Case], 15 Yokohama kokusai hogaku 69, 70 (2007)

[20] Henry G. Manne, Mergers and the Market for Corporate Control, 73 J. Pol. Eco. 110 (1965).

[21] Subject to the qualification Easterbrook & Fischel note below.

over current market value. They willingly pay that premium because they believe the firm will be worth more under their control. Because the outsiders will offer a premium, current investors will sell. And the outsiders will then run the firm in the way that they think will raise its value. As Judge Frank Easterbrook and Professor Dan Fischel put it:[22]

> Prospective bidders monitor the performance of managerial teams by comparing a corporation's potential value with its value ... under current management. When the difference between the market price of a firm's shares and the price those shares might have under different circumstances becomes too great, an outsider can profit by buying the firm and improving its management.

Such is the theory, and it is also the way things work. Put most basically, the market for corporate control moves assets to their highest valued use, and increases investor welfare in the process. Necessarily, the legal regime that maximizes that investor welfare is the regime that most effectively facilitates a smoothly running market for corporate control.

Shareholders straightforwardly benefit if a hostile acquirer buys a target. When a takeover occurs, note economists Michael Jensen and Richard Ruback, investors in the target sell high, and investors in the acquirer at least do not lose money:[23]

> The estimates of positive abnormal returns to targets of successful tender offers in the month or two surrounding the offer are uniformly positive ranging from 16.9

---

[22] Frank H. Easterbrook & Daniel R. Fischel, The Proper Role of a Target's Management in Responding to a Tender Offer, 94 Harv. L. Rev. 1161, 1173 (1981).

[23] Michael C. Jensen & Richard S. Ruback, The Market for Corporate Control: The Scientific Evidence, 11 J. Finan. Econ. 5, 5 (1983) (ital. in orig. removed).

percent to 34.1 percent .... For targets of successful mergers, the estimated abnormal returns immediately around the merger announcement range from 6.2 percent to 13.4 percent ....

Crucially, shareholders benefit from a smoothly functioning corporate control market even when no acquisition occurs. They benefit because the threat of a hostile acquisition induces incumbent managers to work hard. Because incumbent managers now try harder to increase share values, potential acquirers have less incentive actually to buy those shares. No acqusition occurs, but share prices stay high. As Easterbrook and Fischel put it:[24]

> [S]hareholders benefit even if their corporation never is the subject of a tender offer. The process of monitoring by outsiders poses a continuous threat of takeover if performance lags. Managers will attempt to reduce agency costs in order to reduce the chance of takeover, and the process of reducing agency costs leads to higher prices for shares.

b. Facilitating auctions The error that the High Court and Supreme Court made is a common enough mistake, but a mistake nonetheless. Given that Mitsubishi-Tokyo offered a better deal than Sumitomo, the courts seem to have thought it sensible to let UFJ pursue the Mitsubishi-Tokyo contract. The basic phenomenon happens often: one acquirer bids for a firm, and a rival appears who offers a better deal. From this phenomenon, no less a scholar than Lucian Bebchuk concluded that courts should let managers solicit rival bids.[25]

Unfortunately, this analysis focuses on the ex post, and miss-

---

[24] Easterbrook & Fischel, supra note 22, at 1174.

[25] Lucian A. Bebchuk, The Case for Facilitating Competing Tender Offers, 95 Harv. L. Rev. 1028 (1982).

es the ex ante. It looks at what has already happened, and misses the effect that the proposed rule will have on the future. Ex post (after what has already happened), a rival bid will generate more money for a firm's owners. Ex ante (considering the effect that a proposed rule will have on future bids), a court that lets firms switch to a rival bidder will harm investor welfare. To understand this ex ante effect, note what a court that lets firms entertain rival bids does to an outsider's incentives. Identifying underperforming but "fixable" firms is not a simple process. An outsider company who wants to do this will need to invest substantial resources. It will find the investment worthwhile only if it can acquire the underperforming firm cheaply and "fix it" (increase its performance). Suppose, however, that a court lets managers of an underperforming firm solicit rival offers. The firm that initially identified the underperforming firm will have to pay a higher price to acquire the firm. Indeed, it will face lower odds of acquiring the firm at all.

If firms that identify underperforming but fixable firms cannot buy those firms cheaply, they will spend less effort trying to identify them in the first place. As a result, there will be fewer hostile takeovers -- and, (i) investors in underperforming firms will be less likely to sell their shares at a gain to a hostile acquirer, and (ii) because managers everywhere will face less of a threat of a hostile acquirer, all investors will find their firms run less efficiently.

In explaining this dynamic, Judge Frank Easterbrook and Professor Daniel Fischel first describe the relation between the corporate control market and stock prices:[26]

> The value of any stock can be understood as the sum of two components: the price that will prevail in the market if there is no successful offer (multiplied by the likeli-

---

[26] Easterbrook & Fischel, supra note 22, at 1164.

hood that there will be none) and the price that will be paid in a future tender offer (multiplied by the likelihood that some offer will succeed). A shareholder's welfare is maximized by a legal rule that enables the sum of these two components to reach its highest value.

A legal rule that lets target managers solicit rival bids lowers the expected gain to identifying underperforming firms. In effect, it reduces the second of the Easterbrook-Fischel components —— it reduces the likelihood that any offer will be made.

Professor Alan Schwartz elegantly makes exactly this point:[27]

> Some firms search for and acquire mismanaged companies because a successful searcher can earn the difference between the "maximizing price," the price for which the target's shares will sell when it is run optimally, and the target's lower current market price, which reflects its suboptimal performance. An auction shrinks the difference between these two prices because other firms will overbid initial offers that are close to the low current price. Consequently, auctions reduce the returns to search for mismanaged companies; the less search there is, the less effective is the takeover sanction in causing managers to maximize share values. Hence, auctions are inefficient.

Delaware courts make much the same mistake that the UFJ courts made. Professor Stephen Bainbridge describes the Delaware approach:[28]

> [Target firm boards] may expressly retain a right ...

---

[27] Alan Schwartz, Search Theory and the Tender Offer Auction, 2 J. L. Econ. & Org. 229, 230 (1986).

[28] Stephen M. Bainbridge, Corporate Law, 2d ed. 351 (New York: Foundation Press, 2009).

to solicit other offers or to negotiate with other bidders if its
fiduciary duties so require. The most potent version relieves
the target board of its obligation to recommend the initial
offer to the shareholders if a better offer is made or permits
the target to terminate the merger agreement if a higher offer is received.

Indeed, in *Omnicare v. NCS*,[29] the Delaware Supreme Court
held that the target board should have retained the right (practicing
lawyers call it a "fiduciary out" clause) to renege on its contractual duties to the initial acquirer and sell the firm to a rival offering a higher
price instead. In dissent, Justice Norman Veasey nicely noted the way
that the court had focused on the ex post, and missed the ex ante consequences of its approach.[30] Unless the first acquirer had been able
to negotiate what it thought was a binding contract with the target, it
never would have made a bid at all. If the target board "had insisted
on a fiduciary out," the first acquirer would never have offered a high
price, and the later rival would never have offered the even higher
price. "Thus, the only value-enhancing transaction available would
have disappeared."

解 説　COMMENT　大手銀行の救済に関する買収の協議禁止条項の効力

　本件は，著名な大手銀行間のビジネス上の争いが最高裁まで行ったという日
本ではめずらしい事案である。また，M&A の基本合意書に定める独占交渉権
の期間が 2 年近くと長期であったため（通常は数か月程度である），差止めの仮
処分をめぐって最高裁まで争われることとなり，この点でもめずらしい事案

---

[29]　Omnicare, Inc. v. NCS Healthcare, Inc., 818 A.2d 914, 938 (Del. 2003).
[30]　Omnicare, 818 A.2d at 941 (Veasey, J., dissenting).

である。本件紛争については，最高裁で敗訴した債権者に同情する見方が学界では少なくない（石黒一憲『契約の神聖さ　住友信託 vs. UFJ 銀行』〔信山社，2010〕，岩原紳作ほか編『会社法判例百選（第 3 版）』〔有斐閣，2016〕196 頁〔神谷高保〕参照）。また，本件の後の UFJ グループの三菱東京フィナンシャル・グループとの統合における種類株式を用いたディール・プロテクションの仕組みが学界の一部では強く批判されるなど，いろいろな意味で UFJ 銀行の救済劇は話題となった（中東正文編『UFJ vs. 住友信託 vs. 三菱東京 M&A のリーガルリスク』〔日本評論社，2005〕参照）。

　本件では，最高裁は，仮の地位を定める仮処分（民事保全法 23 条 2 項）における被保全権利と保全の必要性という民事保全法上の法律問題について粛々と判断し，被保全権利についてはその有無を判断せず，保全の必要性についてこれを否定し，原審決定の結論を維持した。保全の必要性を判断するに際して，債権者側に生じる損害と債務者側に生じる損害とを総合考慮してこれを否定したことが重要である（調査官解説である『最高裁判所判例解説（民事篇）平成 16 年度（上）』〔法曹会，2005〕528 頁〔志田原信三〕参照）。

　ラムザイヤー教授の説くような見解はアメリカの学界の一部で有力であるものの（ただし，ラムザイヤー教授ご指摘のように，アメリカの裁判例において受け入れられているとはいえない），日本では，学界においても実務界においても，ほとんど紹介もされておらず，支持する見解が見当たらないことが不思議である（日本での議論の例として，たとえば，藤田友敬編著『M&A 契約研究』〔有斐閣，2018〕CHAPTER 1 参照）。ただ，いずれにせよ，M&A における各種の契約条項は，アメリカと日本とでは少なくとも現在は同じではなく，日本における法律問題については，今後さまざまな議論が続くものと思われる（たとえば，前掲の藤田友敬編著『M&A 契約研究』の Part 1 を参照）。

[Apamanshop Derivative Litigation]

2091 Hanrei jiho 90 (Sup. Ct. July 15, 2010).

アパマンショップ事件
(最判平成 22 年 7 月 5 日判例時報 2091 号 90 頁)

1 The facts

Apamanshop Network ran a chain of real-estate rental brokerage firms. It developed a business formula, and transformed it into a franchise. It dictated the brand and operating protocol, and served as franchisor. Independent firms that agreed to operate by its formula served as franchisees. By 2001, it had attracted over 400 firms as franchisees.[1]

Network ran several other businesses through subsidiaries as well. Through Apamanshop Monthly, it competed in the market for furnished month-to-month rental apartments. It held 66.7 percent of Monthly's stock, and key franchisees held the rest.

In early 2006, Network decided to reorganize its holdings. It would transform affiliated corporations like Monthly into wholly owned subsidiaries, and rename itself Apamanshop Holdings. Under Japanese corporate law, it could freeze-out dissenting shareholders through a "share exchange."[2] It worried, though, that some Monthly

---

[1] Apamanshop Network, 2001 securities law filing, available at http://www.apamanshop-hd.co.jp/ir/portfolio_pdf/011218.pdf
[2] Kaisha ho [Corporate Code], Law No. 86 of 2005, Secs. 767-768.

233

shareholders might resent its forcing them to transfer their shares. Given that these shareholders were key franchisees within its national network, it preferred to buy their shares through consensual trades.

In May 2006, the Network president worked with two inside directors who functioned as his advisory committee and decided on a plan: they would offer to buy Monthly shares at 50,000 yen per share. Worried about possible legal challenges, they asked an attorney about the price, but he demurred. As the shares were not listed on an exchange, they had no actual market price. The firm had recently lost money, but the investors had paid 50,000 yen when they had bought the shares upon the firm's incorporation in 2001. The board members decided to stick with 50,000.

At the same time, the Network directors worried that one of the Monthly shareholders would refuse to sell. They had become embroiled in a acrimonious dispute with him. Rather than hope that he would sell voluntarily, they decided to acquire his stock through a forced "share exchange." They consulted two appraising firms about the price to pay. One suggested an exchange ratio that came to 9,709 yen per share. The other suggested a range between 6,561 yen and 19,090 yen per share.

On June, 2006, Network proceeded with its reorganization. It froze-out the estranged shareholder at an exchange equivalent to 8,448 yen per share. It bought the stock of the other Monthly shareholders at 50,000 yen per share, and renamed itself Apamanshop Holdings.

2 The decision

Several Network shareholders sued derivatively to challenge the 50,000 yen price. In buying the stock at so high a price, they claimed, Network directors violated their duties of loyalty and care. They could have bought the stock for 8,448 yen per share, but paid

234

50,000 instead. Necessarily, they owed Network the excess —— about 130 million yen.

The Tokyo District Court dismissed their claim,[3] but the High Court reversed.[4] The directors could not justify the high price, the High Court announced. They could show no rational basis for what they had done. The company paid 50,000 per share when it could have bought the shares for 10,000. By causing the firm to over-pay so egregiously, they breached their duty of care.

In turn, the Supreme Court reversed the High Court. Network might have acquired the stock for less than 50,000 yen per share, but the directors could reasonably worry about about the goodwill of its key franchisees. Given those concerns, they could reasonably decide to pay an amount within a price range that included 50,000 per share. The Court explained:[5]

> This is the kind of issue that should be left to the profesional judgment of managers. They can evaluate its impact on future prospects of the firm .... When structuring and pricing the transaction, directors consider a wide range of factors —— the asessed value of the shares, the need for the acquisition, any financial burden on [Network], the need to carry out the transaction smoothly, and so forth. Unless the process or content of the decision-making is extremely unreasonable, a director who does this does not breach his duty of care as a prudent manager.

---

[3] [No names given], 1304 Kinsho 33 (Tokyo D. Ct. Dec. 4, 2007).

[4] [No names given], 1304 Kinsho 28 (Tokyo High Ct. Oct. 29, 2008).

[5] [No names given], 2091 Hanrei jiho 90 (Sup. Ct. July 15, 2010). I take the translation from Masakazu Iwakura & J. Mark Ramseyer, M&A Keesu & Materiazu [M&A Cases & Materials] (Tokyo: Shoji homu, forthcoming 2015).

∃ Duty of care

a. Board incentives   The Supreme Court was right. Born in 1965, Network president Koji Omura had held the biggest block of stock in Network. He had co-founded the firm in 1999 and successfully guided it to a Nasdaq Japan listing. As of 2006, he still owned more shares in Network than anyone else: 19.6 percent.[6] If the firm paid more for Monthly shares than it needed to pay, he paid a fifth of that excess himself. The notion that he might carelessly overpay is just implausible on its face.

Corporate law professor Daniel R. Fischel nicely explains some of the incentives that lie behind the deference toward business decisions that the business judgment rule embodies. On the one hand, he notes, most corporate officers —— exactly like Omura —— face strong incentives to make business decisions correctly:[7]

> Senior managers typically have a large percentage of their wealth in the shares of their firms; moreover, executive compensation agreements link compensation of senior managers to the performance of the firm. Thus, managers who make correct decisions on how much information to acquire and thereby increase the value of the firm will be rewarded, and those who do not will be penalized.

For every 10,000 yen that Network overpaid for Monthly stock, Omura lost 2,000. By contrast, a judge has no incentive to make good corporate decisions:[8]

> The much-heralded independence of judges, ... al-

---

[6]   Toyo keizai, ed., Kaisha shikiho [Corporate News] 1674 (Tokyo: Toyokeizai, 2006 I).

[7]   Daniel R. Fischel, The Business Judgment Rule and the Trans Union Case, 40 Bus. Law. 1437, 1442-43 (1985).

[8]   Fischel, supra note 7, at 1443.

though desirable for other reasons, makes judges particularly poor candidates to make business decisions because it frees them from the contractual and market mechanisms that encourage sound decision making.

If Omura makes the wrong decision, he loses his own money. If the High Court makes the wrong decision, it simply moves on to the next case.

b. The Trans Union debacle The High Court decision resembles nothing so much as the 1985 Delaware case of *Trans Union*.[9] Businessman Jay Pritzker had offered to buy the firm of Trans Union at a 45 percent premium over the market price. He insisted that the Trans Union board reply to his offer within three days. The directors met, they discussed his offer, and they decided to accept it. Seventy percent of the shareholders approved the sale.

Dissatisfied shareholders sued the directors, and the Delaware Supreme Court held for the plaintiffs. The Trans Union directors had deliberated for two hours, but they could have talked longer. They had faced a deadline, but maybe they could have convinced Pritzker to extend it. They obtained a price 45 percent above the market price, but maybe they could have negotiated one higher still.

The court held the Trans Union directors personally liable for the difference between the price Pritzker paid, and the hypothetical price they might have obtained if only they had bargained harder. For the state of Delaware, a disaster ensued. Suddenly, Delaware firms could not convince experienced business executives to serve on their boards. Successful senior executives do not need board jobs. They have their savings; they do not need the income. They have

---

[9] Smith v. Van Gorkom, 488 A.2d 858 (Del. Sup. Ct. 1985).

things to do; they do not need help staying busy. They know how to be honest, and do not worry about courts holding them liable for self-dealing. They do worry about courts holding directors liable for negotiating a price that is "only" 45 percent over the market price. Rather than take that risk, successful senior business executives decided to retire and play golf instead.

To induce experienced executives to serve on the board of Delaware firms, the state legislature had to undo *Trans Union*. It did so by adding Sec. 102(b)(7) to the Delaware corporate code.[10] Under the new section, corporations could amend their charter to "opt out" of the duty of care. They could add:

A provision eliminating or limiting the personal liability of a director to the corporation or its stockholders for monetary damages for breach of fiduciary duty as a director, provided that such provision shall not eliminate or limit the liability of a director: (i) For any breach of the director's duty of loyalty to the corporation or its stockholders; (ii) for acts or omissions not in good faith or which involve intentional misconduct or a knowing violation of law ....

Among large Delaware firms, the 102(b)(7) amendments have become, in the words of corporate law professor Stephen Bainbridge, "nearly universal." After *Van Gorkom*, "[m]ost public corporations have amended their charters to include such provisions."[11]

After the Delaware court's decision to hold directors liable for violating their duty of care, in short, virtually no directors of Delaware public corporations owe their shareholders any duty of care at all.

---

[10] Del. Corp. Code, Sec. 102(b)(7).

[11] Stephen M. Bainbridge, The Story of Smith v. Van Gorkom, in J. Mark Ramseyer, ed., Corporate Law Stories 197, 198 (New York: Foundation Press, 2009).

4 The underlying dispute

Through the 1990s, Omura had worked in the Fukuoka real estate market with one Keiji Kaida. As one of their business entities, the two men ran a firm called Marui kenso. Toward the end of the decade, Omura decided to expand their business formula through a national franchise model. To do so, he created Network in 1999 and became its president. In turn, Kaida became president of Marui. Kaida personally bought stock in Network, however, and ran Marui as a Fukuoka-area Network franchisee.

Around the middle of 2005, Omura and Kaida turned bitter enemies. Quite what caused the rift is not clear. But by the time Omura decided to reorganize his Apamanshop firms in early 2006, Network and Marui were locked in bitter litigation. Marui owned 150 (4.5 percent) of the 3,310 Monthly shares not held by Network. And it was this Marui —— still run by Omura's one-time confidant Kaida —— that Network forced out at 8,448 yen per share while it paid the other shareholders 50,000.

This derivative suit apparently stems from that underlying fight between Omura and Kaida. The suit was filed by Kaida's lawyers —— the same lawyers who filed trademark-domain claims on behalf of Marui against Network.[12] If so, the real force behind this derivative suit may not be the "extra" 130 million yen that Monthly paid to its shareholders. Instead, it may be that undisclosed quarrel between the two former partners. Perhaps, in other words, the plaintiffs did not file this derivative suit to recover any overpayment. Per-

---

[12] http://www.google.co.jp/url?sa=t&rct=j&q=&esrc=s&source=web&cd=10&ved=0CFAQFjAJ&url=http%3A%2F%2Fwww.wipo.int%2Famc%2Fen%2Fdomains%2Fdecisions%2Fword%2F2006%2Fd2006-0288.doc&ei=XaHTVK6WBoemNrCVgeAl&usg=AFQjCNGNHj49oGR5ZoWO8Gfqaa7SuAnPZA&bvm=bv.85464276,d.eXY

haps they simply filed it to as part of a broader harassment campaign against Omura.

If this derivative suit did not promote shareholder interests, that would not distinguish it from U.S. derivative suits. Possibly (the point is controversial), derivative suits in the U.S. rarely —— if ever —— promote shareholder interests. Roberta Romano was one of first corporate law scholars to investigate shareholder claims empirically.[13] She studied all shareholder suits (both derivative and class action) brought against a random sample of about 5,000 corporations between the late 1960s and 1987. She found "scant evidence that lawsuits function as an alternative governance mechanism" to ensure appropriate decision-making by the board. Instead:

> [W]hile most suits settle, the settlements provide minimal compensation. There are financial recoveries in only half of settled suits, and per share recoveries are small. ... Settlements requiring structural relief ... tend to propose only cosmetic changes.

Apparently, derivative suits do not compensate shareholders for board misbehavior in the U.S. Instead, they give strategic parties (and attorneys) a way to extort funds from the firm by harassing corporate officers and directors. Without knowing the underlying dispute between Kaida and Omura, it is hard to know what Kaida' s lawyers hoped to obtain by filing this suit. A good guess, though, is that it had nothing to do with anything they argued in court.

---

[13] Roberta Romano, The Shareholder Suit: Litigation without Foundation?, 7 J.L. Econ. & Org. 55, 84, 85 (1991).

| 解 説 COMMENT | 経営判断の法理 |

　本件は，本書所収の会社法に関する事案3件のうちで最高裁判所民事裁判例集に掲載されなかった判例である。その意味で，この判例集の編集者は本件最高裁判決をあまり普遍性のない事例判決であると考えた可能性がある。しかし，実際には，本件で最高裁が述べた法理がその後の会社実務や下級審裁判所の裁判に与えた影響は大きいように見受けられる。

　アメリカの経営判断原則と大きく異なる日本の特徴として，本件で最高裁が定式化した「取締役の判断の過程と判断の内容の両方において著しい不合理性がない」かぎり取締役の善管注意義務違反は否定されるという日本版経営判断原則では，判断の内容についても裁判所が審査をする点があげられる。その意味で，経営判断原則といっても，アメリカと日本とでは大きく異なる（森田果「わが国に経営判断原則は存在していたのか」商事法務1858号4頁参照）。なお，日本では，どの範囲で本件最高裁が述べた日本版経営判断原則の適用があるのかについては，必ずしも明らかとなってはおらず，今後に残されている問題である。

　ラムザイヤー教授ご指摘の本件紛争の背景事情は，判決文からだけはわからない。株主代表訴訟一般についていえば，日本で提訴される株主代表訴訟がどのような背景を有しているかについては，学界においていくつかの興味深い研究はあるものの（Mark D. West, Why Shareholders Sue: The Evidence from Japan, 30 Journal of Legal Studies 351 (2001); Tomotaka Fujita, Transformation of the Management Liability Regime in Japan in the wake of the 1993 Revision, in Curtis Milhaupt, Hideki Kanda and Kon-Sik Kim (eds.), Transforming Corporate Governance in East Asia 15 (Routledge, 2008) 参照。なおアジア諸国について，Dan W. Puchniak, Harald Baum and Michael Ewing-Chow (eds.), The Derivative Action in Asia: A Comparative and Functional Approach (Cambridge University Press, 2012) 参照），株主代表訴訟が会社および株主全体の利益を向上させるものかについては，今後の研究にゆだねられているといわざるをえない。ただ，日本では，取締役側が敗訴して会社に対する巨額の損害賠償責任を負う事案がいくつか見られることが特徴的である（大阪地判平成12・9・20判例時報1721

アパマンショップ事件 [Apamanshop Derivative Litigation]

CASE
19

241

号 3 頁〔大和銀行。控訴審で和解〕，最判平成 18・4・10 民集 60 巻 4 号 1273 頁〔蛇の目ミシン〕，東京地判令和元・5・16 裁判所ウェブサイト〔オリンパス〕。もっとも，法令違反が認定されることが通常である），また，アメリカと異なり，社外取締役や監査役等の責任が肯定された事案も見られる（たとえば，大阪高判平成 27・5・21 判時 2279 号 96 頁〔セイクレスト〕）。

　日本の会社法にはデラウエア州会社法 107 条 2 項 b 号に相当する規定はなく，定款等によって取締役の対会社責任についておよそ軽過失の場合を免責して重過失の場合に限定することは認められない。もっとも，事後的には，株主全員の合意（会社法 424 条参照）がなくても，株主総会または取締役会決議によって善意で重過失がない場合の取締役の責任の一部免除を決定することが認められ（会社法 425 条・426 条），また，非業務執行取締役等については，定款によって善意で重過失がない場合の責任の一部免除をあらかじめ会社と契約することが認められ（責任限定契約）（会社法 427 条），後者は実際にも広く使われている。日本にはデラウエア州会社法 107 条 2 項 b 号に相当する規定がないにもかかわらず，日本で業務執行取締役へのなり手に不足しないのはなぜかというのはやや不思議なことではある。また，非業務執行取締役について責任限定契約が認められる範囲は責任の一部にすぎないが（原則として年間の報酬額の 2 年分相当額を超える額），それでもこの点を理由として非業務執行取締役へのなり手がいないとの声は聞かない。D&O 保険の実務を含めて，なお，アメリカと日本の違いをよく研究する価値はありそうである（こうした問題についての比較法的研究として，山中利晃『上場会社の経営監督における法的課題とその検討——経営者と監督者の責任を中心に』〔商事法務，2018〕参照）。

7 PART

労 働 法

CASE	
20	高知放送事件
21	秋北バス事件
22	電通事件

K.K. Kochi hoso v. Shiota

120 Saiban shu min 23 (Sup. Ct. Jan. 31, 1977).

高知放送事件
(最判昭和52年1月31日集民120号23頁)

1 The facts

Born in 1942, by 1967 the plaintiff read the news for the Kochi hoso radio station. The station employed five announcers, and rotated them through three shifts. On the morning of Feb. 23, 1967, he had nearly finished his night shift. At 6:00 a.m., he was to read a 10-minute version of the morning news. Alas, he overslept, missed his cue, and caused the station to go dead for 10 minutes. He reported his mistake to the firm, and apologized.

On March 8, however, the announcer overslept again. This time he did manage to report the news for the last 5 minutes of the segment. But rather than report his mistake, he tried to avoid responsibility.

Upon discovering what the announcer had done, Kochi hoso dismissed him. His supervisors claimed their labor contract gave them grounds to fire him through a disciplinary discharge (*chokai kaiko*). After all, he had missed two broadcasts and hidden one mistake besides. Out of compassion (they explained), they discharged him through a ordinary dismissal (*futsu kaiko*) instead.

The announcer sued to establish his employment status.

244

2 The decision

The Kochi District Court and Takamatsu High Court held for the announcer,[1] and the Supreme Court affirmed. The radio station may have had a right to dismiss the plaintiff, but in dismissing him under these circumstances it abused that right. The question, explained the Supreme Court, turned on whether the dismissal comported with the "common sense of society." Here it did not.

The announcer had done nothing egregiously improper, explained the Court. To be sure, he overslept. But he overslept negligently rather than maliciously (never mind that he misreported the second misstep). He was not the only person at fault; the employee charged with calling him also overslept (never mind that on the second occasion the nightwatchman did awaken him, but he rolled over and went back to sleep). The station was only off the air for a few minutes. The announcer confessed to the first incident immediately (never mind that he did not confess to the second). The station had not dismissed any employee for such transgressions in the past. And the announcer did not have a history of misbehavior.

3 Discussion

a. On the abuse of "abuse of rights" Unfortunately, in applying the "abuse of rights" theory[2] to labor cases, the Court missused the theory itself. Pre-war courts had imported the theory from continental jurisprudence. Typically, they applied it in one of two situations, both of which involved negotiation problems. The first class of

---

[1] K.K. Kochi hoso v. Shiota, unpublished (Kochi D. Ct. Mar. 27, 1973), aff'd, 304 Hanrei taimuzu 196 (Takamatsu High Ct. Dec. 19, 1973).
[2] Now incorporated into Sec. 1(c) of the Civil Code.

245

cases concerned bilateral monopolies.[3] For (a very classic) example, suppose an owner sued to remove a pipe laid inadvertently on his land. In fact, the pipe caused the owner only trivial harm but its removal would entail large costs. Given property law, however, the landowner could sue to remove the pipe —— and "hold up" the infringer for a large settlement.

The negotiations between the land and pipe owners were hard because they involved a "bilateral monopoly." By way of contrast, suppose A wanted to buy a used car. He could go to a dealer, find the car he wanted, and negotiate a price. If the dealer refused to accept a reasonable offer, he could go to one of ten other used car dealers in the city. If A refused to buy at a reasonable price, the dealer could sell the car to one of ten other buyers who would visit his dealership over the next several days. A could buy a car from other dealers; the dealer could sell his car to other buyers. Necessarily, (in the absence of fraud) any agreement they reach will occur at a price most people would consider fair.

From these negotiations between A and the car dealer, negotiations within a bilateral monopoly differ fundamentally. Return to the pipe case. Suppose B owns a plot of land, and C owns a pipe laid inadvertently on that land long ago. B and C would like to resolve their dispute privately, but without a "market" alternative the negotiations can readily break down. If the car dealer proved unreasonable A could turn elsewhere; if A proved unreasonable, the dealer could turn elsewhere. B and C have no such "elsewhere." Inextricably locked into their relationship, they cannot turn to an outside market. They cannot avoid their fundamentally problematic negotiation. Through doctrines like "abuse of rights," courts can sometimes impose

---

[3] Shinagawa v. Kurobe tetsudo, K.K.,14 Hanketsu minshu 1965 (Sup. Ct. Oct. 5, 1935)(Unazuki onsen).

246

sensible outcomes on these bilateral monopolies.

The second class of abuse of rights cases involved negotiations among large numbers of parties. The cases might, for example, concern the rights of rice farmers or hot-springs owners to a communal resource. Suppose the farmers and owners all use a given stream of water or steam. Sometimes, such streams can support existing uses but not a new paddy or hot-springs hotel. In theory, the various farmers and owners could assemble and privately negotiate the efficient level of use for each. When a stream passes many potential users, however, the contracting process can turn intractible. Faced with these difficulties, the courts can impose sensible outcomes by limiting each claimant's use to efficient levels.[4]

The labor market presents neither set of negotiating problems. When firms and workers agree to a labor contract, they do so within a competitive market. The worker can choose among multiple competing employers; the firm can choose among multiple competing workers. The firm will hire the worker who offers the best expected performance at the lowest price; the worker will choose the firm that presents the most attractive package of work, contractual terms, and pay.

In selecting an employment contract, firms and workers will select the contract that benefits them both. Suppose a firm wanted a contract that imposed disagreeable terms on its workers. A worker who chose between this firm and a competitor with more pleasant terms will opt for a job at the disagreeable firm only if it pays a salary high enough to compensate for those disagreeable contractual terms. When firms and workers select "disagreeable" contracts, in other words, they select them only if (a) the firm pays the worker a

---

[4] J. Mark Ramseyer, Water Law in Imperial Japan: Public Goods, Private Claims, and Legal Convergence, 18 J. Legal Stud. 51 (1989).

salary high enough fully to offset the "disagreeableness," and (b) the firm finds the disagreeable terms sufficiently valuable to justify that compensating salary.

Return to the *Kochi hoso* case. Transacting across a competitive labor market, the two parties selected a contract that gave Kochi hoso the right to fire its announcer for irresponsible behavior. The parties could have negotiated a contract that denied Kochi hoso that right —— but Kochi hoso would have offered a lower salary. The announcer agreed to give Kochi hoso this right because he wanted the higher salary he could then earn.

It is no answer to say that workers do not choose among employers. To the extent that some workers do not have a choice, the problem results from restrictions that courts (*e.g.*, limits on dismissals) and legislatures (*e.g.*, minimum wage) impose on the labor market. But whatever the case with other workers, the announcer would have had a wide variety of choices. According to information elsewhere on the Internet, he had recently graduated from Keio University. Some young workers may have trouble finding jobs, but Keio graduates face a panoply of firms eager to hire them.

Necessarily, when judges rewrite the terms of a labor contract, they impose inferior terms. The announcer and Kochi hoso had deliberately agreed to terms that gave Kochi hoso the right to fire him for misbehavior. They had strong incentives to choose the contract that best fit their respective preferences. Although the contract gave Kochi hoso the right to fire him, the announcer agreed to it —— presumably because Kochi hoso offered other employment terms (like salary) attractive enough to offset the right to fire him.

In effect, the Supreme Court banned the choice that Kochi hoso and its announcer mutually desired. In the process, it raised the costs (and lowered the benefits) to firms of hiring workers. Predictable consequences follow —— which I detail below.

248

b. Other termination restrictions The courts do not just limit discharges for misconduct; they also limit dismissals for economic reasons. In the 1975 *Omura nogami* case, for example, the Nagasaki District Court invoked the abuse of right doctrine to articulate the reasons for which an economically distressed firm could dismiss its employees. If it failed to meet the court's four-part test, the dismissals were void:[5]

> Whether a firm has abused its right in dismissing employees as part of a restructuring effort depends primarily on the following factors: *First*, the need to dismiss employees must have been so acute that a failure to do so would have threatened its very survival; *second*, the firm must have tried to reduce the number of surplus workers by less painful means (*e.g.*, transfers, temporary furloughs, solicitation of voluntary retirements); *third*, it must have explained its circumstances to the labor union and to its employee representatives and tried to obtain their consent, and it must have tried to obtain the consent of its workers to the timing, scale, and method of the planned dismissals; and *fourth*, it must have accomplished its reorganization and chosen the employees to dismiss through standards that were objective and rational.

---

[5] Hamada v. Omura nogami, K.K., 813 Hanrei jiho 98, 100 (Nagasaki D. Ct. Dec. 24, 1975).

For an excellent empirical study of this four-factor test, see Daiji Kawaguchi & Ryo Kanbayashi, Yon yoken handan no tokei teki bunseki [A Statistical Analysis of the Four Factors], in Ryo Kanbayashi, ed., Kaiko kisei no ho to keizaigaku [The Law & Economics of the Regulation of Dismissals] ch. 5 (Tokyo: Nihon hyoron sha, 2008). Other sophisticated analyses include Ryo Kanbayashi, Saibansho ni okeru kaiko jiken [Dismissal Cases in Court], in Kanbayashi, supra, at ch. 6; Ryo Kanbayashi & Junko Hirasawa, Hanrei shu kara miru seiri kaiko jiken [Economic Dismissals from Reported Cases], in Kanbayashi, supra, at ch. 3; Hisashi Okuno & Masato Hara, Seiri kaiko saibanrei no bunseki [An Analysis of Economic Dismissal Cases], in Kanbayashi, supra, at ch. 4.

In effect, some courts let firms dismiss workers for economic reasons only if they otherwise would fail. More recent opinions suggest the courts may not go quite that far.[6] Yet the restrictions on lay-offs remain severe: in the words of Professor Takashi Araki: "Japanese caselaw sets stringent restrictions on economic dismissals."[7] As Professor Araki nicely explained, courts require employers "to exhaust most alternatives before resorting to economic dismissals and there are many alternatives." As a result, the employer must first try to avoid dismissals by "reducing overtime, reducing mid-term recruitment, transferring or farming out redundant workers, not renewing fixed-term contracts or contracts of part-timers, curtailing regular hiring, reducing executive and managerial salaries, temporarily stopping operation with reduced pay, and soliciting voluntary retirements."[8] Ultimately, Professor Araki thoughtfully concludes, "dismissals must be the last resort to cope with the economic difficulties."[9]

c. **Implications for hires** Given these court-imposed limits on their ability to dismiss workers, firms will hire fewer employees. Consider separately the *Kochi hoso* limits on disciplinary discharges, and the *Omura nogami* limits on economically driven dismissals. First, if a firm cannot fire workers who misbehave, it will earn a lower expected benefit from hiring them. To the extent that technology can substitute for human beings, it will use more technology. To the ex-

---

[6] See Takashi Araki, Corporate Governance Reforms and Labor and Employment Relations in Japan: Whither Japan's Practice-Dependent Stakeholder Model?, 1 U. Tokyo J.L. & Pol. 45, 66 (2004).

[7] Takashi Araki, A Comparative Analysis: Corporate Governance and Labor and Employment Relations in Japan, 22 Comp. Labor L. & Pol'y J. 67, 80 (2000).

[8] Takashi Araki, Corporate Restructuring and Employee Protection: Japan's New Experiment, in Roger Blanpain & Manfred Weiss, eds., Changing Industrial Relations and Modernisation of Labour Law 27, 29 (The Hague: Kluwer, 2003).

[9] Araki, supra note 7, at 81.

tent that it finds its existing employees satisfactory, it will work make them longer hours rather than take the risk of hiring new employees.

Second, if a firm cannot fire misbehaving workers, it will screen potential hires more carefully. Rather than risk an otherwise promising hire with traits that correlate (however imperfectly) with problematic behavior, it will stay with safer applicants. It will shun applicants who misbehaved in school. It will avoid applicants with police records. It may even avoid recent university and high-school graduates simply because —— being still unemployed —— they cannot demonstrate a history of faithful work performance.

Third, if a firm cannot freely layoff workers during slack times, it will not hire as many workers during peak demand. Firms understand that business activity rises and falls. Even if they need more workers now, they realize that they will need fewer in the future. If they cannot dismiss their workers during recessions, they will not hire extra workers during boom times.

Fourth, if the inability to dismiss employees causes a firm to hire fewer workers during peak demand, it will compensate for the labor shortage by causing existing employees to work longer hours. The occasional "deaths from overwork" (karoshi) follow. Firms demand overtime because they do not hire enough new workers, and they do not hire new workers because judges restrict lay-offs. "Death from overwork" is not a problem judges need to regulate; it is a phenomenon in part that judges caused.[10]

d. Comparative studies   Other scholars have reached similar conclusions about Western Europe and Latin America. Edward Lazear,[11] for example, studies the effect of dismissal restrictions

---

[10] See Case 22; Mark D. West, Law in Everyday Japan: Sex, Sumo, Suicide, and Statutes (Chicago: University of Chicago Press, 2005).

(particularly, mandated severance pay) on a cross-section of countries. He finds that 59 percent of the increase in unemployment in France between 1956 and 1984 resulted from changes in termination restrictions.[12] More generally, using data from 22 countries over three decades, he concludes:[13]

> The best estimates suggest that moving from no required severance pay to three months of required severance pay to employees with ten years of service would reduce the employment-population ratio by about 1 percent.

Disproportionately, moreover, he concludes that young workers bear the brunt of these effects.

With co-author Carmen Pages, Nobel laureate James Heckman[14] uses data from Latin America and the Carribean to explore the differential effect of labor market regulation. He too concludes that the regulation harms the newest, youngest workers:[15]

> In the face of a negative shock and declining marginal value of labor, a firm may want to dismiss some workers, but it has to pay a mandatory dismissal cost. This cost has the effect of discouraging firms from adjusting their labor force, resulting in fewer dismissals than in the absence of such costs. Conversely, in the face of a positive shock firms may want to hire additional workers but will take into account that some workers may have to be fired in the future if

---

[11] Edward P. Lazear, Job Security Provisions and Employment, 105 Q.J. Econ. 699 (1990).

[12] Lazear, supra note 11, at 700.

[13] Lazear, supra note 11, at 724-25.

[14] James J. Heckman & Carmen Pages, The cost of Job Security Regulation: Evidence from Latin American Labor Markets, NBER Working Paper No. 7773 (June 2000).

[15] Heckman & Pages, supra note 14, at 8-9.

demand turns down, and this is costly. This prospective cost acts as a hiring cost, effectively reducing creation of new jobs in good states. The net result is lower employment rates in expansions, higher employment rates in recessions and lower turnover rates as firms hire and fire fewer workers than they would in the absence of these costs.

The regulation of employment termination, Heckman concludes:[16]

> reduces aggregate employment and ... [has] the greatest adverse impact ... on youth and groups marginal to the workforce. Insiders and entrenched workers gain from regulation but outsiders suffer. As a consequence, job security regulations reduce employment and promote inequality across workers.

e. Implications for growth When judges stop firms from dismissing employees and thereby —— indirectly —— discourage them from hiring new employees during peak demand, they also slash the rate of economic growth. To demonstrate this effect on Japanese data, Professor Hiroko Okudaira and her co-authors distinguish court opinions that facilitate dismissals from those which block them. They then combine that data with information on judicial personnel assignments to explore the effect that judges can have on economic growth.

More specifically, Prof. Okudaira:[17]

> first created a judgment indicator by coding adjustment dismissal precedents into pro-worker or pro-employer

---

[16] Heckman & Pages, supra note 14, at 2 (ital. in orig.).

[17] Hiroko Okudaira, The Economic Costs of Court Decisions Concerning Dismissals in Japan: Identification by Judge Transfers 4 (2009) (Osaka Univ. Inst. Social & Econ. Res., Discussion Paper 733).

judgments. Then, by using this variable, [she] examined how the direction of judgment affects the labor market performance in a prefecture-level panel model.

She found that:[18]

[T]he employment rate is reduced significantly —— by approximately 1.5% —— if a prefecture has a greater number of "pro-worker" judgments in a certain year as compared with those that are "pro-employer."

Thus, she concludes:[19]

[S]trict employment protection significantly reduces the employment-to-population ratio by approximately 1.4 log points, after controlling for observable and unobservable prefecture characteristics. [These conclusions] are also robust to instrumental variable estimations. ... Stringent employment protection not only deprives employment opportunities to potential workers but also requires the incumbent workers to accept a decline in their hourly wages. ...

Prof. Okudaira and her co-authors also use her earlier study to explore the effect of labor law on other aspects of a prefecture's economic performance. They find:[20]

[P]ro-worker judgments significantly reduce growth rates in firms' total factor productivity and labour productivity ....

f. Implications for sub-contracting In addition, judicial limits on dismissal increase the odds that a manufacturer will buy its com-

---

[18] Okudaira, supra note 17, at 4.

[19] Okudaira, supra note 17, at 29.

[20] Hiroko Okudaira, Miho Takizawa & Kotaro Tsuru, Employment Protection and Productivity: Evidence from Firm-Level Panel Data in Japan, 456 Appllied Econ. 2091 (2013)

ponents from sub-contractors rather than make them in-house. Some manufacturers "vertically integrate" : they make most of their product's component parts in-house. Other manufacturers subcontract —— they buy those component parts from independent suppliers. GM makes many of its automotive components in-house; Toyota famously buys its components from subcontractors, and those subcontractors in turn buy sub-components from sub-subcontractors.

The barriers to dismissal push a firm away from vertical integration, and toward subcontracting. Suppose a firm faces decreased demand during cyclical downturns. To dismiss unneeded employees, judges will push it to demonstrate that the layoffs are what Prof. Araki calls a "last resort." A major producer like Toyota or Nissan could rarely do that: a diversified manufacturer with thousands of employees will find it hard to convince a judge that it cannot move its redundant workers somewhere else. A small sub-subcontractor could convince the judge easily: it may have 15 employees who stamp Corolla door handles, but if Toyota drops its door-handle order it will not stay in business if it must pay all 15.

In effect, subcontracting increases a firm's flexibility over its workforce. If the firm makes all its components in-house, it will find it hard to shrink its workforce during cyclical downturns. It will try to maintain flexibility by hiring some of its staff as "irregular" workers with no expectation of long-term tenure. As hard as it tries, however, it will find itself paying wages to employees for whom it has little or no work. If it buys components from suppliers who in turn buy sub-components from sub-suppliers, it avoids those empty wages. Because its suppliers (being small) can readily dismiss workers they do not need, they can produce the components at a lower cost than the manufacturer itself would have to pay.

Given judicial limits on dismissals, in other words, producers who make components in-house (vertically integrated firms) have higher

K.K. Kochi hoso v. Shiota 高知放送事件

costs during cyclical downturns than producers who buy components from suppliers. During cyclical downturns, the vertically integrated firm must pay workers with little or nothing to do. The firm that buys its components from suppliers does not face that cost. Because its suppliers (and sub-suppliers) can more easily dismiss their workers, they can manufacture the component parts more cheaply than a vertically integrated firm forced by courts to keep idle workers on its payroll.

g. **Culture** Nothing about any of this is distinctly Japanese. Mean job tenure is long in Japan, but it follows union violence and judicial policy rather than anything peculiar about Japanese culture. Japanese firms dismissed workers readily before World War II, and workers readily quit. When firms tried to dismiss workers during the post-war occupation, the hyper-militant socialist- and communist-affiliated unions launched violent strikes (detailed in the **Case21**).[21] When the employees sued, the courts threatened to vacate the dismissals. In the 1970s, the economy slid into recession, and firms again tried to dismiss extra workers. The employees again sued, and the courts again vacated the dismissals.

Worker tenure in Japan is not long by tradition. It is not long because of any distinctively Japanese work-place culture. And it is not long because of any implicit contract between a firm and its employees. It is long because labor unions in the 1940s and 1950s turned violent, and judges refused to let firms dismiss misbehaving or redundant workers.[22]

---

[21] Detailed in J. Mark Ramseyer, Second-Best Justice: The Virtues of Japanese Private Law chap. 6 (Chicago: University of Chicago Press, 2015).

解説　　解雇規制

　解雇規制は，その国の雇用システムを決定づける重要性を持つ。先進国の中で最も解雇規制が緩やかといってよい国がアメリカである。アメリカでは，解雇に正当事由は不要で，解雇は（差別禁止事由に該当する場合と公序違反のような例外的場合を除くと）自由である。意のままに雇い，意のままに解雇できるというこの随意的雇用（at will employment）が，今日でも維持されているのかについては大論争があった。しかし，2015年にまとめられたアメリカ法律協会（American Law Institute）の雇用法リステートメント（一流の法律家が，判例を中心とした現在の法理論状況を法典の形で文章化し，注釈を加えたもの）では，異なる合意がなされない限り，この解雇自由（随意的雇用）がアメリカの雇用関係を支配する原則的ルールであることが確認された。

　解雇が自由で雇用保障のない雇用システムでは，雇用関係に労働市場機能が直接に作用する。解雇には正当事由が不要であるので，企業は労働力需給の変化に応じて，余剰人員は解雇し，人員不足となれば新たに労働者を雇い入れることが可能となる。労働者は，企業に特有な技能（企業特殊的技能）を時間とエネルギーを使って習得しようとはせず，企業も，労働者が転職すれば訓練投資は無駄となるため，教育訓練インセンティブを持ちにくい。教育訓練は労働者が自ら費用を負担して行うべきものとなり，使用者は既に必要な技能を持った労働者を雇い入れることになる。企業は労働条件を引き下げる必要があれば，単に労働条件引下げを提案し，これに同意しない労働者は適法に解雇できる。次項目で検討する秋北バス事件判決のような労働条件変更のための法的ルールも不要となる。労働者は，現在の労働条件に不満があれば，使用者に労働条件

K.K. Kochi hoso v. Shiota　高知放送事件

▼22　Observers often use the term "life-time employment" (shushin koyo) to characterize what they consider the distinctive Japanese workforce. In fact, the term was invented to translate the book of a young American anthropologist (James Abegglen; he would soon become a business consultant) who attributed Japanese labor practices to assorted stereotypes about Confucian culture. The book fit nicely into the booming 1960s market for the ethnocentric Nihonjin-ron literature, and sold extremely well. See generally Ramseyer, supra note 21, at chap. 6.

を上げてくれなければ転職すると提案したり，あるいは実際によりよい労働条件の企業に転職する。こうしたシステムが労働者にとっても有効に機能するためには，転職によって容易に適職を選択できるという流動的労働市場が備わっていることが重要となる。

アメリカのような雇用システムにおいては，例えば，リーマンショック時には失業率が高騰するが，景気が回復すれば失業率もめざましく改善するというダイナミックな展開を見せる。アメリカの活力の一つはこのような市場機能を大胆に活用している点に見いだすことができよう。

日本でも，民法はアメリカと同様，解雇には正当事由を要求しない解雇自由の制度を前提としていた。すなわち，民法627条は，当事者が雇用の期間を定めなかった場合，「いつでも解約の申入れをすることができ」，この場合，「雇用は，解約の申入れの日から二週間を経過することによって終了する。」とし，雇用契約の解約（使用者の解雇も含む）に何ら正当事由を要求していない。しかし，日本の裁判所は，戦後，労働市場に求職者が溢れ，雇用を失うことが本人そしてその家族に甚大な影響を与える状況の中，解雇に制限を課すルールを模索することとなった。すなわち，権利の濫用は許されないという民法の基本原則（民1条3項）に依拠して，使用者は確かに解雇権を持っているが，客観的合理的理由を欠き社会通念上相当として是認されないような解雇権行使は，権利濫用として無効とするという裁判例を積み重ねた。これが最高裁でも昭和50年の判決（日本食塩事件・最判昭和50・4・25民集29巻4号456頁）および昭和52年の高知放送事件判決で確認され，いわゆる「解雇権濫用法理」が確立するに至る。このルールは長い間，判例法理にとどまっていたが，2003年の労働基準法改正で明文化され（当時の労基18条の2），現在では労働契約法16条に明記されている。

諸外国と比較してみると，アメリカのように解雇の自由を維持している国は極めて例外的な存在で，ほとんどの先進国では正当事由や客観的合理的理由を欠いた解雇を違法とする解雇制限規制を導入している。

しかし，ラムザイヤー教授は，自由に解雇できない雇用システムの種々の問題点を指摘する。使用者は採用に慎重になり，雇用を減少させる，若年雇用に悪影響を及ぼす，解雇規制によって守られた労働者と，解雇規制ゆえに職を得ることができない失業者の間の格差を拡大させる等で，こうした問題は国際比

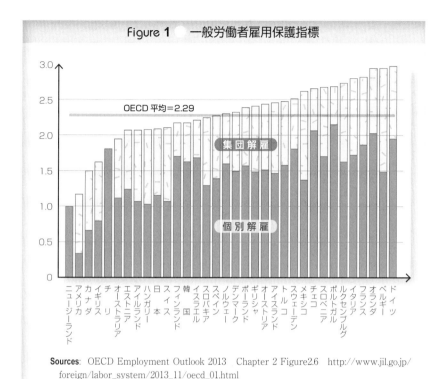

Sources: OECD Employment Outlook 2013 Chapter 2 Figure2.6 http://www.jil.go.jp/foreign/labor_system/2013_11/oecd_01.html

較研究からも裏付けられるとされる。

　解雇規制が労働者にとって，さらには経済や社会一般にとって有益か否かをめぐっては様々な議論がある。ラムザイヤー教授の指摘するような解雇規制の負の側面を指摘する立場が主張される一方，交渉力の強い使用者や予測の付かない市場変動から労働者を守り，労使双方が長期的投資を行える環境を整備することが経済効率化にも資するとして雇用保護規制を支持する立場も主張されている（例えば，World Bank, World Development Report 2013, p.258 以下）。

　OECDでは，解雇規制の程度を指標化・数値化して各国の比較を行っている。この雇用保護指標は，高知放送事件のような労働者側に起因する「個別解雇」と，経営側の事由による整理解雇ないし「集団解雇」の双方の強度を併せて評価したものである（法律家の目から見ると，OECDの数値化自体に問題がないわけではないが，ここでは立ち入らない）。2008年のOECD雇用保護指標では，ア

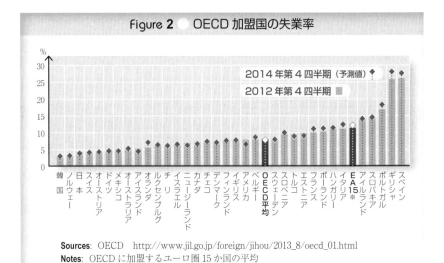

Figure 2 ● OECD加盟国の失業率

Sources: OECD http://www.jil.go.jp/foreign/jihou/2013_8/oecd_01.html
Notes: OECDに加盟するユーロ圏15か国の平均

メリカが最も解雇規制が緩やかな国とされていたが，2013年雇用保護指標では，ニュージーランドについで2番目となっている。他方，2013年の雇用保護指標で最も解雇規制が厳しい国は，ドイツである（Figure 1）。しかし，ドイツの失業率は低い方から数えて6番目であり，日本は3番目である（Figure 2）。解雇規制が厳しければ失業率が高まる国もあるが，ドイツはそうではないし，日本はアメリカ，カナダ，イギリスなど解雇規制が緩やかなアングロ・サクソン国よりも失業率は低い。解雇規制と失業率とは相関するとは限らない。経済学者からも，「解雇規制が失業率や雇用率に及ぼす影響は不確定（inconclusive）であるというのが，多くの専門家によって共有されている知見であろう」と指摘されている（今井亮一「解雇規制のマクロ分析」神林龍編『解雇規制の法と経済』〔日本評論社，2008〕297頁）。

厳しすぎる解雇規制は，現在雇用されている者を過度に保護し，結果として，失業者・新規学卒者等，労働市場に参入しようとする者の雇用機会を奪う弊害があるという認識は一般化してきているが，同時に，緩すぎる解雇規制も市場競争力のない労働者の保護を奪い社会の不安定化をもたらすなど問題があるとして，要は，解雇規制をするかしないかという問題ではなく，規制の程度が問題であり，適度な解雇規制を模索する立場が有力となってきている。

いずれにしても，ラムザイヤー教授の議論からは，解雇規制を論ずるに当たっては，解雇から労働者を守ることが全面的に正しいという単純なことではなく，その規制が，雇用されている労働者よりも，さらに弱者である失業者，新規学卒者，非正規労働者などに不利に作用する可能性があること，また，雇用が流動化し労働市場が活発になることは，雇用が不安定となり問題があるようにも見えるが，他方で，労働者が現状の雇用に不満がある場合に容易に転職することができ，そのことが使用者に対する交渉力をも高める作用があることなど，様々な視点から検討すべき問題であることに気づかされるであろう。

アメリカから見ると，日本は解雇規制のより厳格な国であるが，欧州諸国と比較すると，解雇規制の緩やかな国とも位置づけられる。これからの解雇規制・雇用システムを考える上でも，グローバルな視点から各国の状況を観察し，異なる雇用システムにはそれぞれのメリットとデメリットがあることを謙虚に認識し，検討していくことが必要であろう（荒木尚志「労働法政策を比較法的視点から考える重要性」日本労働研究雑誌659号98頁参照）。

Yoshikawa v. Shuhoku Bus, K.K.

22 Saihan Minshu 3459 (Sup. Ct. Dec. 25, 1968).

秋北バス事件
(最大判昭和 43 年 12 月 25 日民集 22 巻 13 号 3459 頁)

1 The facts

Noriharu Yoshikawa joined Shuhoku Bus in the fall of 1945 at the age of 44. Local bureaucrats had ordered 13 local transportation firms to consolidate operations during the war, and the firms had formed Shuhoku in response. Shuhoku ran buses in northeastern Akita prefecture. The eponymous dogs came from there too, of course, and in time the firm would run a "Hachi-ko" bus, named after the Akita dog that had waited so patiently for his master at Shibuya station.

Hachi-ko had come from Odate city, and it was there that Hogawa worked. He helped run the local branch office, and held Shuhoku stock as well. Most Japanese employees at the time worked under "at-will" contracts, and so did Hogawa. He would later claim the firm had promised him a job for life, but the court found no evidence. Hogawa held his job "at the will" of the firm and himself: the company could dismiss him when it wanted, and he could quit when he wanted.

In the late 1940s, labor unions in Japan were demanding restrictions on dismissals, and so was Shuhoku's union. In 1951, it won the restrictions from the firm. Workers could continue to quit when they wished, but Shuhoku could dismis them only if it could prove

262

unacceptable performance or if business were so bad as to make dismissal unavoidable. The price the union paid: mandatory retirement.

In 1957 Shuhoku extended that mandatory retirement to its managers. Being part of the 1951 union bargain, the earlier terms had applied only to union members. As management, Hogawa had not been not subject to them. Now, Shuhoku decided to force its managers to quit at 55. As Yoshikawa was over 55, the firm told him to retire (though it offered to hire him back under a new contract).

Yoshikawa sued to keep his position as a regular employee. The District Court found in his favor, but the High Court reversed this decision and the Supreme Court affirmed: the mandatory retirement was effective policy.[1] Because employers need uniform workplace rules, workers cannot pick-and-choose among a firm's policies. Provided the rules embody rational policy, they bind all workers —— regardless of what a worker might want, and regardless even of whether a worker knows of the rules. Here, the rules imposed mandatory retirement. Retirement rules are rational and Yoshikawa was over the age at which the rules required retirement, so Yoshikawa needed to retire.

2 Employment practice

Before World War II, Japanese workers had negotiated at-will contracts. Workers could quit when they wanted, and firms could dismiss them when they wanted —— for any reason or for no reason at all. The contracts offer huge efficiency advantages.[2] They let

---

[1] Yoshikawa v. Shuhoku basu, K.K., 542 Hanrei jiho 14 (Sup. Ct. Dec. 25, 1968), affirming 15 Romin 1137 (Sendai High Ct. Oct. 26, 1964), reversing 295 Hanrei jiho 40 (Akita D. Ct. Apr. 16, 1962).

[2] Richard A. Epstein, In Defense of the Contract at Will, 51 U. Chi. L. Rev. 947 (1984).

employees watch for better alternatives, and quit when they find a job that more closely fits their preferences. They let firms cut their labor costs when demand for their product falls. They let firms dismiss substandard workers without incurring the procedural costs of proving fault in court or in an administrative proceeding. And because the risk of dismissal gives workers incentives to perform at higher levels, the contracts increase productivity and earn workers higher wages.

To be sure, firms and workers do not always want at-will contracts; sometimes they prefer more restrictive employment terms. Workers may value job security highly enough to take the pay cut necessary to induce a firm to offer it. Firms may want a workforce with the stability that contracts with job security bring. Sometimes firms and workers will find at-will contracts mutually beneficial, in other words, and sometimes not. Basic principles of "freedom of contract" let them conclude these arrangements when indeed beneficial, and avoid them when not.

After the war, firms and workers continued to negotiate at-will contracts. Simultaneously, however, the far left began massive organizational campaigns. Both the Japan Communist Party and the Japan Socialist Party ran these operations. They formed unions, recruited workers. A year after the end of the war, they had enlisted 4 million.

When firms tried to dismiss the workers they had hired under these at-will contracts, the fringe-left unions struck. In the new post-war era, they ran fiercely violent strikes. Saboteurs who may or may not have had union connections (the crimes have remained largely unsolved) wreaked national havok. When the national railroad tried to cut over-staffing, groups of saboteurs derailed one train after another, killing people as they did. In June 1949 they apparently murdered the company president (some observers called it a suicide) and left him dead on the tracks. In July they ran an unmanned train into a suburban

264

Tokyo station and killed six people. And in August they derailed yet another train, and killed three more.[3]

The chaos mounted. In January 1946, the fringe-left unions organized 64 strikes involving 36,000 employees. That October they organized 109 strikes involving 269,000. And by 1952, they were organizing 1,200 strikes a year. Not only did they strike, they cammandeered factories. Over the course of 1946, 170 unions and 140,000 workers threw out management and took over the factories. Typically, they commandeered 20 a month.[4]

Soon, courts began stopping firms from meeting reduced demand by dismissing employees too. Not until the 1970s would they settle on the rigid rules that would cripple the labor market and so badly damage the economy (see discussion at Case**20**). During the 1950s, they still left the question of whether a firm could lay off workers unsettled. Already, however, some judges were starting to intervene and void dismissals.[5]

∃ Mandatory retirement

Shuhoku (and many other Japanese firms) imposed the mandatory retirement policies in a response to the dismissal limitations imposed by the violent unions and the courts. On the one hand, the limits do not explain mandatory retirement generally. As explained in Section (a) below, many firms impose mandatory retirement to let them adopt "back-end-loaded" wage profiles and raise worker productivity. Instead, the limits on dismissal explain the mid-career "retire-

---

[3] J. Mark Ramseyer, Second-Best Justice: The Virtues of Japanese Private Law chap. 6 (Chicago: University of Chicago Press, 2015).

[4] J. Mark Ramseyer, supra note 3, at chap. 6.

[5] See the history of the employment law in Ramseyer, supra note 3, at chap. 6.

ments" that Shuhoku and so many other Japanese firms adopted. As explained in Section (b), the firms introduced these early "retirement" policies to recover the labor-market flexibility that the dismissal limitations had so badly damaged.

a. Mandatory retirement generally Absent limits on dismissals, many firms would still adopt mandatory retirement policies —— but at ages close to those at which their workers would retire voluntarily. Labor economist Edward Lazear explained the logic.[6] In order to induce their employees to work harder, firms adopt "back-end-loaded" wage profiles that load compensation onto a worker's last years. They want their employees to work hard and conscientiously for the good of the firm. In turn, the employees want to earn the higher wages that the higher productivity would warrant.

If workers earned only their marginal product, however, they would have little reason to work conscientiously. Given that they earn what they produce, if dismissed they could readily replace their pay at another firm. To induce employees to work harder, firms and workers instead use a pay scale that forces workers to post a portion of their earnings as a bond. They post a fraction of their earnings during the early years as a bond with the firm which they then collect at the close of their career —— but only if the firm does not dismiss them for non-performance. And because this incentive will induce them to work harder throughout their life, the firm will pay them higher lifetime wages.

Through this strategy, firms pay their workers according to

---

[6] Edward P. Lazear, Why Is There Mandatory Retirement?, 87 J. Pol. Econ. 1261 (1979). For an excellent discussion of the logic in Japanese, see Atsushi Seike, Nenko chingin wa donaruka [What Will Happen to Age-based Wages], 525 Nihon rodo kenkyu zasshi 26 (Apr. 2004).

a wage profile that climbs steeply with age. In Lazear's words:

> [A] wage profile which pays workers less when they are young and more when they are old will allow the worker and firm to behave in such a way as to raise the present value of marginal product over the lifetime. For example, by deferring payment a firm may induce a worker to perform at a higher level of effort. Both firm and worker may prefer this high wage/high effort combination to a lower wage/lower effort path that results from a payment scheme that creates incentives to shirk.

If a firm adopts this wage profile, it will also need to adopt mandatory retirement. In equilibrium, it will pay its workers lifetime wages that equal their lifetime marginal product. Because the firm "back-end loads" the pay, however, workers will earn more than their marginal product during their later years. This in turn will reduce their incentive to retire as planned. Even if they otherwise would have preferred to retire at (for example) age 65, given their high wage they may choose not to quit. Yet if they do not retire, then the firm will find itself paying its workers lifetime wages greater than their lifetime marginal product.

By imposing mandatory retirement at the age at which a worker would otherwise retire anyway, the firm can safely use a wage profile that pays high wages to its older workers. Through this contract, employees work harder than otherwise. Because they work harder, they earn higher wages. And they retire at the age at which they would otherwise have retired at anyway.

b. Retirement at 50   Lazear's logic does not explain the Shuhoku retirement plan (retirement at 50 or 55, depending on the worker's position), and does not explain the similarly early retirement plans at its contemporary firms. The logic explains mandatory retirement at the age at which a worker would choose to retire anyway. It does not explain retirement at 50 or 55. Even in the 1950s (with its lower life expectancies), 50 was not an age at which most workers would have chosen to retire. Many would not yet have saved enough money, and would have been healthy enough not to want to stop working anyway. Indeed, when forced to retire, many looked for a second career at another firm. Lazear's logic explains why firms might impose mandatory retirement at 65 or 70. It does not explain why —— even in the 1950s —— firms would impose it at 50 or 55.

Part of the reason for the very early retirement ages instead lies in the limits on dismissal. Firms know that the demand for their product can fall. Most do not expect it to fall, and none want it to fall. But firms understand that the risk exists.

When product demand falls, firms need to reduce production. They will need to shrink their work force, and at-will employment lets them do it. Mandatory retirement at an extremely early age offers an alternative way to maintain that ability to shrink the work force. If workers must retire at an early age, a substantial fraction will quit each year. The firm can then match its workforce to product demand by adjusting the number of the new people it hires to replace those who retire.

Take an example. A firm needs a given number of workers. It does not anticipate having to retrench, but worries that it might need to do so from time to time. If it could hire its workers on at-will contracts, it would happily keep them until age 65. If it needed to retrench, it would dismiss them —— but without that need to retrench (and it does not expect to need to retrench), it will happily keep them until age 65.

Suppose now that the union (or the court) limits the firm's ability to dismiss. If demand falls and the firm retains its full labor force, it will badly lose money. To retain the necessary flexibility, it

268

can instead accelerate its mandatory retirement age. Suppose it hires its workers at age 25, and they in turn would otherwise (in the absence of mandatory retirement) retire at 65. In any given year, it would lose 2.5 percent (1/40) of its workers. If it instead requires retirement at 50, it will lose 4 percent (1/25) of its workers each year. In effect, the earlier retirement age increases the flexibility it has to respond to fluctuations in the demand for its products.

Note the cost this policy imposes on both firms and employees. Firms would like their experienced and conscientious workers to stay until they can no longer work productively (say, age 65). Those employees would like to stay until age 65. The firm does not expect demand for its product to fall, and provided it does not fall would happily retain those employees until age 65.

But the firm understands that bad things happen. Product demand might fall. With at-will employment contracts, it can face those contingencies by dismissing a fraction of its workers as necessary. With limits on dismissal (whether imposed by the union or by the courts), it no longer has that flexibility. To retain the basic flexibility, many firms in the 1950s instead dismissed *all* employees at age 50 or 55, and responded to product demand by hiring replacements as needed.

c. The costs of dismissal restrictions What judicial and union-imposed restrictions on dismissals do, in other words, is to cause firms to retire workers whom they would prefer not to retire and who themselves do not want to retire. Under the guise of "retirements," it —— entirely unnecessarily —— increases worker dismissals.

As noted in the discussion to **Case20**, these restrictions cripple the labor market in a wide variety of ways. First, if firms cannot dismiss regular employees, they will hire many workers on fixed-term contracts. Second, if courts stop them from dismissing fixed-term workers whose terms they renew, they will not renew their fixed-term workers at the end of the contract.[7] Third, if they cannot lay off their employees when times are bad, they will not hire when times are good. Instead, they will force existing workers to handle the increased demand by working longer hours.[8] Fourth, if they cannot readily dismiss their workers, they will subcontract production to smaller firms that can easily show that they have no choice but to dismiss. The pervasive use of subcontracting in Japanese production follows, and many potential employees no longer have the chance to work in big firms with more stable demand. Instead, they turn to small and unstable subcontractors.[9]

4 Changes to workplace rules [10]

The Supreme Court presents the case as involving the validity of amendments to work-place rules: if a firm changes the terms of employment, do the new terms govern incumbent employees? The Court apparently considers it a hard problem, and surveys a range of legal theories. It concludes that the terms bind as long as they are "rational."

The problem is entirely artificial, and indeed self-inflicted. Were the Court willing to recognize the at-will contract for what it is —— a mutually value-enhancing contract that rational parties select in competitive labor markets —— the problem would not exist. Yoshikawa worked at Shuhoku under that at-will contract. He had agreed to no obligation to stay at Shuhoku, and had negotiated no right to stay.

---

[7] On use of "irregular" employees at Japanese firms, see Ramseyer, supra note 3, at ch. 6.

[8] As explained in Case 22.

[9] As explained in Case 20.

▼10 The notion that Japanese firms and employees implicitly contract for "lifetime employment" is part of a larger hypothesis that Japanese firms employ a distinctive "Japanese employment system" and "Japanese governance system." Professor Yoshiro Miwa and I examine these widely held beliefs in a series of publications. On the widely discussed "lifetime employment" contracts, we find that commentators largely confuse misguided judicial and union-demanded requirements for voluntary choice. See generally Yoshiro Miwa & J. Mark Ramseyer, The Fable of the Keiretsu: Urban Legends of the Japanese Economy 159-60 (Chicago: University of Chicago Press, 2006); Yoshiro Miwa & J. Mark Ramseyer, The Myth of the Main Bank: Japan and Comparative Corporate Governance, 27 Law & Social Inquiry 401 (2002); Ramseyer, supra note 3, at ch. 6.

Commentators assert wide-spread cross-shareholding arrangements in Japan, but almost always cite second-hand survey results as evidence for the phenomena. When Prof. Miwa and I examine actual shareholding patterns on a firm-by-firm basis, we find almost no cross-holding. See generally Yoshiro Miwa & J. Mark Ramseyer, Nihon keizai ron no gokai: "Keiretsu" no jubaku kara no kaiho [Misunderstandings about the Japanese Economy: Escaping the Spell of the "Keiretsu"] ch. 3 (Tokyo: Toyo keizai shimpo sha, 2001); Miwa & Ramseyer, Fable, supra, at ch. 2; Yoshiro Miwa & J. Mark Ramseyer, "Keiretsu no kenkyu" no keiretsu no kenkyu [Research on the Keiretsu in "Research on the Keiretsu"], 67-2 Keizaigaku ronshu 36 (2001), 67-3 Keizaigaku ronshu 68 (2001); Yoshiro Miwa & J. Mark Ramseyer, The Fable of the Keiretsu, 11 J. Econ. & Mgmt Strategy 169 (2002).

Modern board composition requirements seem to derive from a failure to take economic theory seriously. See generally Yoshiro Miwa & J. Mark Ramseyer, Keizaigaku no tsukaikata: Jisshoteki Nihon keizai ron nyumon [The Usage of Economics: An Introduction to the Empirical Study of the Japanese Economy] chs. 10-11 (Tokyo: Nihon hyoron sha, 2007); Miwa & Ramseyer, Fable, supra note, at ch. 5; Yoshiro Miwa & J. Mark Ramseyer, 2014 kaisha ho kaisei, "koporeto gabanansu kodo" to "shagai torishimariyaku" [The 2014 Amendments to the Corporate Code, "the Corporate Governance Code," and "Outside Directors], 28 Osaka gakuin daigaku keizai ronshu 15 (2015); Yoshiro Miwa & J. Mark Ramseyer, Who Appoints Them, What Do They Do? Evidence on Outside Directors from Japan, 14 J. Econ. & Mgmt Strategy 299 (2005).

Professor Miwa and I also find that the claims of delegated bank monitoring rest on a paucity of evidence. See generally Miwa & Ramseyer, Nihon keizai ron, supra note 10, at chs. 5-6; Miwa & Ramseyer, Keizaigaku no tsukaikata, supra note, at chs. 7, 12; Yoshiro Miwa & J. Mark Ramseyer, Does Relationship Banking Matter? The Myth of the Japanese Main Bank, 2 J. Empirical Legal Stud. 261 (2005); Yoshiro Miwa & J. Mark Ramseyer, Conflicts of Interest in Japanese Insolvencies: The Problem of Bank Rescues, 6 Theoretical Inquiries in Law 301 (2005); Yoshiro Miwa & J. Mark Ramseyer, Ginko torishimari yaku no zenkan chui gimu to "mein banku" shinwa [The Myth of the "Main Bank" and the Fiduciary Duties of Bank Directors], 1871 Hanrei jiho 3, 1872 Hanrei jiho 9 (2004).

If Shuhoku told him to retire, it violated no contractual right of Yoshi-kawa's. Yoshikawa had no right to stay anyway.

解 説　COMMENT　解雇権濫用法理と就業規則の合理的変更法理

　日本の雇用システムを規定している二大判例法理が，解雇権濫用法理と就業規則の合理的変更法理であり，両者は密接に関連している。解雇権濫用法理は，アメリカのように解雇が自由な雇用システムと比較すると，雇用量の柔軟な調整を制約することとなる。そこで，日本の最高裁は，秋北バス事件大法廷判決で，雇用の量的調整の柔軟性を補完する法理として，労働条件の柔軟な調整を認める法理を生み出した。すなわち，同大法廷判決によって，就業規則の不利益変更は，それが合理的なものである限り，変更に反対する者を含めて事業場の全労働者に対して拘束力を持つというルールが形成された。

　100 人の労働者が雇用されているとしよう。企業が不況時に人件費を 10％カットする必要性に迫られた場合，①労働者の数を 10％減らすために 10 人を解雇する，という方策もあるが，②労働者の解雇は回避して全員の雇用を維持し，彼らの賃金を 10％削減するという方策もある。アメリカでは，労働組合が存在する場合でも，先任権制度（seniority rule）といって，勤続年数の長いものは保護され，勤続年数の最も短い者から解雇するルールが定着している。つまり①の方策がとられ，90 人は賃金カットされずにすむが，10 人は雇用を失う。これに対して，日本では，不況の負担を 10 名が解雇という形で全面的に被り，残りの 90 人が何らの負担も負わないという①の処理より，全員が等しく賃金削減を受け入れて，全員の雇用を守る②の措置の方が公正妥当な解決だと考えられた。このような対応を可能とする法理が，就業規則の合理的変更法理である。

　労働条件の不利益変更は，労働者にとって避けたい事態である。したがって，これに同意しない者も当然出てくる。しかし，統一的な労働条件変更が必要な場合や，全員の雇用を守るために同意しない者を含めて，労働条件を不利益に変更せざるを得ない場合など，個々の労働者の同意がなくとも労働条件変更を成就させるルールが必要となる（さもなくば，変更に同意しない労働者は解雇

して，変更を実施するということになる）。そこで，最高裁は，就業規則の不利益変更が合理的なものである限り，変更に同意していない労働者をも拘束する，というユニークな法理を確立した。これは，合意がなければ契約条件を一方的に変更できないという契約原理を修正するものである。しかし，継続的契約関係においては，将来の契約条件に同意しない場合，契約の解約が可能であるという契約原理が，解雇権濫用法理によって，労働条件の一部の変更に反対するというだけでは労働者を解雇できないとして修正されている。それゆえに，労働条件の統一的変更の必要性はあるが，変更に反対する者の解雇も認められないという状況下では，変更に合理性がある場合という限定を課した上で，契約法理を修正した拘束力を認めることも正当化されるとの学説による理論的支持が表明された（菅野和夫『労働法（初版）』〔弘文堂，1985〕93 頁，荒木尚志『雇用システムと労働条件変更法理』〔有斐閣，2001〕249 頁以下）。その後，この就業規則の合理的変更法理は最高裁で何度も支持されて判例法理として確立することとなる。最高裁は，解雇権濫用法理による雇用量調整の制限（柔軟性の欠如）を補完する労働条件調整の柔軟性を日本の雇用関係に導入する重要なルール定立を行ったと評価できる。

　雇用関係における柔軟性というと雇用量の柔軟な調整，すなわち量的柔軟性（numerical flexibility）のみを指すと考えると，これを制限する解雇規制は不効率をもたらすと考えがちである。これに対して，日本は，雇用関係に量的柔軟性ではなく労働条件調整の柔軟性（いわば質的柔軟性）を導入して，雇用保障（security）と雇用関係の柔軟性（flexibility）の調和を模索したといえる。

　柔軟性を欠いた雇用関係は雇用を取り巻く環境変化に対応できない。欧州諸国は労働者保護に厚い法制度を持っているが，その反面として，労働市場を硬直化させ，高い失業率をもたらしてしまったという反省が生じた。そこで，2000 年代の欧州や OECD では Flexibility と Security の調和を目指すべく，この二つの語を合体した "Flexicurity" という造語が作られ，労働政策のめざすべき方向とされた。ただ，そこで奨励されたデンマーク・モデルの Flexicurity は，経済的解雇規制は緩和し，国家が失業保険と職業訓練という Safety net を提供するというもので，外部市場型 Flexicurity であった。これと比較すると，日本のそれは，内部労働市場（企業内）において Flexibility と Security を調和させようとする内部市場型 Flexicurity であるという点に特色がある。そして，2007

年の労働契約法制定の際に，秋北バス事件判決で確立された就業規則の合理的変更法理は，労働契約法9条，10条として法律上明記されることとなった。

アメリカは極めてFlexibilityに富んだ雇用システムを持っている。随意的雇用（at will employment）により，雇用量の調整も自由である。そして，労働条件変更も極めて柔軟である。解雇が自由であるので，使用者は労働条件を不利益に変更するためには，単に，労働条件を引き下げる提案をし，労働者がこれに同意しなければ，この労働者を適法に解雇できる。解雇されたくない労働者は，不利益変更に合意するしかない。このように解雇が自由なアメリカでは，ラムザイヤー教授が指摘するとおり，労働者が同意しない場合にどのようにして労働条件を変更するかという問題はそもそも生じないし，労働条件変更法理も必要ない。使用者の提示する労働条件では雇われる者がいなければ，使用者は提示労働条件を引き上げざるを得ない。つまりアメリカでは労働条件の妥当性も労働市場が判断する。このように雇用量も労働条件もflexibleに調整できるアメリカの雇用システムは，使用者にとっては効率的なシステムだが，労働者にとってはあまりに不安定でsecurityに欠けることが問題とならないのか，外部労働市場が活発であれば，労働者は転職することによって問題が解消されることになるのか，さらに検討してみることも有益であろう。

なお，本件で問題となった主任以上の者に対する55歳（主任未満は50歳）定年についてのラムザイヤー教授の分析は，解雇制限のために雇用量の調整ができないリスクを回避するために，本来の65歳等の引退年齢よりもずっと早期の定年制が設けられたとするものである。しかし，本件定年制が設けられた1957年当時の平均寿命は63.24歳であったこと，当時日本は高度成長期でむしろ労働力不足が深刻な状況であったこと，それでも生じうる循環的景気変動に対応する雇用量調整のためには，有期契約労働者等の非正規雇用が自由に利用でき，実際に雇用調整要員として位置づけられていたこと，などを考えると，当時の50歳，55歳定年の位置づけについては異なる評価も可能であろう。

また，戦後の混乱期に生じた下山事件・松川事件・三鷹事件については，いまだに真相は不明とされている。松川事件では，一審で起訴された全員が有罪（死刑5人を含む）となったが，最高裁では全員が無罪とされた。今日からは想像しがたい当時の状況について，読者各自が調べてみられるのも良いであろう。

Oshima v. K.K. Dentsu

54 Saihan minshu 1155 (Sup. Ct. Mar. 24, 2000).[1]

電通事件
(最判平成 12 年 3 月 24 日民集 54 巻 3 号 1155 頁)

1 Suicide and overwork

a. MIT   It lies 5 km downstream from Harvard along the Charles River, the finest science, math, and engineering school in the world. Its students have long lived by the motto, "work hard, play hard." And play hard MIT (the Massachusetts Institute of Technology) students do. One night several years ago, they placed a police car atop the domed building at the center of campus. They stole the landmark canon from the rival California Institute of Technology and drove it across the country to MIT. They wired colored lights along the outside of a campus skyscraper, and programed them to play the video game "Tetris."

MIT students also work hard. Indeed, they work ruthlessly hard. Professors assign interminable "problem sets" (students call them "p-sets") every week, and deliberately give problems that most students cannot solve. Where "grade inflation" has shifted the median grade at Harvard College to an A- and the modal (most common) grade to an A,[2] MIT allegedly grades by a ruthlessly classic curve.

---

[1] Affirming 1646 Hanrei jiho 44 (Tokyo High Ct. Sept. 26 1997), affirming 1561 Hanrei jiho 3 (Tokyo D. Ct. Mar. 28, 1996).

275

Administrators warn incoming students during orientation that many will receive Fs. For the next four years, students pray frantically for a B-.

The work pays massive dividends. In 2015, among all U.S. universities, the standard ranking placed MIT first in Math, first in Physics, first in Chemistry, first in Biology, first in Computer Science, and first in Engineering. Professors win prizes —— among the American schools, only Harvard, Columbia, and the University of Chicago (all bigger than MIT) can claim more Nobel prizes. Graduates take their pick of the highest paying, most attractive employers.[3]

But the work extracts a brutal cost. From March 2014 to May 2015, six MIT students and one professor killed themselves.[4] The number probably hides many more who tried to commit suicide, but found themselves rescued by friends. Seven in a year was high, but not egregiously high. MIT has long had one of the highest suicide rates of all American universities.

At MIT as elsewhere, most suicides follow from depression. In turn, depression results in part from a chemical imbalance in the brain that causes unusually low levels of serotonin. Anti-depressant drugs can raise these serotonin levels. Yet low serotonin levels alone do not cause depression. Instead, people with that chemical precondition experience a major depressive episode when they encounter a high-stress "trigger." For an MIT student, that trigger

---

[2] Matthew Q. Clarida & Madeline R. Conway, Harvard Official: A- is Median Grade and A Most Common Grade Across All Three FAS Divisions and SEAS, Harvard Crimson, Dec. 5, 2013.

[3] The U.S. News rankings, available at: http://premium.usnews.com/best-graduate-schools.

[4] Lynn Jolicoeur, After Suicides, MIT Works to Relieve Student Pressure, nprEd, May 2015, at: http://www.npr.org/sections/ed/2015/05/14/406727576/after-suicides-mit-works-to-relieve-student-pressure.

276

might include the tension that comes from leaving home. It might include learning that he is no longer the smartest person in the class. It might follow from a professor's harsh words.

A student who works through the night only makes matters worse. Sleep deprivation aggravates depression, and MIT students routinely work late into the night. Faced with impossibly hard p-sets, they refuse to surrender and go to sleep. In the process, they pile that sleep deprivation and frustration onto their stress, and deepen any depression.

Notwithstanding the brutality, high school graduates fight hard for the chance to compete at the school. In 2015, 18,000 students applied for the 1,500 admission spots at MIT. They could have enjoyed a quiet four years at any one of the other fine schools. Instead, they opted for the chance to compete at MIT.

b. Google Recent U.S. university graduates regularly rank Google their most coveted employer.[5] Every year, more than 2 million apply for a job there, but the firm hires scarcely 1 in every 130.[6] Google pays high salaries, to be sure. It also offers famously lavish perquisites.[7] It supplies gourmet meals prepared by professional chefs, three times a day (for free). It offers unlimited

---

[5] See generally Louis Lavelle, Fifty Most Popular Employers for College Students, Bloomberg Business, May 11, 2012. http://www.bloomberg.com/bw/slideshows/2012-05-11/fifty-most-popular-employers-for-college-students#slide2. Peter Jacobs, College Students Want to Work for These Companies When They Graduate, Business Insider, Mar. 25, 2014, at: http://www.businessinsider.com/students-companies-most-ideal-employers-2014-3. United States of America's Most Attractive Employers, Universum. Available at: http://universumglobal.com/rankings/united-states-of-america/.

[6] Stan Phelps, Cracking Into Google, Forbes. Available at: http://www.forbes.com/sites/stanphelps/2014/08/05/cracking-into-google-the-15-reasons-why-over-2-million-people-apply-each-year/.

snacks. It plans evening parties, complete with alcohol. In some locations, it supplies state-of-the exercise facilities; elsewhere, it subsidizes gym memberships. It offers free massages, manicures, showers, video game consoles, pingpong tables, places to nap.

Google does not offer all this out of charity. The perquisites cost money, and by basic market economics it could have skipped the benefits and paid its employees higher salaries in their place. Instead, it deliberately supplies the perquisites to encourage a nearly obsessive devotion to the firm. As one article put it: [8]

> Google features full showers and locker rooms, enabling googlers to work as hard as they want, potentially for days at a time. A former contractor for Google noted that many of the engineers and sales teams 'are always pushing themselves and each other. I saw a lot of really determined, competitive people there,' to the point that they would stay on campus for several days at a time. Brilliantly, Google has designed all of its offices so its employees can stay at work overnight, without having to worry about a thing —— such as their hunger, health, or hygiene. ... Working at Google is a choice to eat, sleep, and breathe Google.

And although Google pays well, it pays for performance. The employees who do best at Google are those who do indeed devote themselves to the business. They are the employees who "eat, sleep, and breathe Google."

Notwithstanding the commitment it extracts, Google

---

[7] James B. Stewart, Looking for a Lesson in Google's Perks, N.Y. Times, Mar. 15, 2013, at http://www.nytimes.com/2013/03/16/business/at-google-a-place-to-work-and-play.html?_r=0; Kelly Clay, What It's Really Like to Work at Google, Locker Gnome, at Jan. 16, 2012; available at: http://www.lockergnome.com/social/2012/01/16/what-its-really-like-to-work-at-google/.

[8] Clay, supra note 7.

apparently offers a formula many college graduates want. After all, millions applied for the job. Many of these could have enjoyed a quieter job at a less demanding employer. Instead, they fought fervently for the chance to compete at Google.

2 The case

Upon graduating from the law department of Meiji Gakuin University in 1990, Ichiro Oshima took a job with the large advertising firm Dentsu. He worked in the radio division. He worked hard, and early on pleased his supervisors. They found him "keen and positive in his work," the Supreme Court would later observe.[9] Oshima continued to devote his life to the firm, and worked longer and longer hours. By August 1990, he routinely returned home after 1:00 or 2:00 a.m. He began staying at Dentsu overnight.

By July of 1991, Oshima showed signs of clinical depression. As the Supreme Court put it, he was "not lively, pessimistic, pale."[10] He had trouble sleeping. He told his group leader "he was not confident of himself, did not understand what he himself was saying."[11] Finally, in August that year he went into the bathroom and hung himself.

In their capacity as his heirs, Oshima's parents sued Dentsu. During his first year, they calculated, he had worked over 3500 hours. The overwork caused the depression, and the depression had caused the suicide. In letting this happen, Dentsu violated the duty of care it owed its employees. The Tokyo District Court agreed, and the High

---

[9] As posted on the Supreme Court of Japan internet site, www.courts.go.jp. Translation credited to the Sir Ernest Satow Chair of Japanese Law, University of London.

[10] Id.

[11] Id.

Court and Supreme Court affirmed: Dentsu owed Oshima's parents damages for wrongful death.

3　Did Oshima die from overwork?

a. Long hours and suicide　Major depressive episodes typically require two prerequisites: a stressful "trigger," and an underlying chemical imbalance. Dentsu may have created a stressful environment, but stress alone seldom causes depression. Rather, stress leads to depressive episodes only among people with low levels of serotonin.

Nor do many people find long working hours the most stressful employment-related crisis they might face. To the contrary, most instead find unemployment —— zero working hours —— far more stressful. Of the 25,427 Japanese who committed suicide in 2014, 15,163 (60 percent) had no job.[12] Neither do aggregate data show any systematic connection between mean work hours and suicide rates. In **Figure 1**, I couple the shift in suicide rates over time with mean annual working hours. In **Figure 2**, I couple suicide rates by prefecture with mean annual working hours. In neither figure do the curves show any obvious connection. Across time, suicide rates do not correlate with mean working hours. Across Japan, suicide rates do not correlate with mean working hours.

Even among college-age men and women, grueling school competition may not be the most stressful crisis they can face. The suicide rate at MIT may be higher than among its peer universities, but it is not significantly higher than among non-students. Over the last ten years, the rate (per 100,000) at MIT was 10.2; over the last five

---

[12]　Naikaku fu jisatsu taisaku suishinshitsu, Sanko zuhyo [Reference Tables and Graphs], Mar. 12, 2015.

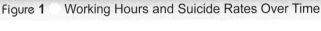

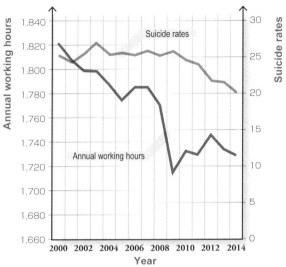

Notes: Suicide rates (per 100,000) on the right axis, from http://www8.cao.go.jp/jisatsutaisaku/toukei/pdf/h26joukyou/zuhyo.pdf. Mean annual working hours on the left axis, from the OECD at https://stats.oecd.org/Index.aspx?DataSetCode=ANHRS.

years, it has been 12.5.[13] Among U.S. college students generally, the suicide rate is about 6.5; among the general population (matched for sex and age), it is 12.6.[14]

b. Labor law and long hours Although Dentsu apparently assigned its workers massive amounts of work, that workload followed directly from Japanese labor law. As explained in **Case20**, Japanese courts refuse to let large employers respond to demand

Oshima v. K.K. Dentsu 電通事件

---

[13] Matt Rocheleau, Suicide Rate at MIT Higher Than National Average, Boston Globe, Mar. 17, 2015, at https://www.bostonglobe.com/metro/2015/03/16/suicide-rate-mit-higher-than-national-average/1aGWr7lRjiEyhoD1WIT78I/story.html.

[14] Allan J. Schwartz, College Student Suicide in the United States: 1990-1991 Through 2003-2004, 54 J. Am. College Health 341 (2006).

281

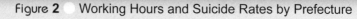

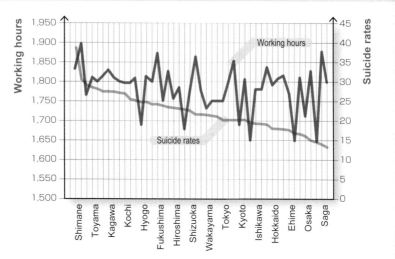

Notes: Suicide rates (per 100,000) on the right axis, from http://www8.cao.go.jp/jisatsutaisaku/toukei/pdf/tsukibetsu_zanteichi.pdf. Mean annual working hours on the left axis, from http://ehime-roudoukyoku.jsite.mhlw.go.jp/library/ehime-roudoukyoku/Library/kantoku/201512794716.pdf

shocks by cutting their labor force indiscriminately.[15] If customers decide to buy less output, a firm cannot freely lay off employees it no longer needs. To be sure, it can (and many firms do) respond in part by hiring "irregular" employees for limited periods of time, and then not renewing the contract.[16] A regular employee, however, a firm can lay off only if the dismissals are what Professor Takashi Araki nicely described as the "last resort."[17]

Firms know that demand both rises and falls. If demand

---

[15] For excellent analyses of this case law, see Ryo Kanbayashi, ed., Kaiko kisei no ho to keizaigaku [The Law & Economics of the Regulation of Dismissals] (Tokyo: Nihon hyoron sha, 2008).

[16] As described at length in J. Mark Ramseyer, Second-Best Justice: The Virtues of Japanese Private Law ch. 6 (Chicago: University of Chicago Press, 2015).

[17] As quoted and discussed in Case 20.

spikes, a firm might want to hire additional staff to respond to the demand. But it knows that demand which rises in February might fall in March. Staff it hires today might be redundant tomorrow. If it could lay off those unnecessary staff tomorrow, it might choose to hire now. Under Japanese labor law, it cannot necessarily do so: large firms face severe limits on their ability to respond to lower demand by reducing their payroll.

Facing restrictions on layoffs during slack demand, Japanese firms respond to high demand in part by increasing hours per worker rather than the number of workers itself.[18] Because they cannot lay off workers when demand falls, they demand longer hours from each worker when demand rises. As Dean Mark West explained:[19]

> Beginning with a series of cases in the 1950s, Japanese courts regulated the employment market to such an extent that it became practically impossible for most businesses, or at least large ones, to fire workers. As a consequence of the inability to dismiss workers legally, large Japanese firms hired a smaller number of workers than were necessary. Large employers rely on the working hours of this undersized cadre of workers ... as a buffer. In bad times, the size of the work force makes dismissal unnecessary. In good times, workers are forced to work long hours.

The problem at Dentsu is not just a problem of firm greed, if it is a problem of greed at all. It is in part a problem that the courts created.

---

[18] I discuss the use of "irregular" contract workers in Japanese firms in Ramseyer, supra note 16, at ch. 6.

[19] Mark D. West, Employment Market Institutions and Japanese Working Hours, Dec. 12, 2003 (SSRN Working Paper 479882), at 3.

c. Foreseeability Although Japanese courts impose a labor law regime that causes firms to demand brutally long hours during peak demand, employees do not usually kill themselves. Dentsu has 22,000 workers. It may work them very hard. Many of them may complain about the hours. But few commit suicide. They skirt suicide for a simple reason: they do not have the serotonin imbalance that transforms stressful triggers into major depressive episodes.

The Supreme Court claimed that Dentsu ignored clear signs of Oshima's trouble, and without that claim its holding becomes legally odd. As Japanese Civil Code professors regularly note, the drafters incorporated into Sec. 416 the well-known *Hadley v. Baxendale*[20] rule, and the courts routinely apply it to tort disputes. Under this rule, a tortfeasor is liable only for those damages that would "ordinarily arise" from the tort, or those that it and the victim could reasonably foresee. Long hours do not "ordinarily" cause suicides.

4 Should courts discourage hard work?

The Supreme Court treats Dentsu's long hours and competitive pressure as straightforwardly undesirable. And indeed, to the extent that the phenomena follow from labor law opinions (see Case**20**), they are phenomena that neither Dentsu nor its employees freely chose. Probably, both would have preferred that Dentsu hire additional staff during peak demand. Because of that case law, however, Dentsu found it hard to do so —— and had little choice but to demand the hours that it did.

Yet sometimes competition, long hours, and the resulting stress can earn striking returns. Smart students do not have to

---

[20] 9 Ex. 341, 156 Eng. Rep. 145 (1854).

attend MIT. They can choose instead from among other top-tier universities that demand much less of them. Those who nevertheless choose MIT choose it because they want to study math, science, and engineering at the highest level. They know that learning at that top level requires excruciatingly hard work. They choose MIT despite that work because they want the knowledge that they know the work will let them acquire.

Smart graduates do not have to work at Google. Other firms offer reasonably close levels of pay. Those who choose Google choose it because of the excitement they enjoy by participating in technological discovery. They do not want a safe and steady job. They want to work at the technological frontier, and Google offers them the chance to do that. They know that producing at the frontier requires them to devote their lives passionately to their work. They choose Google despite the hours because they want to participate in transformative technological discovery.

5 Should firms sort applicants by mental health?

If courts hold firms liable for work-triggered suicides, firms will respond by sorting (even more than they already do) applicants and employees by their susceptibility to depression. A firm can safely demand long hours from the vast majority of its employees. Long hours will trigger major depressive episodes only among those few employees with an underlying serotonin imbalance. Hold the firms liable for their suicides, however, and the firms will respond by trying (more than they already do) to identify those applicants and employees most susceptible to depression.

When firms try to sort people by their susceptibility to depression, several unfortunate results follow. First (and most trivially), firms will waste resources. The person with the best information about his susceptibility to depression is not his employer. It is the employee himself. Employers can only haphazardly and at great cost learn about any chemical imbalances among their employees. Each employee, by contrast, is far more likely to know about his susceptibility to depression. With it, he can (if he wishes) instinctively choose the workplace that lets him best avoid any stress he hates.

Second (and more seriously), once employers identify the job applicants most susceptible to depression, they will try not to hire them. Hold firms liable for employees who commit suicide, in other words, and firms will respond by discriminating against applicants with any trace of mental disability. The logic is simple: to hold a firm liable for a suicide is to raise the costs of hiring people susceptible to clinical depression; to raise the costs of hiring such people is to push firms to avoid hiring them.

In short, if a court holds a firm liable for employees who commit suicide, it increases the firm's incentive to avoid those applicants most prone to mental illness. Faced with the potential liability, firms will try not to hire anyone who has consulted a psychiatrist in the past. They will try not to hire anyone using anti-depressant drugs. They may even try to avoid anyone with a family member who suffered from depression.[21]

Third, if firms discriminate against those applicants most

---

[21] On discrimination against patients who suffer depression, see generally Nikkei medikaru, Feb. 27, 2006, available at: http://medical.nikkeibp.co.jp/inc/all/hotnews/archives/423365.html; Pint Story, Apr. 25, 2015, available at: http://leapsjapan.com/story/%E7%AC%AC%E4%BA%94%E5%9B%9E%E4%BA%94%E6%9C%88%E7%97%85%E3%81%86%E3%81%A4%E7%97%85%E5%BE%8C%E3%81%AE%E5%B0%B1%E8%81%B7%E3%83%BB%E8%BB%A2%E8%81%B7%E6%B4%BB%E5%8B%95%E3%81%9D%E3%81%AE%E2%91%A3%E3%80%8C/; .Shakai sanka ya jushinkikaki ga ubawareru utsubyo kanja heno sabetsu ga jocho [Social Participation and Opportunity for Treatment Stolen, as Discrimination Against Depression Patients Rises], Daimond online, available at: http://diamond.jp/articles/-/32449.

286

susceptible to depression, people with potentially serious depression will avoid medical care. Consider, again, MIT. Faced with high suicide rates, the school offers its students an extraordinarily generous range of high-quality mental-health counseling —— and encourages them to make use of it.[22] At least some troubled students, however, are said to avoid that counseling deliberately. According to student rumor, a student who seeks counseling will be told to withdraw from school for the rest of the semester, to go home, and to recover. When he tries to return to school, however, the school (again, according only to student rumor; this is definitely not the school's position) may deny readmission on the grounds that he has not yet recovered. As some students apparently (and perhaps inaccurately) perceive the situation, if they consult a university psychiatrist about their depression, they will be told to withdraw —— and then potentially never be readmitted. Rather than take that risk, some deeply troubled students apparently avoid obtaining the very health service they so badly require.

After cases like Dentsu, a patient in Japan who consults a physician for mental health care incurs an increased risk. Perhaps a firm will ask him directly about his medical history. Perhaps his neighbors will gossip. Perhaps an estranged girlfriend or wife will leak the information. Whatever the route, if he seeks medical care for depression he increases the risk that a potential employer will learn about his condition. If firms discriminate against applicants with the potential for depression, then —— necessarily —— more people who need the medical care will do without it.

---

[22] Allison Pohle, After a Tough Year of Suicides on Campus, MIT Aims to Improve Mental Health Culture, Boston.com, Sept. 1, 2015, available at: http://www.boston.com/news/education/2015/09/01/after-tough-year-suicides-campus-mit-aims-improve-mental-health-culture/Gv6q0XaqjxpjTmkm2XxapO/story.html.

解説 COMMENT 過労死

Karoshi という言葉は英語辞書にも掲載されるほど国際的に知られるように
なっている。電通事件は，健康かつ明朗快活，素直な性格で責任感が強く完璧
主義だった青年が長時間労働の末にうつ病に罹患し，異常な言動が見られるよ
うになったが，会社は特段の措置をとらずにいたところ，自殺に至ったという
いわゆる「過労自殺」の事件である。本件では，過労自殺が労働災害に当たる
かという問題が争われたのではなく，[1] 使用者が労働者の心身の健康を損なうこ
とがないように注意する義務（安全配慮義務ないし不法行為法上の注意義務）に
違反したとして遺族が会社に損害賠償を請求した。一審は会社の安全配慮義務
違反を認め，約 1 億 2600 万円の損害賠償請求を認めたが，二審は，本人のうつ
病親和的性格や家族の対応等を勘案して，過失相殺により損害額の 3 割を減額
した。しかし，最高裁は，過失相殺を行った点は誤りとして，原審を破棄し差
し戻した（差戻審では 1 億 6800 万円の支払で和解が成立したようである）。

ラムザイヤー教授の議論では労働時間の中央値の推移と自殺率の相関のなさ
が指摘されている。しかし，厚生労働省が医療専門家の議論を踏まえて過労死・
過労自殺と長時間労働の業務関連性について採用している基準は，法定労働時
間を超える法定時間外労働数が発症前 1 ヶ月間に概ね 100 時間を超えた場合，
又は発症前 2 ヶ月ないし 6 ヶ月間に 1 ヶ月当たり概ね 80 時間を超えた場合であ
る。つまり，過労死・過労自殺で問題となる長時間労働とは，法定時間外労働
が月 80 時間とか 100 時間を超える場合（月労働時間が 256 時間とか 276 時間を
超える場合）であるので，労働者全体の労働時間の中央値と自殺の相関関係で
議論することには異論があるかもしれない。

それはともかく，ラムザイヤー教授の議論の特徴は，過労自殺問題もその原
因（の一端）は解雇が制限されていることにあるとする点である。日本では企

---

[1] 過労死・過労自殺問題については，当初の行政の労働災害に当たらないとの判断が裁判所
で取り消され，行政が過労死・過労自殺の認定基準を緩和して，より広く労働災害認定をす
るという展開があった。土田道夫・山川隆一編『労働法の争点』（有斐閣，2014）135 頁［水
島郁子］，137 頁［上田達子］参照。

業は業務量の増加に応じて追加人員を採用すると，業務量が減少した場合に自由に解雇ができない。そこで，追加人員採用は手控え，長時間労働で対応せざるを得ない。つまり解雇制限が長時間労働をもたらしているとされる。確かに，日本では時間外労働が多く，労働投入量を削減する際に，時間外労働数を削減することで対応可能である。この時間外労働数による調整が，不況時にも正規雇用労働者の雇用自体を縮小せずに終身雇用制の維持を可能としてきたことは，しばしば指摘されている。もっとも，雇用量の調整のためには日本では有期契約労働者や派遣労働者等の利用が可能であり，企業もこれら非正規雇用労働者を雇用調整要員として使ってきた。したがって，解雇制限が時間外労働を要請したとするのは，やや過大評価のきらいがある。むしろ，アメリカの公正労働基準法では時間外労働の割増率が50％とされているのに対して，日本の労働基準法では原則として25％（月60時間超の時間外労働には50％）であり，採用コストや仕事をこなせるようにするための教育訓練コスト等も考慮すれば，新規採用よりも割安であることが，長時間労働をもたらすより大きな要因となっている可能性がある。

　ところで，本件で問題となった労働者は，クリエイティビティが重視される一流広告代理店の正規従業員として入社した者である。入社後1年半という仕事を覚える過程での長時間労働は，工場労働のように業務量が増えたから追加要員を雇用して対応するような問題ではあるまい。その意味では，本件労働者は，ラムザイヤー教授が示されたMITの学生やGoogleの従業員と共通する問題に直面していたともいえる。

　ラムザイヤー教授の議論には，個人の自由な選択として，MITやGoogleのような厳しい長時間の勉学・労働に身を置くことを選んだ者に，国家・裁判所が規制をかけるべきではないとの考え方が反映されているようである。精神疾患を発病しやすい，ストレス脆弱性のある者の発症に対して企業に責任を問うことになれば，企業はそうした者の採用を控える行動をとるであろうこと，MITの例では大学の用意した診療プログラムを利用すれば，その後，通常の就学の妨げられかねない（とのうわさがある）ことなどから，精神疾患を発病しやすい者がそもそも受けるべき診療を回避する行動を引き起こしかねないこと等，規制の負の側面が指摘されている。

　ラムザイヤー教授の指摘する問題と共通する問題が，実は，日本でも指摘で

きる。使用者が労働者に対して負う安全配慮義務を高度化すれば，使用者は労働者の健康状態や基礎疾患をより詳細に把握するようになり，発症可能性の高い労働者には時間外労働を命じない，ストレスフルな責任の重い仕事や配置転換などは命じないなどの対応をとることになる可能性がある。ここでは，病気など本人のプライバシーに関する情報を使用者がどこまで取得して良いのかという問題とともに，安全配慮義務の高度化によって，本人の職業キャリア発展にとって重要な機会を奪われかねないという問題が提起されている。

ラムザイヤー教授の議論は，労働者を救済するための規制が，人々の行動に影響し，長期的にはかえって救済対象者にとっても望ましくない事態を生じさせる可能性に気づかせるものである。そういう問題を認識した上で，法は個人の選択に介入を控え，市場の調整に委ねるのが望ましいか，別の法規制のありようで対処する途はないのか（例えばフランスでは，使用者が労働者個人の健康情報を直接取得することを禁止し，中立的専門家である労働医に管理させることとし，労働者の健康・プライバシー保護と企業の必要の調整を試みている）など，深く考察すべき課題が提起されている。

PART 8
経済法

CASE

| 23 | 三井住友銀行事件 |
| 24 | 石油カルテル事件 |

In re K.K. Mitsui Sumitomo Ginko, Fair Trade Commission Recommendation Decision

Kankoku 20, Dec. 26, 2005.

三井住友銀行事件
(公取委勧告審決平成17年12月26日公取委審決集52巻436頁)

1 The case

The Sumitomo Mitsui Bank (known in Japan as the Mitsui Sumitomo Bank) lent money to small firms. Apparently, it often lent the money under adjustable-interest-rate contracts. On these loans, it pegged the rate at a premium over the short-term prime rate. According to the Fair Trade Commission (FTC), it sometimes bundled with the loan an interest-rate swap. Under the terms of these swap contracts, the borrower paid its counterparty a fixed interest rate. In return, it received a payment that fluctuated according to the short-term market rate. It then could forward that amount to Sumitomo Mitsui as interest on its adjustable-rate loan.

Effectively, the swap turned Sumitomo Mitsui's adjustable-rate loan into a fixed-rate loan.[1] Many borrowers —— especially small borrowers —— prefer to borrow at fixed rates. Larger firms may have the resources with which to hedge the risk of interest-rate fluctuations. Small firms often lack those funds. Many banks respond

---

[1] The transaction is nicely explained in Zaimu kaikei no kantan burogu [A Simple Finance Accounting Blog], available at: http://zaimupro.livedoor.biz/archives/50449266.html.

by lending these smaller firms money at fixed interest rates. Sumitomo Mitsui apparently responded by adding an interest-rate swap that transformed its adjustable-rate loan into a fixed rate contract.

Through interest-rate swaps, in short, firms can transform adjustable-rate contracts into fixed-rate contracts —— and vice versa. Under the terms of the swap, one firm will agree to pay its counterparty fixed amounts. The counterparty will agree to pay amounts keyed to the fluctuating market interest rate. The two will set the amounts they pay at levels such that the present value of the payments that the one party makes exactly equals the present value of the other party's payments. As one writer put it: [2]

> A floating to fixed rate swap allows an Issuer with variable rate debt to hedge the interest rate exposure by receiving a variable rate in exchange for paying a fixed rate, thus decreasing the uncertainty of an Issuer's future net debt service payments ....

The FTC declared that Sumitomo Mitsui violated the Antimonopoly Act by bundling swaps with its loans.[3] Never mind that Sumitomo Mitsui could have accomplished the same result by offering borrowers fixed-rate loans. The antitrust statute bans "unfair trade practices" (Sec. 19). At the time of this case, the FTC had listed tied products and services as an unfair practice in an order,[4] and such ties now appear as an unfair practice in the Act itself (Sec. 2 (ix)(v)).

Sumitomo Mitsui dominated the small firms, reasoned the FTC. Those firms wanted loans. The bank would lend them the

---

[2] Douglas Skarr, The Fundamentals of Interest Rate Swaps (Cal. Debt & Investment Advisory Com., Oct. 2004), at 1 (ital. in original removed).

[3] Shiteki dokusen no kinshi oyobi kosei torihiki no kakuho ni kansuru horitsu [Law Regarding the Prohibition of Private Monopoly and the Maintenance of Fair Trade], Law No 54 of 1947.

[4] Fukosei na torihiki hoho [Unfair Trade Practices], Kokuji 15 of 1982.

money only if they also bought an interest-rate swap. In tying the swaps to the loans, the bank engaged in an unfair trade practice.

2 Discussion

a. Introduction On any set of facts, Sumitomo Mitsui did not harm its customers. If the bank lent its funds in a competitive market, it did not harm its customers. If it lent to firms over which it had some monopoly power (as the FTC claimed), it still did not harm them. To understand the logic involved, consider the two possibilities separately: the case where banks and borrowers lend on a competitive market, and the case where the bank has some monopoly power.

b. A competitive market Suppose first that firms borrow on a competitive market. After all, Japan still has over 100 banks, and more if one includes the agricultural and other cooperatives. What is more, 21st century borrowers rarely complain about any credit shortage. Rather, banks fight to attract borrowers. Routinely, bankers complain about insufficient demand. "Anyone working in the financial sector," wrote one economist at the Nomura Research Institute, "is well aware that Japan suffers from an acute shortage of borrowers."[5]

A firm looking to borrow money will search for the best terms available. Suppose it wants (as many small businesses want) a fixed rate loan. It will search for the lowest interest rate. Note that searching for the lowest rate is equivalent, analytically, to searching for the stream of interest payments with the lowest total present val-

---

[5] Richard C. Koo, The Holy Grail of Macroeconomics: Lessons from Japan as Great Recession (Singapore: John Wiley, 2009); see also Mitsui Sumitomo shobun, obieru ginko kai [Banking World Shaking in Wake of Mitsui Sumitomo Disposition], Jcast nyuusu, May 2, 2006, available at: http://www.j-cast.com/2006/05/02001221. html?p=all (banks looking for borrowers).

ue.

The firm will choose from among three types of loan contracts. Bank 1 will lend the money at a fixed rate. Over the life of the loan, it will charge interest payments with a total present value of F_1. Like Sumitomo Mitsui, Bank 2 offers an adjustable-rate loan coupled with an interest-rate swap. Over the life of the loan, it will charge interest payments with a total expected present value of A_2. For the swap contract, it will charge a net price of S_2. Bank 3 will offer the firm an adjustable-rate loan with present-valued interest payments totaling A_3. This bank does not offer a swap contract. To convert the adjustable-rate payments to fixed-rate payments, a firm would need to buy an interest-rate swap on the market at the competitive price of S_c.

In choosing among the three banks, the firm will compare the total present-valued cost of the three proffered contracts: F_1, A_2+S_2, and A_3+S_c. It will then borrow under whatever contract results in the lowest total present-valued payments. If A_2+S_2 is less than F_1, the firm will borrow from Bank 2 rather than Bank 1. It does not care that Bank 2 will force it to buy a swap. It wants to pay the lowest total charges, and if paying the least requires it to buy a swap from Bank 2 it will buy the swap. If $A_3 + S_c$ is less than A_2+S_2 and F_1, the firm will borrow from Bank 3. It will need to buy a swap on the market, but if the total is less than the total it would pay Bank 1 or 2, it will buy a swap on the market.[6]

In this competitive market, Sumitomo Mitsui cannot harm its customers by tying swaps to its loans. It cannot charge borrowers more than they would pay to borrow from a rival bank offering a fixed-rate loan —— because borrowers would switch to the rival bank.

---

[6] And of course those firms that prefer an adjusted-rate loan will simply borrow from Bank 3.

Neither can it charge more than borrowers would pay if they borrowed from a rival bank at an adjustable rate and bought a swap on the competitive market.

In fact, Sumitomo Mitsui does not seem to have tried to earn extra profits through the swaps anyway. One observer, for example, noted that the bank's total costs "appeared not to be very different" from the total costs other banks charged.[7] And when the government told Sumitomo Mitsui to survey its customers about its tying practice, few complained. The bank wrote to the 18,162 firms with whom it had the swap contracts, and successfully obtained information on 2,200. Only 68 of the 2,200 contracts showed any possibility that Sumitomo Mitsui might have abused any dominant position. Only 17 showed serious evidence that it actually did.[8]

c. Monopoly power Now suppose, as the FTC posited, that Sumitomo Mitsui exercises some power over its small borrowers. These borrowers cannot, argued the FTC, cheaply switch to another lender. Over them, the bank has monopoly power.

A rational monopolist will sell to its customers at its profit-maximizing price. Should it sell at a lower price, the cheaper margin on all its sales will cause it to earn lower revenue. Should it sell at a higher price, the fall in the number of customers will cause it similarly to earn less.

---

[7] See Zaimu, supra note 1.

[8] Kinri suwapu hanbaini kakaru yuetsuteki chii no ranyo ni tsuite no chosa hokokushho [Survey Report on the Abuse of Dominant Potion Regarding the Sale of Interest-Rate Swaps], Apr. 27, 2006, available at: http://www.smbc.co.jp/news/html/j200048/j200048_02.html ; see also Toru Kishida, Fushigi no rensa wo yobu "Nishikawa zen todori he no shobun" ["Disposition of the former CEO Nishikawa," Calling Linked Mysteries], May 17, 2006, available at: http://kishida.biz/column/2006/20060516.html.

The latter point is crucial: a monopolist's profit-maximizing price is higher than the price that would prevail in a competitive market, but not infinitely high. As the monopolist raises its price, consumers will buy less of its product or service. As Sumitomo Mitsui raises the price of its loans, some firms will abandon the projects they hoped to undertake with the money they borrowed. Some firms will turn to other sources (e.g., family members, trade partners, friends) for the money. And some firms will pay the extra costs involved in switching to other banks and borrow the money there. In short, even if a bank has some monopoly power, it does not maximize profits by raising its prices to infinity. Instead, it does best by raising its prices to exactly the price beyond which the profits on the smaller amount of money loaned offset the increase in the additional revenue earned per loan.

Now consider three strategies that a bank with monopoly power might take. First, it could lend at a fixed rate. Let the present value of all interest payments on the fixed-rate loan equal F_m. Second, it could (as Sumitomo Mitsui did) tie an adjustable rate loan to a swap. Let the present value of the adjustable rate payments on the tied loan equal A_t, and the net cost of the tied swap equal S_t. Last, it could lend at an adjustable rate, and let borrowers who want fixed rate loans buy interest-rate swaps on the competitive market. Let the present value of the adjustable rate payments equal A_m, and the competitive net price of a swap equal S_c.

In deciding whether to borrow from the bank, a firm will (as in a competitive market setting) consider the total charges involved: F_m in the case of the first strategy, A_t+S_t in the second, and A_m+S_c in the third. Necessarily, the firm will care only about the total price it pays. It will choose the fixed-rate loan over the adjustable-swap package if the former is cheaper than the latter; it will choose the adjustable-swap package over the fixed-rate loan if the package is cheaper than the fixed-rate loan. And in pricing the adjustable-swap package, it will not care whether the bank couples a cheap loan with an expensive swap or an expensive loan with a cheap swap. Necessarily, it will care only about the total.

In turn, the bank will gauge the relative profitability of the different strategies by totaling the present-valued revenue it would receive. In the first and third strategies, it would earn revenue of F_m and A_m. In the second, it would earn $A_t + S_t$. Again, note that a bank would not care whether it it earns a large profit on its loan and a small profit on its swap, or a small profit on its loan and a large one on its swap. Given that it sells the two as a package in strategy 2, it would care only about the total.

Crucially, even a bank with monopoly power cannot increase its monopoly returns by bundling swaps with its loans. Recall that a monopolist will price its products or services at a discrete, profit-maximizing price. Should it raise prices further, consumers will reduce the quantity they buy —— and reduce it by amounts that more than offset the higher per-item revenue the monopolist receives. First, suppose a bank lends at a fixed interest rate. If it sets that interest rate at the profit-maximizing level, it will not earn higher profits by raising the rate further. By hypothesis, it already lends at the profit-maximizing level.

Second, suppose a bank lends at an adjustable interest rate. If it prices its adjustable rate at the profit-maximizing level, it cannot earn additional profit by raising the interest rate further. Neither can it earn additional monopoly profits by bundling a swap. Its customers care about the total charge —— the sum of the interest rate and any swap price. The bank already prices its adjustable-rate loan at the profit-maximizing level. If it tried to charge more than the competitive price S_c for its swap, it would effectively raise the total price on its bundled package beyond that profit-maximizing level —— and lower profits.[9]

Economists often refer to the principle by the aphorism: "there's only one monopoly rent." If a firm earns a monopoly return on one product, it cannot increase those monopoly returns by tying a second product to the first. After all, it can earn its entire monopoly return on the first. If it tries to earn any extra monopoly return on the tied second product, it will simply raise the price of the total tied bundle beyond the profit —— maximizing point —— and the fall in consumer demand will lower total revenue.

Nobel laureate George Stigler explained this logic in the context of "block-booking" at movie theaters. Traditionally, U.S. studios bundled popular movies with less popular ones. When the government attacked the practice as as an antitrust violation, Stigler explained why it was wrong. Suppose, he suggested, the studios had some monopoly power with respect to the popular film. Suppose further that they bundled the unpopular films with the popular ones. Whatever their reason for doing this, it was not to increase their monopoly returns.[10]

> Consider the following simple example. One film, [Supreme Court] Justice Goldberg cited *Gone with the Wind*, is worth $10,000 to the buyer, while a second film, the Justice cited *Getting Gertie's Garter*, is worthless to him. The seller

---

[9] The FTC makes much of the cases where Sumitomo Mitsui sold swaps for periods longer than the term of the loan —— what it calls "over-hedging." This is of course equivalent simply to charging a higher price for the swap.

[10] George J. Stigler, United States v. Loew's Inc.: A Note on Block-Booking, 1963 Sup. Ct. Rev. 152, 182-83 (1963). For various complications, exceptions, and extensions, see generally Dennis W. Carlton & Michael Waldman, Upgrades, Switching Costs and the Leverage Theory of Tying, 122 Econ. J. 675 (2012); Michael D. Whinston, Tying, Foreclosure, and Exclusion, 80 Am. Econ. Rev. 837 (1990); Dennis W. Carlton & Michael D. Waldman, Robert Bork's Contributions to Antitrust Perspectives on Tying Behavior, 57 J.L. & Econ. S121 (2014), and the literature cited in these articles.

CASE

299

could sell the one for $10,000, and throw away the second, for no matter what its cost, bygones are forever bygones. Instead the seller compels the buyer to take both. But surely he can obtain no more than $10,000, since by hypothesis this is the value of both films to the buyer.[11] Why not, in short, use his monopoly power directly on the desirable film? It seems no more sensible, on this logic, to block-book the two films than it would be to compel the exhibitor to buy *Gone with the Wind* and seven Ouija boards, again for $10,000.

Sumitomo Mitsui could have lent money under fixed interest-rate contracts. For reasons never explained, it preferred to bundle adjustable-rate loans with swaps. Borrowers did not care. After all, the adjustable-loan-swap bundle yielded the same result as the fixed-rate loans. Sumitomo Mitsui preferred the bundle to the fixed rate loan. Whatever the reason,[12] it did not thereby increase its monopoly returns. Neither did it impose on its customers additional costs.

---

[11] This is of course exactly the situation of those firms that prefer to borrow under an adjustable-rate contract. For them, the swap contract (even at competitive market prices) is equivalent to a second movie they do not want.

[12] The FTC suggests that accounting rules may have triggered the practice. The Commission does not say, but regulatory rules may have driven this concern with accounting profitability.

Sumitomo Mitsui may also have believed that its smaller borrowers could not handle the interest-rate risk created by adjustable-rate loans. Even where the firms claimed to prefer an adjustable-rate loan, the bank may have worried that the adjustable rates increased the risk that the borrower would default to a level that it (as creditor) was unwilling to take.

解説　優越的地位

　日本独禁法の優越的地位濫用規制はアメリカにはない考え方であるとされているが，その背景には幾重もの要素があり，それを解きほぐしながら彼我の異同を理解する必要がある。

　まず，日本法にいう「優越的地位」の基準を広く取った場合には，取引先が行為者と取引することが必須でなく行為者が他の事業者と依然として競争を行っている場合にも「優越的地位」が存在することになり，そのような規制に対する違和感は大きくなる。平成 21 年改正によって優越的地位濫用に課徴金を導入したあと初めて法的判断を示したトイザらス事件の公正取引委員会審決（平成 27 年 6 月 4 日）における「優越的地位」の基準は，その例であろう。それに対し本件（三井住友銀行事件）では，他の銀行にスイッチできない中小企業のみを取引先として観念しているので，三井住友銀行には「monopoly power」があることになり，アメリカから見た違和感の原因は別のところに求められることになる。

　次に，「中小企業のうち三井住友銀行に囲い込まれたものだけを対象とする融資の市場」というサブマーケットを，「中小企業一般に対する融資の市場」という大きな市場とは別に観念するという発想それ自体に馴染めない論者が多い。「中小企業一般に対する融資の市場」においてさほど強いわけではない三井住友銀行が違反者になることを「絶対的優越がなくとも優越的地位は認定される」などと表現する例は根強く存在する。しかしこれは，そのような論者の論理性の問題であり，そのような文献しか参照しない外国論者の姿勢の問題である。「解説」は，公正取引委員会の認定における三井住友銀行の立場を「monopoly power」と表現しているように，さすがにこの水準は軽々とクリアしている。

　最後に，サブマーケットであるか大きな市場であるかは別として（そのような区別をすること自体が論理性のなさを示しているのであるが），とにかく市場において強い立場に立っている（「monopoly power」がある）者による取引先に対する濫用行為を問題とすることそれ自体に対する違和感が，アメリカには強く存在する。市場における強者による取引先に対する濫用行為は，EU 競争法においても「搾取型濫用（exploitative abuse）」として EU 機能条約（TFEU）102

条違反行為の一つのカテゴリーとなっており，このような EU 競争法の搾取型濫用規制は，日本独禁法の優越的地位濫用規制と同様のものであるといえる（白石忠志「支配的地位と優越的地位」日本経済法学会年報 35 号）。そのようなものは競争法（独禁法）の問題ではないとするアメリカ的な考え方を明確に示しているという意味で，ラムザイヤー教授の「解説」は貴重な資料である。そこにはまず，暗黙のうちに，独占者が独占利潤（利潤最大化価格による利潤）を得るのは当然に許される，という前提があり，そのうえで，独占者が不要なものを抱き合わせて売っても独占者が得る独占利潤の量に変化はないのであるから問題とするに値しない，ということになる。

EU 競争法においても，1990 年代から 2000 年代にかけては，アメリカ法の影響を強く受け，搾取型濫用が正面から議論されることは少なかった。しかし 2010 年代に入って，ロシアのエネルギー企業 Gazprom による過剰高価格設定（excessive pricing）を問題とするなど，搾取型濫用が脚光を浴びている。アメリカにおいても，特許権を自ら実施せず権利行使だけをする PAE（patent assertion entity）の問題が盛んに重視されているところ，権利行使のターゲットとなる事業者と PAE とは競争関係にないため，これを競争政策的に問題とするというのであれば，実質上，アメリカ法も搾取型濫用・優越的地位濫用の考え方に一歩踏み込まざるを得ない。EU 競争法や日本独禁法のような立場が世界の多くの国の競争法で採用され，この問題は競争法の問題ではないとする主要国は競争法の母国アメリカなど僅かである。反トラスト法（antitrust law）でなく競争法（competition law）が世界の共通語となってしまった現代において，アメリカ法がどのような展開を見せるのかが，むしろ注目される。

CASE 24

Kuni v. Idemitsu kosan, and Kuni v. Sekiyu renmei

33 koukeishu 511, and 33 koukeishu 359
(Tokyo High Ct. Sept. 26, 1980). [1]

石油カルテル事件
(東京高判昭和 55 年 9 月 26 日高刑集 33 巻 5 号 511 頁, 高刑集 33 巻 5 号 359 頁)

1 The case [2]

In 1973, a coalition of Arab nations chose Yom Kippur, the holiest of the Jewish holidays, to launch an invasion. The Israel Defense Force fought back and drove deep into Egrypt and Syria. Faced with the humiliating Arab defeat, OPEC (joined by Egypt, Syria, and Tunisia) declared a boycott of all countries that had supported Israel. That included Japan.

Japan depended heavily on Arab oil. It produced virtually none domestically, and most of the oil it bought it imported from the Mideast. With those imports unavailable, it spun into recession. Where GDP grew 10.3 percent in 1970 and 8.4 percent in 1972, by

---

[1] Kuni v. Idemitsu kosan, 985 Hanrei jiho 3 (Tokyo High Ct. Sept. 26, 1980), transl'd in J. Mark Ramseyer, The Oil Cartel Criminal Cases: Translations and Postscript, 15 L. Japan 57 (1982), aff'd in part and rev'd in part, 1108 Hanrei jiho 3 (Sup. Ct. Feb. 24, 1984); Kuni v. Sekiyu renmei, 983 Hanrei jiho 22 (Tokyo High Ct. Sept. 26, 1980), transl'd in Ramseyer, supra.

[2] See generally J. Mark Ramseyer, Japanese Antitrust Enforcement after the Oil Embargo, 31 Am. J. Comp. L. 395 (1983); J. Mark Ramseyer, The Costs of the Consensual Myth: Antitrust Enforcement and Institutional Barriers to Litigation in Japan, 94 Yale L.J. 604 (1985); Note (Ramseyer), Trustbusting in Japan: Cartels and Government-Business Cooperation, 94 Harv. L. Rev. 1064 (1981).

1974 it fell 1.2 percent. Manufacturing production fell 21.4 percent.[3]

In the ensuing chaos, Japanese petroleum refining companies agreed to slash production and boost prices. They competed with each other to buy raw pretroleum from the Mideast, and they competed with each other to sell their refined products. They hoped to mitigate the damage caused by the embargo by allocating production quotas among each other.

Yet the allocation presented a problem. The firms could not just agree to production cuts. The antitrust statute bans such cartels,[4] for good reason. Firms always have an incentive to negotiate them, because if successful the cartels let them charge more than the market price and pocket the monopoly rent. The statute bans them, because they generate welfare losses attributable to the lower consumption caused by the higher prices.

To gain legal cover and enforce compliance on each other, the firms negotiated their agreement under the aegis of the Ministry of International Trade & Industry (MITI). They asked MITI to use "administrative guidance" to enforce its terms. MITI agreed.

The Fair Trade Commission (FTC) would have none of it. Charged with enforcing the antitrust statute,[5] the FTC saw the agreement as a straightforwardly criminal cartel. It raided the offices of the oil firms.[6] And by February 1974, it launched criminal prosecutions against the refining firms, their executives, and the industry

---

[3] J. Mark Ramseyer, Second - Best Justice: The Virtues of Japanese Private Law ch. 6 (Chicago: University of Chicago Press, 2015).

[4] Shiteki dokusen no kinshi oyobi kosei torihiki no kakuho ni kansuru horitsu [Law Concerning the Prohibition of Private Monopolies and the Maintenance of Fair Trade], Law No. 54 of 1947, at Secs. 3 (cartels by firms), 8 (cartels by trade associations).

[5] Antimonopoly Act, supra note 4.

[6] Ramseyer, Japanese Antitrust, supra note 2, at 398.

trade association."▼7 In response, the defendants invoked their legal cover: they were merely complying with MITI instructions. MITI's involvement, they argued, absolved them of criminal responsibility.

In 1980, the trial court acquitted the trade association, but convicted twelve oil companies and fourteen of their top executives of criminal antitrust violations. Four years later, the case hit the Supreme Court. The Court acquitted two of the firms and one of the executives, but affirmed all other convictions.

2 The context

Several firms colluded to cut production and fix prices. They asked for the government's blessing, but the agency charged with enforcing the antitrust law refused to defer. It filed criminal charges, and the courts convicted.

Such is the gist of this case, and at that level it is simple and straightforward. To understand the turmoil it caused, consider the context. Politically, the public found the prosecution enormously popular. When the FTC filed its charges, people cheered —— literally. As the agency announced its indictments, protestors from the "Housewives Federation" shouted "banzai."▼8

Intellectually, many in the chattering classes had not yet accepted the notion that standard price theory applied in Japan. Senior MITI bureaucrat Naohiro Amaya attacked the trial court decision with an article in *Bungei Shunju* that celebrated the cartel as a reflection of the primordial "ethic of harmony" (*wa no rinri*) behind Japanese village society.▼9 As noted in **Case 6**, Harvard and Hitotsubashi economists Henry Rosovsky and Kazushi Ohkawa could still describe

---

▼7 Antimonopoly Act, supra note 4, at Sec. 89(a).
▼8 Ramseyer, Costs, supra note 2, at 619 n. 86.

Japan as "the only capitalist country in the world in which the Government decides how many firms should be in a given industry, and then sets about to arrange the desired number." [10] And —— again as noted in Case 6 —— even future Nobel laureate Paul Krugman could dismiss Japan as "a fuzzy kind of society" where firms behaved out of "habits of deference to central authority." [11]

Legally, the defendants argued that MITI's involvement forestalled a conviction. Section 35 of the Criminal Code precluded punishment for conduct "pursuant to law or in the course of proper activities." [12] MITI's involvement rendered the cartel "pursuant to law," argued the defendants, or at least a "proper" activity. The court disagreed. It was illegal for firms to fix prices, it was illegal for government bureaucrats to tell firms to fix prices —— and MITI only said what it said under pressure from the industry anyway.

In turn, Section 38 of the Criminal Code precluded punishment where a defendant lacked "criminal intent." The defendants argued that MITI's involvement at least vitiated that intent. On this, the court drew a line among the defendants. Apparently because of differences in the extent to which the defendants had pressured MITI to enforce the cartel, the court convicted the firms and their executives, but acquitted the industry trade asociation.

---

[9] Naohiro Amaya, Wa no rinri to Dokkinho no ronri [The Ethics of Harmony and the Logic of the Antimonopoly Act], 58 Bungei shunju, Dec. 1980, at 176.

[10] Kazushi Ohkawa (Hitotsubashi) & Henry Rosovsky (Harvard), Japanese Economic Growth: Trend Acceleration in the Twentieth Century 223 (Stanford: Stanford University Press, 1973).

[11] Paul Krugman, The Age of Diminishing Expectations: U.S. Economic Policy in the 1990s, at 139-140 (3d ed., 1997).

[12] Keiho [Criminal Code], Law No. 45 of 1911, Sec. 35.

3 Government compulsion

a. The prisoners' dilemma The firms wanted MITI to enforce the terms of their cartel. With any such cartel, members face a prisoners' dilemma. They do best collectively if they all cooperate (and abide by its terms), but each individually does best if it cheats on the cartel (and discounts prices) while the others abide by the cartel terms. If the members could force each other to follow those terms, they could maximize their collective welfare. But if they cannot enforce those terms, they each face an incentive privately to cheat on the cartel. They all do best collectively if they follow the cartel's terms; they each do best individually by cheating on the cartel; they all cheat, and the cartel disintegrates.[13]

The oil firms wanted MITI to prevent this disintegration by enforcing the cartel. Under the terms of the antitrust statute, they could have organized a "recession cartel."[14] By those terms, however, they could not bind each other.[15] They needed a way to force each other to comply —— and eliminate the corrosive logic of the prisoners' dilemma. That enforcement the recession cartel could not offer.

Under the terms of the Petroleum Industry Act, MITI did have some power over the industry. It had the power to propose prices and quantity restraints.[16] Again, however, it could not dictate compliance. The Act did not give it power to decree terms that bound.[17]

---

[13] The observation derives from the classic article, George J. Stigler, A Theory of Oligopoly, 72 J. Pol. Econ. 44 (1964).

[14] Antimonopoly Act, supra note 4.

[15] Yoshiro Miwa & J. Mark Ramseyer, Capitalist Politicians, Socialist Bureaucrats? Legends of Government Planning from Japan, Antitrust Bull., Fall 2003, at 595, 615.

[16] Sekiyu gyo ho [Petroleum Industry Act], Law No. 128 of 1962, Secs. 10, 15.

Under the law in effect at the time, MITI also had the power to allocate foreign exchange. After all, the legislature did not deregulate foreign exchange market until the 1980s. Already in 1969, however, the Tokyo District Court had held that MITI could not use its control over this allocation to force firms to comply on unrelated matters.[18] It thus could not enforce an oil cartel through foreign exchange. It could not, as the Japanese aphorism put it, take Edo's revenge in Nagasaki.

b. **Administrative guidance** (see Musashino case) Nonetheless, the firms went to MITI and asked it to enforce the terms of its cartel anyay. Firms had asked this of the ministry through the 1960s —— albeit always without success. The steel industry had asked it to enforce its cartel, for example, and in 1965 MITI tried to do just that with Sumitomo Metals. Sumitomo refused to comply with the terms of the industry cartel, and insisted on producing more than its allocated amount. MITI ordered it to comply, but Sumitomo refused. It threatened to sue, and MITI acquiesced.[19] In 1966, MITI tried to

---

[17] Despite the conventional wisdom to the contrary, MITI and the Ministry of Finance did not have the ability to allocate loans on a preferential basis. See generally Yoshiro Miwa & J. Mark Ramseyer, Directed Credit? The Loan Market in High-Growth Japan, 13 J. Econ. & Mgmt. Strategy 171 (2004); Yoshiro Miwa & J. Mark Ramseyer, Nihon no keizai seisaku to seisaku kenkyu [Japanese Economic Policy and Policy Research], 52 Keizai kenkyu 193 (2001). Neither was the Ministry of Finance able to use tax subsidies in a way that altered fundamental economic choices. See generally Yoshiro Miwa & J. Mark Ramseyer, The Legislative Dynamic: Evidence from the Deregulation of Financial Services in Japan, in Dan Foote, ed., Law in Japan: A Turning Point 153 (Seattle: University of Washington Press, 2007).

[18] 1969 nen Hokkyo jokai Nihon kogyo tenran kai v. Japan, 560 Hanrei jiho 6 (Tokyo D. Ct. July 8, 1969).

[19] Miwa & Ramseyer, supra note 15, at 598, 608-20; Yoshiro Miwa & J. Mark Ramseyer, Sangyo seisaku ron no gokai: kodo seicho no shinjutsu [Misunderstandings about Industrial Policy: The Truth about High Grow] (Tokyo: Toyo keizai shimpo sha, 2002).

enforce the terms of a petroleum industry cartel on Idemitsu kosan. Again, Idemitsu refused to comply with the industry cartel, and insisted on producing more than its allowed share. MITI once more pleaded with Idemitsu to comply, Idemitsu refused, and MITI deferred.[20]

In the wake of the Arab oil embargo, the petroleum firms tried to enlist MITI in their cartel anyway. Faced with an industry that wanted a cartel, but with no legal power to order one, MITI turned to "administrative guidance." Unfortunately for MITI and the industry, the legal basis for this practice would start to disintegrate very soon.

The litigation began in suburban Tokyo.[21] As the bed-room communities ringing Tokyo grew, suburban governments tried to force developers to contribute to the local infrastructure. As detailed more fully in **Case6**, the governments tried to require the developers to help pay for the community facilities that their apartments and condominia necessitated. Unfortunately, the governmnts had no statutory basis for the practice. Faced with that legal powerlessness, they simply ordered the developers to comply —— they used "administrative guidance."

The developers refused. One non-compliant developer sued a local government in 1975. The government had refused to process his application unless he complied with its "administrative guidance," he explained. By 1985, the Supreme Court would find in his favor.[22] Indeed, by 1978 the Tokyo prosecutor's office initiated criminal prosecution of the Musashino mayor for using administrative guidance against uncooperative developers. The Tokyo District Court convicted the

---

[20] Miwa & Ramseyer, supra note 15, at 619-20; Miwa & Ramseyer, supra note 19.

[21] See generally J. Mark Ramseyer, Rethinking Administrative Guidance, in Finance, Development and Competition in Japan: Essays in Honor of Hugh Patrick 199 (Masahiko Aoki & Gary Saxonhouse, eds., Oxford: Oxford University Press, 2000).

[22] Tokyo v. G.G. Nakaya honten, 39 minshu 989 (Sup. Ct. July 16, 1985).

mayor in 1984,[23] and the Supreme Court affirmed the decision.[24] Administrative guidance was not just illegal. It was a crime.

＊　　＊　　＊

The petroleum refining firms wanted to avoid criminal antitrust sanctions by enlisting MITI. But the terms they wanted to enforce were the terms of a cartel. Like all cartels, this one benefited the industry incumbent firms. They could not transform the illegal agreement into a legal practice by contacting MITI. They could not avoid criminal intent by contacting MITI. And they could not even enforce the terms of the cartel on each other through MITI.

解 説　COMMENT　行政指導と独禁法

本件は，事業所管官庁による行政指導がある場合に独禁法がどのように適用されるのかに関する古典的な著名事例である。

石油連盟が被告人となっている事件は，石油連盟の会員である石油精製会社らの原油処理量を石油連盟が調整した行為に関するもの（いわゆる生産調整事件）である。出光興産等が被告人となっている事件は，出光興産等の石油元売会社が，石油製品の価格を協定した行為に関するもの（いわゆる価格協定事件）であり，この「価格の会合」には「石連事務局推薦の営業委員及び同局職員は出席せず」と認定されている（高刑 33 巻 5 号 543 頁）。両判決は，同じ 5 人の裁判官によるものである。被告人が異なる別々の裁判手続であるから厳密に同じとはいえないものの，相当程度に共通した事実認識・法解釈のもとでのものであると受け止めることができる。当時は，独禁法違反の刑事事件は，東京高裁を第 1 審とし，5 人の裁判官によって審理された（平成 17 年改正前の独禁 85

---

[23] Kuni v. Goto, 1114 Hanrei jiho 10 (Tokyo D. Ct. Hachioji Branch Off. Feb. 24, 1984).

[24] Kuni v. Goto, 1328 Hanrei Jiho 16 (Sup. Ct. Nov. 7, 1989).

310

条, 87条)。生産調整事件の東京高裁判決がそのまま確定したのに対し, 価格協定事件は, その後, 著名な最高裁判決となっているが（最判昭和59・2・24刑集38巻4号1287頁）, 行政指導に関する最高裁判決の判示は東京高裁判決と似通っているので, 同じ日の2件の東京高裁判決を並べるのは一つのわかりやすい比較の仕方である。

　生産調整事件は無罪, 価格協定事件は有罪, と明確に結論が分かれたわけであるが, 重要なのは理由付けである。いずれの判決も, 簡単にいうと, 一般論として, 独禁法の究極目的等に反していない共同行為を促す行政指導に従った共同行為は, 独禁法違反ではなく, あるいは, 刑法35条によって違法性が阻却されることを前提としている。そうしたところ, 生産調整事件では, それを超えた行政指導が通商産業省（当時）によって行われており, 石油連盟はそれに従った, と認定された。価格協定事件では, 通産省の行政指導は独禁法違反ではないような共同行為を促すのみであったが石油元売会社がそれを超えた共同行為をした, と認定された。その結果, 生産調整事件では, 石油連盟の行為は独禁法違反であり刑事法上の違法性があるが通産省の行政指導に裏付けられていたのであるから違法性の意識がなく責任が阻却されるとされ（刑38条）, 価格協定事件では, 石油元売会社の行為は独禁法違反であり刑事法上の違法性があって責任阻却の問題もない, とされた。ラムザイヤー教授の解説では, この違いの原因を「Apparently because of differences in the extent to which the defendants had pressured MITI to enforce the cartel」と表現している。

　本件がたまたま刑事事件であったために, 「行政指導と独禁法」の議論は刑事法の言葉が入り交じりながら展開される歴史的運命のもとにあったのであるが, 当然のことながら, 刑法総論が適用されない公正取引委員会の命令事件などにおいても, 「行政指導と独禁法」は問題となり得る。そこでは, 以下の点に注意する必要があろう（白石忠志「行政指導と独占禁止法」髙木光=宇賀克也編『行政法の争点』〔有斐閣, 2014〕）。

　まず, 行政指導が, 独禁法の究極目的等に反していない行為を促すにとどまっていた場合には, 行政指導に従った行為が端的に独禁法に違反するか否かという議論をすることになる。

　他方, それを超えた行政指導が行われており, そのような行政指導に従った行為が問題となった場合には, かりに刑事法上の責任が阻却されるべきである

としても，独禁法違反であることには変わりがない（生産調整事件の東京高裁判決もそのような論理となっている）。そうしたところ，本件などをきっかけとして，昭和52年改正により，日本の独禁法には課徴金制度が導入された。課徴金は，責任が阻却されるような事案でも課されるというのが条文上の建前である。もっとも，課徴金にそぐわない事案でも課徴金を課さざるを得ない公正取引委員会としては，苦慮せざるを得ない。

あとがき

　本書執筆の過程において，私達日本人専門家は，それぞれの専攻する分野の重要判例を選び，それらについての日本法の観点からのコメントを日本語で書いた。しかし，判例に関する英語での分析・解説に関しては，すべて，ラムザイヤー教授ご自身のお考えが述べられており，私達日本人専門家の考えは含まれていない。

　むしろ，本書ができていく中で，私達日本人専門家は，私達がそれぞれの分野における重要判例として選んだものについて，ラムザイヤー教授により，一体どのような分析・解説がなされるかを大いに楽しみに待っていた。その結果，ラムザイヤー教授と私達の間の考え方の差異にびっくりした場合も少なくない。

　以上のような次第であるために，判例を選択した日本人専門家の一人として，誤解を避けるために，ここで再度，以下の点を確認しておきたい。

- 本書における英文の分析・解説の内容がアメリカの研究者の一般的な考え方というわけでは決してなく，あくまでもラムザイヤー教授個人のお考えであること。
- 本書における英語の分析・解説について，私達日本人専門家の考えは反映されておらず，もっぱらラムザイヤー教授のお考えが述べられていること
- 個人のブログやウェブサイト等は，通常の学術論文等においては引用されることはあまりないが，本書では「議論のきっかけ」として引用されていること。

　このような点をご理解の上，読者の皆様には，各法分野における日本の重要判例について，ラムザイヤー教授が果たしてどのように分析するかという点をお読みになられて，同じ判例でも実に様々なとらえ方があるという点を，実感していただければ幸いである。

2019年9月

中 里　実

アメリカから見た日本法
An American Perspective on Japanese Law

2019 年 10 月 10 日　初版第 1 刷発行

著　者	J．マーク・ラムザイヤー 長　谷　部　恭　男 宇　賀　　克　也 中　里　　　実 川　出　敏　裕 大　村　敦　志 松　下　淳　一 神　田　秀　樹 荒　木　尚　志 白　石　　忠　志
発 行 者	江　草　貞　治
発 行 所	株式会社　有　斐　閣

郵便番号101-0051
東京都千代田区神田神保町 2-17
電話(03) 3264-1314〔編集〕
　　(03) 3265-6811〔営業〕
http://www.yuhikaku.co.jp/

組版・田中あゆみ
印刷・大日本法令印刷株式会社／製本・大口製本印刷株式会社
©2019, J. M. Ramseyer, Y. Hasebe, K. Uga, M. Nakazato, T. Kawaide, A. Omura,
J. Matsushita, H. Kanda, T. Araki, T. Shiraishi. Printed in Japan
落丁・乱丁本はお取替えいたします。
★定価はカバーに表示してあります。

ISBN 978-4-641-12591-9

[JCOPY] 本書の無断複写(コピー)は、著作権法上での例外を除き、禁じられています。複写される場合は、そのつど事前に(一社)出版者著作権管理機構(電話03-5244-5088, FAX03-5244-5089, e-mail:info@jcopy.or.jp)の許諾を得てください。

本書のコピー，スキャン，デジタル化等の無断複製は著作権法上での例外を除き禁じられています。本書を代行業者等の第三者に依頼してスキャンやデジタル化することは，たとえ個人や家庭内での利用でも著作権法違反です。